I'm gonna walk in Jerusalem!
I'm gonna talk in Jerusalem!
Sing in Jerusalem!
Be in Jerusalem!
High up! In Jerusalem when I die!

The unabashed exultation of this spiritual likening Jerusalem to heaven has been echoed by mankind for over three thousand years, as befitting the most venerated site on earth. She is made of golden stones, not one of which has remained unturned by scholars and holy men. Everything about her is subjected to sublime glorification, her air, her walls, her valleys, those paths trod by the sandals of prophets and saints, those places of agony, her sacred mount, even the necropolis, her city of the dead. It is said the world has ten measures of beauty and nine of these belong to Jerusalem.

—from *Jerusalem, Song of Songs*
by Jill and Leon Uris

JERUSALEM
Song of Songs

Jill and Leon Uris

BANTAM BOOKS
TORONTO • NEW YORK • LONDON • SYDNEY • AUCKLAND

We wish to acknowledge our appreciation to our associates Betsy Rosenberg of Jerusalem, Lynne Pearce and Brooke Newman of Aspen, Colorado.

JERUSALEM, SONG OF SONGS
*A Bantam Book / published by arrangement with
Doubleday and Company Inc.*

PRINTING HISTORY
*Doubleday edition published October 1981
An Alternate Selection of Literary Guild
Bantam edition / August 1985*

ISBN 0-553-24964-9

Published simultaneously in the United States and Canada

PRINTED IN THE UNITED STATES OF AMERICA

O   0 9 8 7 6 5 4 3 2 1

*This book is dedicated
to Teddy Kollek of Jerusalem,
a man who comes along
once every two thousand years.*

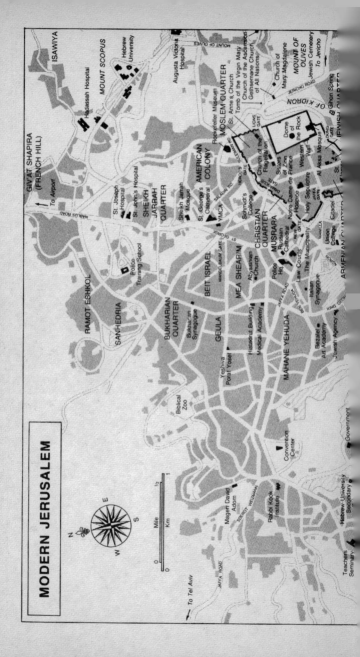

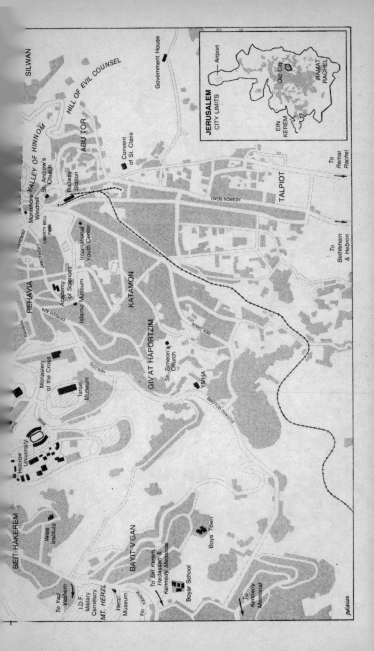

JERUSALEM
THE OLD CITY

MOUNT OF OLIVES

Six-Day War Memorial ■ ■ Tomb of the Virgin Mary
Garden of Gethsemane
St. Stephen's Church ■ Church of All Nations
Gethsemane Church of Mary Magdalene
Jehoshafat's Tower
Absalom's Tomb

OF KIDRON

JERICHO ROAD

Moslem Cemetery

LIONS GATE

GOLDEN GATE

HARAM ESH SHARIF

Dome of the Rock

Church of St. Anne

MOSLEM QUARTER

Antonia

Church of the Flagellation

Rockefeller Museum

SULTAN SULEIMAN

HEROD'S GATE

Indian Hospice

Ecce Homo Arch

VIA DOLOROSA

Austrian Hospice

Sisters of Zion

Church of St. Veronica

Islamic Orphanage

VIA DOLOROSA

Red Mosque

St. John's Hospice

Coptic Patriarchate

Coptic Monastery

Church of the Holy Sepulchre

Jeremiah's Grotto

SALADIN ROAD

St. Stephen's Church

The Garden Tomb

NABLUS ROAD

Schmidt's College

DAMASCUS GATE

Polish Hospice

Ethiopian Monastery

Terra Sancta College

HANEVI'IM (PARATROOPERS)

HATZANHANIM (PARATROOPERS)

CHRISTIAN QU

MUSRARA

Notre Dame de France Hospice

NEW GATE

Church of St. Savior

Church of St. Michael

Christian

Contents

JERUSALEM
Song of Songs

Jerusalem High

I'm gonna walk in Jerusalem!
I'm gonna talk in Jerusalem!
Sing in Jerusalem!
Be in Jerusalem!
High up! In Jerusalem when I die!
Be in Jerusalem!
Swing in Jerusalem!
Shout in Jerusalem!
Pray in Jerusalem!
High up! In Jerusalem when I die!

The unabashed exultation of this spiritual likening Jerusalem to heaven has been echoed by mankind for over three thousand years, as befitting the most venerated site on earth. She is made of golden stones, not one of which has remained unturned by scholars and holy men. Everything about her is subjected to sublime glorification, her air, her walls, her valleys, those paths trod by the sandals of prophets and saints, those places of agony, her sacred mount, even the necropolis, her city of the dead. It is said the world has ten measures of beauty and nine of these belong to Jerusalem.

Jerusalem has known the hosts of thirty-six wars. She has been reduced to ashes seventeen times. She has risen eighteen. She has been sanctified by blood and martyrdom. She knew the hoofbeat of Assyrian war chariot, chilled to the besieging battering machines of Rome, heard the hissing arcs of Saladin's sabers and the rattle of crusader mail...and the tattoo of Israeli paratroop gunfire. She has seen more passion and love and more human savagery than any other place in the world.

Jerusalem has variously been described as the center of the world, the eye of the world and the navel of the world. She is regarded as the halfway house between heaven and earth. Her location, off the commercial beat, difficult for agriculture, in a constant search for sufficient water, without natural wealth, tells us that she should not have a place among those cities considered as great. But Jerusalem is the greatest of the great, for she alone has achieved immortality on moral and ethical grounds.

She rises and rests on hot windy crests of omnipresent stone of which she is made. Stone has given her a constant look for thousands of years. Sun and stone are companions putting on a changing light show from a blinding midday glare to muted golds and purples of sunrise, sunset and moonglow. When winter bites, the dull flat summer sky turns to deep azures and fogs creep through her valleys and rains, driven by desert winds, glisten on the rocks and there comes an occasional thin cloak of white.

The Old City is entered today through seven magic gates leading into a vortex of holy fires, of smells of ancient spices and a cobblestone labyrinth that eventually finds the heart of hearts, the Temple Mount. From this place David, Jesus and Mohammed all made their ascensions to their celestial temples.

The very names of Jerusalem call out to us like poetry heard in distant childhood...Calvary...Ophel...Al Aksa...Gethsemane...the Mount of Olives...Sanhedria ...Via Dolorosa...the Valleys of Hinnom and Kidron... the Pool of Siloam...the Spring of Gihon...the Dome of the Rock...Ecce Homo...Zion.

There are 103 varieties of Jews from 103 separate lands. Jews from Morocco and Yemen and Bukhara and India retain vestiges of their native dress and customs. Other Jewish sects, like the Hasidics, live cloistered in self-imposed ghettos resembling the pales of Russia and Poland of two centuries back. They dress to fit the occasion with wide-brimmed beaver hats and striped kaftans. On the Sabbath the costume becomes the spodik, a fur hat, and long black silk kapotes. They are bearded and earlocked. Their women shave their heads and are bundled, in ultramodesty, in long-sleeved, cheap, sacklike prints.

These mixed with the monks and nuns of Armenia, Greece, Russia, the Franciscans and bedouins and Arabs and just plain folks in jeans and pants suits give Jerusalem the look of a perennial costume ball.

All that holiness notwithstanding, Jerusalem is very much a modern city with traffic jams, working stiffs, rude salespeople, bureaucrats of the nation's capital, surly and rebellious juveniles, a military presence because of unresolved boundaries, trains and buses and donkeys, jittery horn-blowing drivers, magnificent women, decent restaurants and the full kit of civic maladies. She is a city of round-the-calendar holidays and round-the-clock cultural events.

Outside of the walled city we come upon fine old neighborhoods where German, Spanish and American colonies were founded and Jewish enclaves dared venture outside the gates in the middle of the last century. And then a new Jerusalem fans out into the hills, bursting into wide boulevards, zillions of trees and flowers, statuary, big parks and pocket parks, some electrifying architecture, religious institutions, universities, hospitals, memorials, study centers, museums and edifices of government. By night magnificent illuminations show off the principal ancient and modern sites. The beauty of Jerusalem is not exaggerated.

No city's rulers have come from such a variety of places and cultures, from ancient Egypt and Rome to modern Ottoman and Anglo. Yet, with all the wars and heavily traveled passages and all the sacred esteem, Jerusalem has remained exceedingly provincial and in the backwaters of world importance until quite recently.

She has known only two periods of true greatness and these have been separated by two thousand years. Greatness has happened only under Jewish rule. This is so because the Jews have always loved her the most and have remained constant in that love throughout the centuries of their strange dispersion and odyssey. It is the longest, deepest love affair in all of history. The city is a mosaic of strangers speaking different languages, with different alphabets and alien to one another in culture, religion, social life and education. The Jews alone have created conditions and an atmosphere in which all these diverse peoples can thrive in harmony despite the fact it is one of the most volatile locations in the world. Because they have been suffocated for eternities, the Jews let others breathe. Such decency is new in this part of the world.

The tree called Jerusalem was planted before recorded history. Its roots go back to the dawn of civilized man. Civilizations rose because of certain geographic and geological truths. A body of water was essential: the Tigris and Euphrates rivers, the Nile, the Mediterranean. Ancient Israel had none of these. The Hebrews were a hill people who became a nation on an idea, and that made her unique. Jerusalem was the magnificent crown of that idea.

All the mighty kingdoms that once surrounded her have been eclipsed. Nothing but crumbled ruins remain of the mighty Mesopotamian empires. The pinnacle of Egypt's glory was reached twenty-five hundred years ago.

Of all the cities founded by the ancients, Jerusalem alone retains her ancient glory and her special relationship to God. It is here that reality, miracle and illusion all tumble around together, where a lovely touch of madness remains unconquered by man's folly.

THE PEOPLE OF THE BOOK

The general attitude today toward the Old Testament is that it is man's view of God rather than God's view of man. It is acceptable as a reasonable history of the events of an era which is often blurred by the dust storms of time and flawed by human exaggeration and fantasy. The Old Testament is inundated with impossibilities, inaccuracies and contradictions. It depicts a God who speaks directly to man and is often petulant and petty. God involves Himself in the affairs of man like a traffic cop passing out tickets to the offenders and at times demanding brutal and un-Godlike vengeance. At other times He is relegated to being a ringmaster in a circus of the supernatural, continually asserting His authority over man.

The texts show people living to ages over a century and women giving birth fifty years after menopause when life expectancy was scarcely twenty-five years. Seas opened for passage for the good guys and drowned the bad, suns stood still so our side had the right to slaughter the other side, pagan temples were pulled down by hand, walls fell to trumpets, bushes spoke, water poured from rocks and food from heaven and snakes leapt out of rocks. This aspect of the Bible has been attacked by vitriolic outpourings from Tom Paine, who seriously demanded a literal accounting, to George Gershwin, who noted with whimsey that "It Ain't Necessarily So."

Most of what was physically there is gone with the winds or was mud brick melted by the rains, lost forever and shrouded in mystery. The new science of archaeology surfaced in the middle of the last century and brought scores of teams from all over the world in search of a new kind of buried treasure, the truth. As they learned to interpret the levels of civilizations and fire lines of prehistoric tels, stunning confirmations told of city-kingdoms, floods and movements of people just as it had been written.

The issue of biblical accuracy has been clouded and confused as well as helped by the inordinate nit-picking of theological scholars who play word games with every line, word and comma. For example, a volume of the Song of Songs in which the poem itself occupies ten pages of verse is almost lost in seven hundred pages of interpretation.

We are not in the miracle-busting business. The Bible story and its allied writings were compiled centuries after the events occurred. It is a marvelous history of an ancient people grappling for the first time with the great moral issues of the universe, written in the dawn of man's philosophical development. Considering the distant past and the unique ideas, a heavy-handed infiltration of legend, folklore, magic and pagan influence, the biblical exaggerations become understandable. The Hebrews had the courage to take on a strange unknown and unseen force against a backdrop of their longings and aspirations which is manifest in all religion, a submission to a mysterious power to quell our fears and seek answers and comfort for our longings and aspirations. Those who dismiss the Old Testament as fiction as well as those who ponder over every inference seem to miss the point equally, which is neither historical accuracy nor indulgence in scholastic overkill.

The point is that certain eternal truths were first understood by man and these truths took root, emerged and endured. These truths will continue to dictate who we are and what we are so long as man occupies this planet.

The creators of the Bible were men of consummate literary genius, the Old Testament being among the most magnificent volumes of pure prose and poetry ever produced. Within those pages we can find every known story of black villainy and lofty virtue.

Never before was human thought and imagination so fluid and expansive. Sometimes its content is difficult to decipher, owing to hypercharged emotionalism, mysterious symbolisms and embellishment, yet it emerges just as powerfully as the day it was written as man's greatest single source of inspiration. The books of the Old Testament were drawn from scores of sources from an unknown number of contributors who include historians, court scribes, recorders, essayists, rabbis, poets and religious scholars. They cover an enormous expanse of content from history and law to ethics, economy, philosophy, proverbs of ultimate wisdom, poetry of sublime magnitude, prophecy of stunning clarity. What was truly fashioned in these pages were the ethical codes and concepts that are the foundation of Western civilization.

Through this greatest of works, the Jewish people and their unique odyssey became an energy cell of the world. If the cast of characters take on larger-than-life dimensions, the wanderings, tragedies and triumphs of the Jewish people were also larger than life. The makers of this history were not a bunch of namby-pamby psalm singers or quaking holier-than-thous. The old Hebrews loved and worshiped God as He has never been loved and worshiped before but they loved their women too.

If nothing else, the Hebrews were a lusty breed. They came in out of the wilds to create a nation and along the way they lied, cheated, pillaged, slaughtered, thieved, burned and conspired. Even the most noble of the heroes turned coward at times and nearly all practiced deceit and blatant dishonesty. Brother plotted against brother and son committed treachery against father.

This sensual lot delighted in debauchery with their collections of concubines, cavorting with whores, engaging in adultery, rape, sodomy, incest and orgies. The notion that celibacy, virginity and sexual abstinence were outsized virtues certainly didn't come from these folks. Mostly, they were human beings, you, me, all of us, filled with all our human frailties. The awesome concept of a single and all-powerful God pulled them back from the abyss of perfidy, kept them within bounds of decency and allowed them to endure.

Fathers and Sons

\/\/

The curtain of history was raised in Mesopotamia. The stone age was finished and the floods had receded. Man crossed the threshold into civilization with a necklace of city-kingdoms along the Tigris and Euphrates valleys. To the south the pyramids of Egypt had been built and the Nile Valley was the breadbasket of the known world.

Between Egypt and Mesopotamia a land bridge known as Canaan connected Africa to Asia; it was populated by successive waves of tribes from the Semitic families of Arabia and Asia Minor: the Amorites, Hittites, Phoenicians, Jebusites, Ammonites, Moabites, Edomites and Amalekites. The Canaanite civilization was rich and sophisticated and reached back into the dawn of enlightened man with such urban developments as Jericho and Beersheba and Jaffa and Megiddo. Canaan was generally controlled by the dominant power either to the north or south. This land passage of Canaan which became Israel was a geopolitical death trap, then as today, and was predestined to be a battlefield of the ages.

The over-all region known as the Fertile Crescent began at the Persian Gulf, arched west through what is now Iraq and Syria to the Mediterranean and then south to the Nile Delta. Canaan was not only naked to marching armies like a morsel between two jaws of a crocodile, it was the poor cousin of the Fertile Crescent. Most of the land, save for a few valleys and the seacoast, was mountainous, rocky and rain-starved.

It was a time of restless movement of peoples. Tribes swept down from the north and west constantly, downing old empires and creating new ones.

Man has always measured his progress along twin lines, philosophical and technological. As he learned the technical building blocks of civilization the parallel need increased for him to deal with the unknown in daily life and the fear of the unknown beyond mortal life. Craving for immortality was matched by a maniacal fear of death. To cope with the unknown, man placed his fate in the hands of hundreds of idols, believing them to be the force behind wind, fire, rain, sun and storm. There were idols with heads of snakes, dogs, bulls, rams, great birds and fish, all of which needed constant appeasement, often in the form of human sacrifice. The Egyptians became so enraptured with the cult of death that they expended their national energy building tombs to enshrine their human god/kings for the transitional journey. Death, the fear of death and the unknown forces of nature dominated the existence of every culture and civilization. Despite this ponderous preoccupation, idolatry obviously was unable to provide the answers.

The time was ripe and the stage was set for a dynamic new idea to take root and the Old Testament represents the continual discovery and development of man's search for and relationship to God.

When the "big boom" came those billions of years back, God created ten billion galaxies we know of and a hundred billion stars, more or less, in each galaxy. The entire universe is made up of the same life-giving properties. By taking the most minimal figures, reasonable men must conclude that some form of human or intelligent life as we know it exists on at least tens of millions of planets. Millions of these have civilizations millions of years older than the earth. In this century our own infinitesimal little earth will have the technology to confirm life elsewhere in the universe.

Even without this technology, how arrogant it is to believe that earth, out of all the universe, was singled out to contain the only intelligent forms of life. What arrogance to believe that we alone out of hundreds of trillions of planets think we exclusively discovered God and have God's exclusive services. When God put the earth here,

THE FERTILE CRESCENT

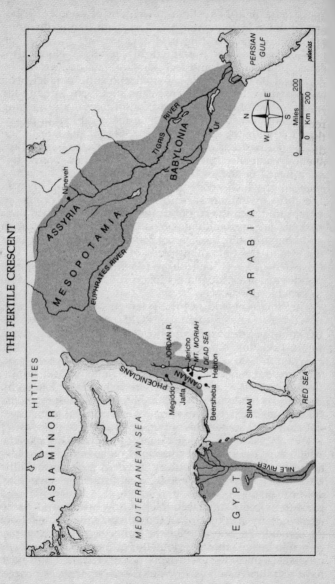

along with all the rest of it out there, He provided all the elements for human survival as well as human destruction. He gave us the gift of the sun, which is the source of all life. Beyond that, man is on his own to survive or perish. God has no need to come down and discover man or to manipulate him into making him a believer. It is entirely up to man to discover God. The Old Testament must be read and viewed as man's search, one in which God remains unseen, unheard and mysterious. Throughout the writing of the Scriptures, man was on the brink of discoveries he could not explain. The easiest and most obvious way out was simply to attribute the unexplainable to "miracles of God." God, after all, probably has as many civilizations in the universe as there are people on this earth. He simply doesn't have all that much time to come down here and put on a command performance for us: If the Old Testament is read as man's exploration for universal truth, the emergence of God becomes crystal clear.

ABRAHAM

The time is considered to have been two thousand years before Jesus and the place given as Ur in Mesopotamia. The man, Abraham, a semi-nomad of some means, perhaps an Amorite. He married his paternal half sister, Sarah, a common practice of the times. Abraham was motivated by an insatiable craving for permanent settlement. His age was said to be seventy-five when he first heard the voice of God promise him a homeland.

The voice Abraham heard was his own, a manifestation of his longings and aspirations. He wanted to achieve a better sense of life, something beyond his given ability under the norms of the times. It took incredible courage to divorce himself from the death cults that consumed and paralyzed the human mind. He smashed the idols of ignorance by taking personal responsibility for his own destiny. He journeyed into the unknown, initiating the first great act of faith by placing his fate in the hands of an unseen God. From Abraham's time onward, the Jews have historically been a forward-moving people, a people of life. Abraham's discovery of God is our first major philosophical achievement, the break with the bondage of paganism. He had come in out of man's darkness.

Aside from his piety, Abraham showed a range of demeanor and characteristics from courage to cowardice. He was no saint, no stricken holy man, no paragon of purity, and thus he established a biblical pattern of human frailty.

For her part, Sarah was smitten with a curse of sterility, a repetitious theme in the Bible. She presented Abraham with a concubine, Hagar, traditional in those times. Hagar bore a son, Ishmael, who later fathered the Arab race. Hagar and Ishmael were cast out in the desert by Sarah, who got caught up by the green-eyed monster of jealousy. During Abraham's wanderings, Sodom and Gomorrah ceased to exist because of "God's wrath" over certain orgiastic carryings-on. Abraham's nephew Lot saw his own wife turned into a pillar of salt for taking that forbidden backward glance. Lot then turned around and sired the patriarchs of the Moabite and Ammonite nations through incest with his daughters, while ostensibly grieving for his wife. This cycle of behavior was early proof that man's imperfections were part of him and not some kind of mutation. While his imperfections may have caused him to seek out God, they were in him whether he sought out God or not. Evil, in other words, was and is an ingrained part of man.

Abraham was finally to become involved in one of the most important discoveries in human events. The Scriptures tell us it was God who summoned Abraham to Moriah, demanding the sacrifice of his beloved son Isaac.

It appears that Abraham was ready and willing to commit an act of murder blindly when an angel of the Lord intervened, suggesting substitution of an animal at the altar. Although substitution of animals for humans constituted a major rupture with paganism, one must seriously contend it was not God who made the suggestion but that man had discovered it in the next logical development in his understanding of God.

Murder is the type of demand one might expect of a demoniac idol of Canaan. Was God merely playing a trick to discover the extent of Abraham's loyalty and obedience? Would God do this through use of terror on a man?

Would God ask a man of proven faith to destroy his son?

Abraham had been intimate with God long enough to realize that human sacrifice was an abomination and a perversion of God's law and he needed no angel to tell him so. Abraham went to Mount Moriah in Jerusalem to demonstrate his own conclusion that both man and God rejected murder. The lesson of Moriah is that *man should not kill. Man should not kill, particularly in the name of God.*

Like most peoples, the Hebrews tended to marry among themselves, yet intermarriage with Canaanite and Egyptian was commonplace. Scratch an Israelite and you were certain to find Amorite, Hittite, Phoenician or Mesopotamian blood. There were five tribal matriarchs. Only two of these were Hebrews.

Racial purity was never a Jewish concept. Much later in the Old Testament the Book of Ruth solidified the acceptance of the outsider. Ruth herself became a direct ancestor of both David and Jesus. Israel never considered God to be its exclusive possession but a universal God belonging to all peoples.

The story of the patriarchs tells us that the Hebrews were a living breed. They took risks, they traveled far, they adored life. They transgressed, sinned, lusted. They were honorable, pious, deceitful. The women were strong, beautiful, ugly, cunning. They were forgiving as Esau forgave Jacob for stealing his inheritance and as Joseph forgave his brothers for selling him into bondage. They were family. They fought each other as families do but their sense of family generally prevailed. This sense of family within Jewish life has been a key to Jewish survival. They were a cult of life in the midst of cults of death.

The cradle of civilization formed in Mesopotamia some seven thousand years ago along the Tigris and Euphrates river valleys. It made great technical advancements culminating in city-kingdoms.

Landless nomads of Semitic stock drifted throughout the region. They became known as the wanderers or "Hebrews." Around four thousand years ago a number of strong leaders arose among them and developed an ethic that set them uniquely apart. Their belief in a single, unseen and all-powerful God was in diametric contrast to the existing idol worship. Extended families, clans and tribes of these Hebrews migrated south into Canaan, which also had a long-standing civilization. Canaan had been peopled by waves of earlier migration and its cities were vassals of the Egyptians to the south. The Hebrews were unsophisticated in contrast to the Canaanites. As shepherds and farmers they remained outside the central cores, continuing always as semi-nomads.

Although these Hebrews could not be formally defined as a people or a nation, they had an indelible unity and infrastructure owing to their concept of God. From time to time they were driven by famine to the more hospitable lands in the eastern delta of the Nile called Goshen. Around seventeen hundred years before the Christian Era, the Hebrews made a major but peaceful incursion into Goshen. Although their numbers are uncertain, some of every tribe must have made the migration. Some of the Hebrews remained in Canaan, which became a sort of hinterland. After a time the fate of those in Goshen changed drastically from welcomed guests to bondage. All of this set the stage for the entrance of the greatest single human being ever to grace the earth...a man named Moses.

THE EXODUS

For several hundred years the Bible story is eclipsed in vagueness. We do know that during this period Egypt went into another period of massive building and during this time the fate of the Israelites changed from that of free men to bondage.

The strata of Egyptian culture placed the Pharaoh at the top as a human god/king. Around him in his court were his generals, priests, scribes, administrators, artisans, architects, physicians, magicians, musicians, artists and landholders. These were few in number but they molded Egypt's glory in tomb and temple, through brilliant royal records, through works of gold and alabaster and miles upon miles of green bountiful farms along the Nile and its delta. Beneath this exquisite society the masses lived in squalor and misery.

Living apart were the strangers, the semi-nomadic

Hebrews, who were neither fish nor fowl in the society, whose fortunes had taken a turn for the worse since their arrival. To feed the building binge, the Hebrews were tapped into a pool of national labor. While life became difficult it was not yet unbearable. The Hebrews were allowed to maintain their separate life style, retain their flocks and fields and, mainly, to preserve their faith so long as they complied with Pharaoh's edicts. Later, nominal bondage degenerated into full-blown slavery.

Pharaonic building took on maniacal proportions, with one Pharaoh outconstructing his predecessor for the purpose of insuring his own immortality. Awestruck by the threat of death, the Egyptians compulsively lived with death. The worship of pagan gods swamped them with a sense of fatalism. Glorification of death became the result of all that grandeur. Their works were magnificent but toward a negative end and true creativity eroded onto a treadmill of repetition. As they climbed to the pinnacle of their greatest era, the taskmaster's whip cracked with increasing fury. The death force of the Egyptians was soon in an inevitable clash with the counterforce of life emanating from their Hebrew slaves. The harder they drove the Hebrews, the more the Hebrews craved freedom. They dreamed of Canaan and reignited the ancient faith of Abraham, and despite their privation they grew in numbers.

What maddened and bedeviled the Egyptians was the ability of the Hebrews to find solace in their mystifying God while their own gods continued to betray them. Egypt's pagan fatalism was being ideologically weakened by the Israelites, who held that the purpose of man lay within man himself. Disharmony with their gods, lack of respect for human life and dignity all foretold the coming downfall of their civilization.

As they began to slip, Egyptian hatred of the Hebrews devoured reason. Despite the fact that the Israelites constituted their major labor force, genocide became the ultimate end of unbridled xenophobia. Pharaoh ordered that all newborn Hebrew males be exterminated. The parallels with Nazi Germany are almost too obvious to record. Egypt, as was Germany, was so consumed by evil that reaching the point of self-destruction became inevitable.

Into this caldron of social upheaval Moses was born. Unlike the allegorical patriarchs, who may or may not have existed, Moses actually lived. From the tribe of Levi, he was numbered among the newborn to be slain but was saved by Pharaoh's daughter. Raised as an Egyptian prince, the facts of his tainted birth were kept secret from the Pharaoh and his court. But Moses had been nursed by his own mother and raised by his sister Miriam, and he knew he was a Levite and seethed in anger over the slavery of his people. It was but a matter of time until his sense of outrage boiled over and he killed an Egyptian taskmaster beating a Hebrew slave. His cover blown, Moses fled.

The flight took him to the Midianites, a tribe of bedouins, where a Midianite priest, Jethro, took him in. Moses married his daughter, the beautiful Zipporah. While tending Jethro's flock, Moses became a stargazer in search of the meaning of God.

As he lay back and saw the desert heavens by day and night, he observed that stars, sun and moon were all in their proper places. Every animal and plant had its place and purpose. The thin crust of desert life functioned with miraculous control, in incredibly predictable cycles. Moses deduced that everything out there in the sky and here on earth was part of an absolute system of universal order and within that system of universal order was the meaning of God. Thousands of years later another Jew, Albert Einstein, was to prove universal order by his equation $E = mc^2$.

In Egypt, Moses reckoned, the architects constructed according to certain known mathematical principles, chemists made their compounds by absolute formulas, astronomers charted the heavens according to long-studied and proved patterns. Those laws of science, Moses deduced, were absolute. A measurement, a compound, a weight, a distance would have the same application anywhere in the world or any place in the heavens.

Life around him consisted of many absolutes. Rain equaled crops, resurrection came in springtime and renewed life, sexual intercourse produced children, fire caused heat and light, wool made cloth. The close inspection of insects, flowers, animal life showed them made up of functional absolutes. All of these were part of the universal system of order.

Moses' lonely search left him to conclude that there were moral laws as well as laws of science and nature.

These laws, however, were unseen by the naked eye nor could they be proved by the addition or subtraction of numbers. It was man's duty to discover what these moral laws were. The task was all the more difficult because they could be defined only from man's mind. Moses knew from Abraham that murder was against God's law. His life in Egypt told him that slavery was against God's law. There were, indeed, certain universal rights and wrongs which were as absolute as day following night.

Moses became the first man we know of to apply the theory of force and counterforce. He knew that every force of evil would be met by a counterforce of good and that these forces would be in eternal conflict. They could and did coexist within a single man, a tribe or an entire nation. Only if a universal moral law could be defined and accepted as absolute could man actually know right from wrong.

The Egyptian monolith was beginning to crumble because it had become a polarized society whose main thrust was to build empty monuments to human vanity. No kingdom built on the backs of slaves could endure. Paganism and human vassalage were contrary to God's universal order of morality.

If Egypt fell, would not the Hittites and Canaanites fall as well? Moses realized that all of mankind must ultimately collapse unless man learned moral law and kept it parallel with the growth of technology. Technology, without the guiding force of morality, was bound to turn into a force of evil as it had in Egypt.

Moses' own people, the Hebrews, had survived not because of any glorious civilization they had created. They were a primitive society by comparison with those who lorded over them. Their survival was through a rudimentary understanding of Abraham's faith which endowed them with superhuman ability to endure debasement, tragedy and genocide.

If Moses was able to move them to liberate themselves

and if he should be able to define for them the meaning of universal morality, then these people would become worthy of bringing God's law to man and be able to face the eternal task of defending that law.

Moses took on the most difficult task ever engaged in by a single human being: to discover the laws of God and to charge a people with keeping them. He was not only alone in the desert but alone in the entire world, with pagan civilizations all around him filled with idol worship, death cults and ritual orgy. He had no books to read, no round table of philosophers to debate with, no precedents in man's history to draw upon. One man's innovations had to change the entire course of human events. He needed no burning bush to outline his task for him. He was Moses, alone, unique, a force of one.

The rumbles for freedom in Egypt didn't occur in a single moment of revelation. The movement had been building for years, if not decades. Some slaves always escape. Unquestionably Hebrew slaves had been escaping through an underground railway. Unquestionably they had some sort of contact with their kinsmen in Canaan. Caravans, smugglers, escaped slaves and desert winds all carry messages. He knew the swell for freedom had risen to epidemic proportions and it was time for him to return. For a moment even the mighty Moses faltered and asked to have his brother Aaron spirited out of Egypt to meet him and assist him. When Aaron escaped Egypt to keep the rendezvous, the Hebrews in Goshen knew that Moses was on the way. If Moses had not returned, they would have invented him. Their longing for freedom and their vision of Canaan were centuries old and they were ready to vote with their feet.

Like all great leaders, Moses was a product of his times and the needs of his people. He was the complete leader, blending compassion, ruthlessness and fury. He possessed all the dynamics and all the wisdom of leadership including those enigmatic qualities of aloofness, petulance and dogmatism. His re-entry into Egypt set the stage for the first great confrontation between slavery and freedom.

It is said that the elders of the tribes balked. That was why they were elders: to restrain the young turks and keep the people from plunging into a disaster. But the elders knew and supported the growing resistance to

Pharaoh. Moses convinced them that what he needed and wanted was time to organize. Despite the Scriptures telling us the Hebrews fled on a single moment's notice, logic compels us to look into the realities of the situation, for it was no fly-by-night operation.

The exact number of Hebrews is unknown, with estimates of several hundred thousand up to two million. One must assume that tens of thousands were strung out in Goshen with a heavy concentration at the city of Rameses being built and named for the Pharaoh.

During his years in the Egyptian court Moses had been able to learn of the enormous organizational effort and manpower required to feed, house, guard and move the armies of slaves. He realized his task would be the largest undertaking of its kind ever to be tried.

Inquire of any military general today what kind of resources are required to move a division of twenty thousand troops any distance. These would be well-trained healthy men with the most modern transport and the best supplies. The logistics of how many rolls of toilet paper, bars of soap, rations, blankets, rounds of ammunition, shoes, medicine and all of the communications and gasoline and spare parts, water, tents... is staggering.

Moses had to contend with old people, infants, cripples and the infirm. Everything had to be carried in crude wooden ox- and ass-drawn carts. Everything, not only for themselves, but for their flocks, their food source, tents, grain and water in cumbersome skins. They had to have weapons to beat off the desert tribes. At best they could make a few miles a day.

Moses needed months to stockpile. It had to be done secretly. Weapons had to be manufactured in clandestine factories just as weapons were secretly manufactured on the kibbutzim by modern Israelis during the British Mandate. The entire tribe, down to small children, were involved in smuggling and security. Section leaders had to be chosen carefully.

Reconnaissance scouts were sent out in advance to find the best routes and to make arrangements with friendly bedouins for encampment sites. Certainly the tides, currents, and shallow crossings of the Red Sea were charted and studied meticulously. Water was jealously guarded in the desert and the Amalekites, a tribe of desert rats descending from Esau, would challenge the way. Along with the logistical headaches, Moses had to organize a military capability to contend with this eventuality. At the same time he was getting all this into shape he had to convince Pharaoh to let his people go. Such a project in those early times could have only been achieved by extraordinary genius.

The Hebrews had been able to keep family and tribal life intact. Over a period of time they learned to protect each other. It was then as it is today in the gulag slave camps of Russia; when a Jew is brought in he is immediately singled out by a watchdog committee of other Jews to protect him. It is the ultimate sense of family that defies being broken.

Pharaoh tried some of everything: beatings, starvation, massacres and genocide of first-born. Everything failed. Pharaoh's failure was his inability to penetrate the family infrastructure of the Hebrews.

W hen Moses returned to Egypt, Rameses II's first impulse was to have him seized and dragged to death behind the wheels of a chariot. Cooler heads in the court prevailed. Moses' death would have undoubtedly triggered a slave revolt. He had been raised as an Egyptian and if any sort of compromise was to be made it could only be done through Moses.

It is said that God invoked "Ten Plagues" on Egypt to make Rameses II see the light. What was plaguing the country was very real and needed no side show from the Lord to convince them they had problems. The brewing Hebrew insurrection was but the latest in a series of calamities that had befallen Egypt. Rameses II had bled his military into exhaustion attempting to regain control of the Mesopotamian provinces. The Pharaoh was to lose control of the vital coastal route, the Via Maris. A migration of "Sea People" had swept in from the Mediterranean. The Mycenaeans of Greece and the Minoans of Crete brought with them the iron age and superior weaponry that took them to the very gates of Egypt before they were turned back and settled the Canaan coast. On Egypt's western borders, the Libyans, then as today, were a constant harassment.

Perhaps some disasters similar to the Ten Plagues did happen to magnify Rameses II's season of disaster. Certainly locust plagues, crop and cattle failures were common facts of life. Certainly the water could become crimson from a red tide that destroyed marine life along the delta outlets to the sea. All these natural phenomena played into Moses' hands. When he came to court he also had the threat of a rebellion. Moses harped on the "supernatural" disasters and promised more of the same. The Pharaoh sagged. Rameses II did not give in in any single explosive moment. He tried to alleviate the pressure by letting go of non-essential slaves, a few hundred this week, a few hundred the next. It was the same method adopted by the Soviet Union today in their attempt to enslave intellectually their Jewish community. Then, as today, the tactic of selective release failed to satisfy the hunger for freedom but merely whetted the appetite. For when the force of freedom is in you, no Pharaoh can stop you.

Work stoppages and slowdowns, smuggling, reduced productivity, sabotage, attacks on guards, raids on stores, all contributed to the deterioration of the situation beyond the Egyptian ability to control it. Week after week the Hebrews' advance party emptied out into the desert and waited for the rest to follow.

The final large group of Israelites were those thousands impounded for the building of the city of Rameses. And then the final disaster came in the form of an epidemic. Egyptians fell by the thousands to some form of ancient disease. Either because of their segregation or a natural immunity built up for generations, the Hebrews were not affected. It was the final blow. Pharaoh told Moses to get them out.

Even as he left Egypt, Moses realized Rameses II's unbalanced state of mind. He had singled out the man Joshua, of the tribe of Ephraim, as his most capable military man and had set up a decoy force under his command. As the main body of Hebrews streamed out of Goshen, Joshua's commandos deliberately laid tracks for the Pharaoh to pursue.

With each passing day Rameses II became more demented. Once Egypt stopped building shrines with slave labor, it had lost its purpose as a culture. By letting the Hebrews go he had sounded the death knell of the empire and his own immortality. Rameses II became Hitler in the bunker, a raving madman. It made no sense to either recapture or slaughter the Hebrews but the force of evil had to play out its final drama by consuming itself. With his judgment shot, Pharaoh fell easy prey to Joshua's trap. The decoy force led the rampaging Egyptian chariots into a preplanned location where a quagmire of quicksand and fast-moving tides wiped them out.

RENDEZVOUS AT SINAI

The crossing out of Egypt was done. The scattered elements reunited on the edge of the wilderness but there was no time for jubilation. The Sea People blocked the coastal route. They were heavily armed with iron weaponry and were becoming edgy about the massive assemblage of Hebrews near their territory. If the Sea People took a notion to sweep in they could surely have massacred the lot of them or captured them and taken them into another period of slavery. It was decided to give them a wide berth.

Inside Egypt the court was enraged by the death of Rameses II at the Sea of Reeds and was in the process of mounting a pursuit expedition. The Israelites were in a nutcracker. Their only choice was to plunge into the merciless desert and put distance between themselves and their enemies. This ragtag band was now to face their first moment of truth and their first hour of agony. Heat on the desert floor flamed to 120°. Food and the most vital commodity, water, was desperately short and disease found an easy mark among the weak. Death was their constant companion and they died glazed-eyed and frothing-mouthed with an omnipresent flock of vultures massed overhead.

It was akin to madness to herd a mob of tens of thousands deeper and deeper into this fearsome furnace of a place but the price of freedom gave them no choice.

Moses knew he had to free them spiritually as he had liberated them bodily. He had to infuse them with purpose, direction, unity and courage or they would die miserably. By alternately coaxing and driving he pressed them ever closer to their immortal rendezvous with God.

His first goal was that magic mountain where he had shepherded the flocks of his father-in-law, Jethro. The place where he had first conceived his ideas of universal moral order. The site would afford water, distance from pursuit, a chance for rest and haven. Ever southward they trudged, farther into the Wilderness of Sin, as the death count reached epidemic proportions with cries of dissent falling on Moses' ears. Cries that even slavery was better than this.

Now the Amalekites came out to challenge the way. This tribe of accursed nomads descended from Esau nipped at their heels until the forays erupted into a full-blown battle. Moses called upon his man and Joshua carried the first of many days of battle. In proving their mettle in combat for the first time the Hebrews blasted the way open to Mount Sinai and Joshua established his place at the side of the great leader.

Three torturous months after the flight from Goshen the Israelites collapsed at the foot of Mount Sinai. They were exhausted, their ranks depleted, a trail of corpses of wives, children and parents in their wake. The agony of what had happened and the terror of what lay ahead crashed down on them and they were consumed by fear. Yet Moses had taken them where he wanted them to be and the moment of moments in man's epoch was at hand.

Certainly this great leader clearly understood their state of mind. A miracle was needed to rally them or the venture was doomed to failure. Unless they found the ability to rise, the option was eternal aimless wandering and death in a hostile land. For months, perhaps years, Moses had been their principal source of strength. He knew he wouldn't live forever and that another source of strength was needed to replace him, a source to give full expression to the righteousness of their longings and aspirations. They needed an ethic, a moral code, a religion

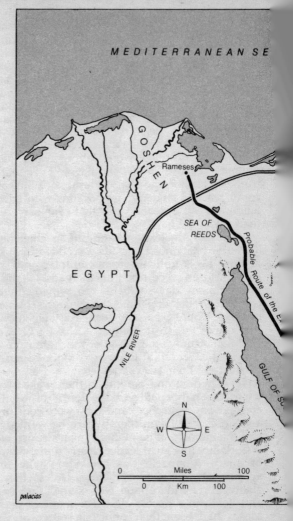

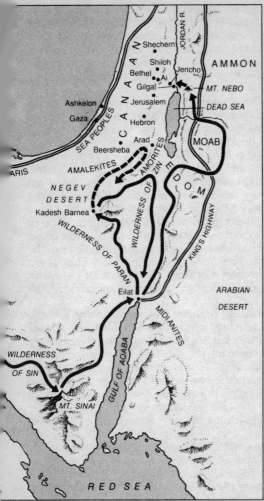

if you please, in order to win the race for survival. Moses was aware of the power he held over them and he used it ingeniously. He had, after all, liberated them and they completely accepted that he had some sort of divine stature. When he informed them that he was going up into the mountain to speak with God, they believed him implicitly.

Moses departed knowing that the people would fall prey to the full horror of their situation. With fear of abandonment by their leader, they would become unbalanced. It can be assumed that Moses deliberately dangled evil temptation before their eyes to set them up and to compromise them. As days passed by with no Moses, confusion and fright swept through them. Panic raged out of control and they skidded into idolatry. Moses selected a moment at the very height of their frenzied debauchery to return. Catching them red-handed abandoning the God of Abraham, he played the outraged father. He alone could and did succeed in sobering and shaming them. Now he could show them how to purge themselves. The lesson and choices were clear. Continue in the path of paganism and destroy yourselves or accept human morality as the truth for man's survival.

Consider the blazing oranges and muted purples of the desert sunset seguéing into a star-filled, comet-strewn night. Consider this ragged sprawl of ancient humanity entering into a compact for the first time with God by acceptance of His laws. It was the scene of the highest order of drama staged by an actor of ultimate genius and no stage would hold its equal again. The eight-century epic of the Hebrew search for and union with God climaxed in the most magnificent single moment man has ever known.

Mosaic law contained all the basic ingredients of humanity. It will exist as long as man exists and it will never be improved upon. Moses, the first freedom fighter, Moses the liberator, Moses the lawgiver, the first great religious and moral philosopher, Moses the brilliant organizer, creator of the priesthood, now founded a nation of former slaves in the wilds of Sinai. And what was more, Moses was the world's first bona fide hero.

THE WAY TO CANAAN

t was time to rest, regroup, heal, restock. A crop needed o be planted and harvested. The gold smuggled out of :gypt which had been made into the calflike idol was nelted down. Trading parties ventured forth and bartered gold for livestock to replenish the herds. Pottery had to be kilned to hold stores of grain and water. Transport carts needed to be shored up. A source of copper needed to be found to smelt weapons. Cloth and sandals needed to be made.

It was a time of personal joy for Moses, who had known poor little of it. He was reunited with his wife and sons. His father-in-law, Jethro, a wise old desert fox, counseled him and underscored the importance of forming a tight administration through the elders. With Jethro's help Moses set up the first-known judiciary.

The Covenant with God was formalized by the building of an Ark to contain the Tablets of the Law, the ten commandments, which were the basis of the Torah. Literally meaning "the doctrine" or "the instruction," the Torah contained the stories of the creation, the patriarchs and the Exodus as well as the three books of the law. The Ark itself was a simple portable wooden structure housing these books, but its meaning was all-encompassing, for it denoted the presence of God among them. As symbol of man's union with God the Ark was the most sacred object on earth. For the first time, the Hebrews held that the written word was sacred.

The Ark was housed in the Tabernacle, a tentlike sanctuary built of indigenous materials of the desert: skins, cloth and some wood. Moses created the priesthood through his brother Aaron and designated his own tribe, the Levites, to serve that priesthood. He defined all the priestly paraphernalia and rituals.

In what was probably the world's first census Moses ordered a tribe-by-tribe count of the available fighting men. The Levites, who had charge of the Ark, were exempted from military duty.

One can only surmise the emotion that engulfed them when they celebrated the anniversary of their liberation.

The first Passover in the Sinai was to be re-enacted fo
over three thousand years as man's first festival of freedom.

A rigid marching order was prescribed with a group
from the tribe of Judah on the forward point. The Levites
came next with the Ark and the Tabernacle, the rest in
fixed positions, with Dan bringing up the rear. The ram's
horn, which had replaced the cow's horn after the golden
calf incident, blasted to herald the coming of Israel. They
forged northward, a far different people than those who
had fled Egypt. When they came to rest, the Levite tents
formed a square around the Ark and Tabernacle. An outer
square was made with each tribe in a set position behind
its own standard, facing the Ark.

About two years after the Exodus they found Kadesh
Barnea, with water and greenery. They were far enough
inland to be safe from the Sea People and some sixty miles
south of the first Canaanite stronghold of Arad.

In their obsession for the promised land they simply
forgot that it was the endless famines of Canaan that had
driven them into Egypt in the first place. Canaan, in
truth, was the poor man's sector of the Fertile Crescent, a
place doomed to know the tramping feet of ancient armies
and the rumble of modern tank treads. It is said in jest
that if Moses had wandered another forty years he might
have come to settle in some oil-rich Persian Gulf state . . .
or, at the least, the Riviera.

Scriptures relate a continued cycle of miracles during
food and water shortages. God either sent relief raining
down from heaven or had it struck from a rock or some
such. During one such incident after the defeat at Arad, it
is written that Moses momentarily doubted the Lord's
power to rescue them and, because of that doubt, God
crashed down on him. God condemned all the Hebrews
alive never to see the promised land, except for Joshua
and Caleb.

It is one of the most senseless and unexplainable passages in the Bible. What possible reason could God have
had to be so utterly cruel to His personal champion,
Moses? Unless, of course, God never made any such
judgment. One would conclude that Moses, a master at
psychological manipulation, deliberately used the incident
to bring home another hard lesson. Moses had come to
the devastating conclusion that the tribes of Israel, in their

present state, were totally incapable of conquering Canaan.

The people at Kadesh Barnea were strong physically from their battles for survival but they still possessed the minds of slaves. They whimpered, they complained, they toyed with idolatry and some even demanded to return to Egypt. Canaan, Moses knew full well, could not be won by slaves. What he needed was another generation to replace these people, a generation to be born and raised in freedom, purged of the mentality of servitude.

There is a parallel in the Jews who returned to Palestine in the middle of the last century from the ghettos of eastern Europe. A hundred years had to pass before Jews were born in Palestine and raised in freedom and dignity. This new breed, the native "sabras," would eventually be called upon and were capable of gaining the independence of modern Israel.

Moses placed himself at the head of those to be sacrificed, never to set foot on the promised land, in order to sustain hope among the others. Whether he told them that the denial of Canaan was a curse of God is highly debatable. What he might have said was, "We aren't ready and if we try before we are ready we shall surely fail. You and I together must come to grips with the possibility that we will not live to see the promised land. Now, let us pull ourselves together and settle down to the task of making sure we prepare our children for their task."

"Forty years" is an often repeated phrase whose literal translation is nebulous. It could refer to a "lifetime" as the life span was in that neighborhood or it could mean "a generation" or "a long time." In this instance, the "forty years" Israel spent in the wilderness is given to mean the replacement of the old generation by the new. During this period Moses knitted a military force, a spiritual force and a national force. He squashed dissent ruthlessly. The old crowd indeed died off, including his brother Aaron and his sister Miriam, while Joshua rose to the undeniable position of Moses' successor.

Joshua now commanded a tough, desert-hardened, disciplined, dedicated force of free men and women. They were the sons and daughters of slaves but knew nothing of slavery themselves. Moses deemed them equal to the task of entering Canaan.

They were moving not only an army but a nation, and

settlement had to accompany conquest. In moving masses of people in behind the army for settlement it was required that a hinterland be built up. Moses settled upon a plan to swing out deeply into the Arabian Desert and then double back to Canaan through the sparsely populated kingdoms of Moab and Ammon on the east bank of the Jordan River. From such a position they could plant the bulk of the population, then move the army into Canaan. The order of implementation was, pick off the easier kingdoms, settle, consolidate and then invade Canaan.

As Israel girded to cross into Canaan, future tribal areas were settled upon. The tribes of Gad, Reuben and part of Manasseh opted to remain on the eastern bank of the Jordan. The day of Moses had come to its end. He realized, with a sense of tragedy, that the conquest and settlement of Canaan would take years, perhaps generations, even centuries. Canaan was not an end but one more beginning of what would be eternal struggle for his people. Israel would have to carry the awesome burden of revealing and defending God in a pagan world. It was a world that would abandon God time and time again down through the ages and would turn on the Jews with varying degrees of rage for having "imposed" God upon them. There was no longer need for Moses nor did he have any desire to cross this threshold into endless ordeal. And so he gave his final sermons. He reviewed their incredible accomplishments, their wanderings and, mostly, the glory of the Covenant. He blessed them and he warned them and he went once more up into a mountain. From the heights of Nebo he could look beyond Jordan to that strangely promised land as below the banners of the house of Jacob were poised to enter.

JOSHUA AND THE BATTLE
THAT NEVER WAS

To Joshua befell the unenviable historical role of succeeding Moses. The moment called for a warrior and he was all of that.

After having made an emotional crossing of the Jordan,

he Iraelites celebrated their first Passover in the promised
and at Gilgal, a whisper away from Jericho, the world's
oldest city. Here the ritual of circumcision, neglected during the desert wanderings, was reinstated. Circumcision
knives hewn from stone have been among the archaeological finds. Circumcision was first imposed by Egyptians at
the slave markets to offer proof a man was a slave. It was
later adopted as proof that a Hebrew was a Son of the
Covenant.

Arrayed before them were the cities and encampments
of Amorites, Hittites and all the rest of the Canaanite
tribal units and their old nemeses, the Amalekites and the
Midianites. Beyond the mountains along the Via Maris the
Sea People, known as the Philistines, grew in rival power.

Archaeological evidence tends to deny that the most
famous siege in history, at Jericho, ever took place. The
second battle at Ai, likewise, appears to be a lovely bit of
Old Testament mythology. What was absolutely certain
was that Canaan knew that Israel had crossed the Jordan.
The country held a complex variety of peoples without a
central authority. Joshua had the definite advantage of
being able to pick and choose his route of assault against a
fragmented enemy without danger of Egyptian interference;
as Egypt had lost control of the province. The initial phase
of the operation was a peaceful infiltration into the
unpopulated areas of the hills away from the cities.

The second stage was assault against the fortified
Canaanite cities. There seems to be little evidence of major
fighting after the battle at Aijalon, where God made the
sun stand still in the hills north of Jerusalem. Areas
around the major cities of Bethel, Shiloh and Shechem
were successfully infiltrated and settled by the tribes of
Ephraim, Manasseh and Benjamin.

It is generally held that the invasion and settlement of
Canaan came in waves of immigration rather than a single
extended campaign. With the central highlands in Israel's
hands, the way south was open. The next phase fell to the
powerful tribe of Judah in alliance with the smaller tribe of
Simeon. There are two schools of thought holding opposing points of view on whether or not Jerusalem was
captured and razed before the swing south. In any event,
Israel did not occupy the city. This became a pattern of the
conquest. The Hebrews were overrunning a vastly superi-

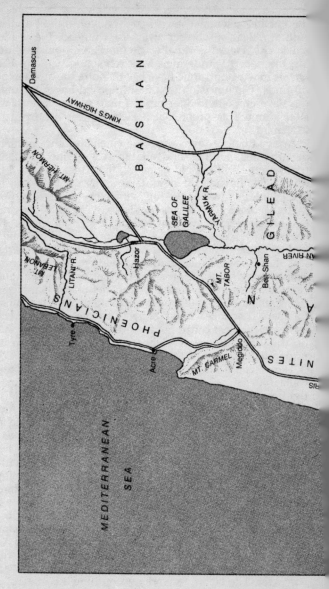

CANAAN

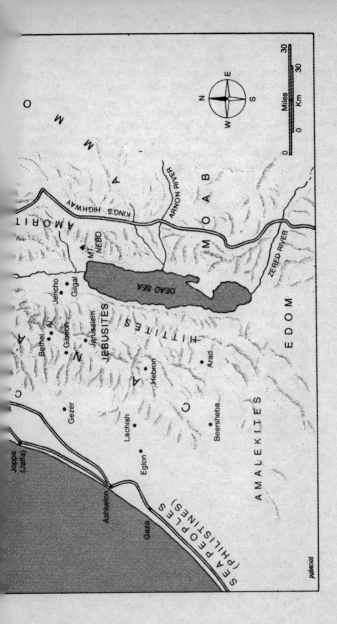

or civilization, they had only just come in out of the desert and sorely lacked the skills and technology to build and operate a sophisticated modern city. One city after another was simply leveled and abandoned.

The Jebusites, a tribe of veiled origin, either rebuilt or reoccupied Jerusalem and for several hundred years it was to remain an enclave in the midst of Israelite settlement. The city was of key geographical importance because it split the northern and southern tribes and slowed any cohesion toward nationalization.

The southern conquest rolled up Hebron, where Caleb and his inheritors settled around the tombs of the patriarchs. Meanwhile, at Mount Ebal the first altar raised to God since Abraham confirmed the presence of God in Canaan.

The final Joshuan stage took place in the north. At the end of this period the Israelites went to their various inheritances from the Litani River in the north some two hundred miles south to Beersheba. There was a distinct split between the northern and southern tribes, one that was to become bitterly permanent in later years.

Joshua of Ephraim installed the Ark within his own tribal bounds at Shiloh. All told, the Israelites lived in, among and about the Canaanites, who continued to operate the large cities and to expose the Israelites to the lures of paganism. Israel's strength of numbers and system of tribal unity made it impossible for the Canaanites to expel them so the two forces were in somewhat of a standoff.

Joshua served his time with great skill and remained a true disciple of Moses and a loyal servant to God.

IN THE TIME OF JUDGES

The post-Joshuan era could be best characterized as one of agonizing transition. For several generations the Israelites had been dominated by two extraordinary no-nonsense leaders, Moses and Joshua. During their wanderings and later on the battlefield the tribes developed a powerful sense of communal unity, family and interdependence. As far back as Egypt they had lived isolated from the rest of the population, were treated as outsiders and therefore insulated from alien philosophical pressures.

After the invasion of Canaan, as they dispersed to their separate territories, they were without an all-commanding leadership or a central authority for the first time in nearly a century. Thinned out, mostly in mountainous terrain, contact became sketchier and the glue that once bound them was loosened. The hill country of Canaan strangely suited them, for they had mastered the tricks of hillside and flash-flood farming in the desert and knew how to finesse every drop of available water. The Judean hills became a man-made masterpiece of giant steps hewn from immense boulders to retain rain and prevent soil slippage. Thousand-foot-deep terraces became a wonder of the ancient world, and many exist and are farmed to this day.

Near the cities the Israelites settled in intimate proximity to the older and more advanced Canaanite society. The Hebrews were totally agrarian in nature, picking up the skills, crafts and trades of the Canaanites slowly and undramatically. With the spartan demands of nomadic life behind them, the temptations offered by the highly developed Canaanites began to assault their beliefs and ultimately brought on a test of their faith.

Baal worship of the Canaanites mixed with and diluted their own religion so there became a continuous struggle with the lures of paganism. Baal penetrated their festivals, their altars, customs and sexual practices until it verged on consuming the Covenant itself. As the Hebrews were assimilated there was an outburst of demon worship, worship of the dead, witchcraft, orgies of food, drink and sex and ultimately human sacrifice reappeared.

The tribe of Simeon, the southernmost at the head of the Negev Desert, began to lose its identity as did Asher in the north by settlement among the Phoenicians. Even mighty Judah underwent a deep infusion of Canaanite blood.

Against this onslaught, the Levite priests formed a thin line of resistance and often kept a very lonely vigil. How was all this possible for the sons and daughters of the Covenant? Loss of central leadership played a primary role. For decades they had been sustained in the Sinai by a dual obsession for land and freedom.

Settlement in Canaan meant that the early goals had been achieved, which caused them to lose a great deal of their religious intensity; and they had left their sense of nationhood out in the desert. Now, settled within tribal pales, disconnected from close contact with each other, they became caught up in their own individual day-to-day problems without a unified goal.

A major factor in any pagan culture stemmed from the rites surrounding agriculture. The early Hebrew longings and aspirations were replaced by the pragmatism of planting and harvesting. The Canaanites offered a highly convenient and wide variety of idols to oversee the crop. There were gods of rain, grain, seed, grape, tree, wind, harvest. The inner erosion that was to come evolved from those kinds of conflicts man has always had within himself.

Externally the Israelites were never to know a day's peace. Their conquest had been only partial. Hostile cities and peoples remained all around them. With Egyptian rule of Canaan completely gone, anarchy reigned on the major highways so that no man was safe beyond the perimeters of his village. There were constant raids, brutal battles and total warfare of unparalleled viciousness. Universal massacre of men, women and children became the norm and the fate of the vanquished on both sides.

The Israelites warred against a revitalized Moab nation, which brutalized the tribes of Reuben and Benjamin. They warred against the Ammonites and against a Canaanite confederation in the north. They warred against the Amorites, who unseated the tribe of Dan from its territory. They warred against the Midianites, who introduced the new and terrifying dimension of camel cavalry. They warred against the Amalekites, always eager to join any alliance against them. They warred against a threat from Mesopotamia and they warred against the greatest menace of them all, the Philistines, the former Sea People.

To counter these threats, Israel had no standing army, no national authority, no capital, no single leader to rally around. Bound in a loose confederation, the tribes met each crisis with a quota of militia. These soldiers had to leave their fields and carry their own weapons and supplies into battle. As ordinary infantry they often had to stand up against the armor-plated chariots which could rip through their ranks like rocket-powered battering rams.

TRIBAL AREAS

Oftentimes one tribe or the other failed to answer an emergency and inner tribal conflicts broke into bloodshed. Brother fought against brother with no less fury than against the common enemy. At one point, retribution against the tribe of Benjamin nearly ended in its extermination.

In this repetitive cycle of war, sin and salvation there arose a series of mini-deliverers known as judges. Each judge in turn contended with one of Israel's enemies and was able to win a period of peace. The judges were an odd assortment. Some probably never existed except in legend, others may not have been Hebrew. Between them and their supporting cast of characters, they broke about every rule in the game. One accomplished his mission by an assassination based on trickery. Another side player, a lady named Yael, did the unpardonable by murdering a guest under the protection of her roof, breaking the ancient canon of sanctuary. One of the judges was the bastard son of a prostitute who ultimately committed human sacrifice of his only daughter and another was an out-and-out whoremonger and reprobate. The half-Hebrew, half-Canaanite son of Gideon murdered seventy of his brothers in an attempt to establish a monarchy.

The deep religious development under Moses was no longer the dominant factor of life. Religion, indeed, had been largely supplanted by the nuts and bolts of survival and by an inevitable route of political development. This political direction was pointed up by two of the most important judges. Deborah, in defeating a Canaanite coalition, and Gideon, in stopping the Midianites from scourging the fields at harvest time, had achieved national victories. They were able to field large forces in which many of the tribes were represented. Tribal unity began to emerge naturally as the best means of coping with the continued threats. The trend toward nationalism became irreversible. Gideon was offered a throne after his victory but refused it.

A unique and important sidelight of the period of the judges was the emergence of Deborah, history's first great woman, the preeminent woman in the Bible and both judge and prophetess of Israel. The Song of Deborah, attributed to her authorship, was the first truly feminist document. Women's liberation can honestly claim it was founded on the battlefields of ancient Canaan.

If a single man could summarize the times and personify the dilemma of Israel, Samson was that man. To understand the parables of Samson one must relate to the desperate situation confronting the tribe of Dan. Its territory placed Dan near the coast, bounded by hostile Philistines. At one point the tribe was forced to up and move north to the present-day boundaries of Lebanon.

Catching it from all sides, the longings and aspirations of the Danites required a Robin Hood, a savior in fact or in fiction. As the predecessor of Superman, Samson's feats of strength require only short recounting. He killed lions barehanded, moved mountains, took on a thousand of the enemy with the jawbone of an ass. But as a man he was totally unqualified to be a judge of Israel. Samson had a weakness for women, Philistine women. Although the Bible affords us a look at only three, if there was a Samson, there were many, many others, for he was a lecher of the first rank.

Backslider that he was, he fell to the pits for his sins. Bereft of his great might, blinded, betrayed, enslaved and ridiculed, Samson was still able to reach inside himself and ascend to an incredible height to gather the ultimate power of faith. Although he surely deserved his fate, he was able to win final redemption through his belief in God.

In bringing down the pagan temple barehanded, Samson allegorically spoke for all of Israel during the time of judges. He, like the children of Israel, had reverted to debauchery. The leaders of the people—and he was one —had behaved miserably. The awesome forces of Baal had given God a run for His money. In the final balance sheet, the Israelites had been infused with enough Mosaic sense of right and wrong to opt for God.

God seemed to understand that even the people bound to the Covenant with Him were only mortals. God displayed enormous patience, enormous forgiveness, enormous compassion, enormous understanding that man was errant and riddled with weaknesses. Man will sin so long as he exists. Man will exist so long as he has the power of redemption. With all that might have been wrong with them, the Israelites were completely married to an idea that would ultimately pull them through. Israel alone prevailed, survived and continued while every culture and society around her faded into a midnight never to emerge again.

THE RELUCTANT KINGMAKER

Yet another example of the "miracle birth" syndrome that repeats in the Bible befell Hannah. In gratitude, she gave the boy, Samuel, to serve the High Priest Eli at the sanctuary at Shiloh where the Ark rested.

By this time the Philistines had increased their dominance dramatically. Massed in five royal cities along the coast, the Philistine coalition held the monopoly on iron weaponry and possessed a massive chariot force. They sallied forth out of Gaza, Ashkelon and their other cities bent on consuming the territories of Benjamin and Ephraim. In desperation, Israel carried the Ark into battle to exhort some sort of divine assist. Instead, the Philistines defeated them ruinously and spirited the Ark off and set it before Dagon, their half-man, half-fish god. When the news of this reached Eli, he dropped dead.

The new High Priest Samuel proved a dogmatic and incorruptible fanatic. With Shiloh destroyed, he operated from his home in Ramah in his tribal pale of Benjamin but his influence crossed tribal boundaries. Even the aloof Judah fell under his sway.

With the sanctuary gone, the Philistines were able to impose vassalage in some Israelite territory with garrisons, governors and taxes, and all of Israel was threatened. There seemed no other option than establishment of a monarchy which could unite all the tribes. Gathering at Ramah, the elders demanded that Samuel anoint a king.

Samuel resisted passionately, seeing a monarchy as a corruption of Hebrew life. He warned of standing armies, bureaucrats, tax burdens and servitude. Yet there were other reasons, personal and institutional, why Samuel deplored the coming of the kings.

From the time Moses and Aaron established the priesthood in the Sinai, its foundation had been based on its claim to unique powers. As custodian of human morality, the institution set itself up as the exclusive intermediary between man and God. Since then all religions have endowed their priesthoods with privilege and have placed them in an exalted position above and beyond the normal society. The people have been willing to pay this price because, as individuals, they have been unable or unwilling to manage their own moral affairs and needed a "big father" to instruct and command them as to what is proper and what is improper.

Whether the rights of priests are man-given or God-given is a subject for debate. The priesthood has always presumed its divine status and its direct link to God. In pursuit of its "priestly powers" it has taken for itself whatever the traffic will bear.

A monarchy comes in direct conflict with the priesthood. A king, any king, automatically is the defender of the faith. He can sustain his rule only so long as his own claim to divine power is upheld by the people and supported, however reluctantly, by the priesthood. Divine power, therefore, is always jointly claimed by both institutions, the monarchy and the religion. Without this assumption of divine rights, neither institution has a power base. It is a mystic power, supposedly from God, and the less ordinary people understand it, the easier the ride for king and priest. Samuel did not want to put another institution into the divinity business to infringe, dilute or share the all-powerful status of the priesthood.

It would be only a matter of time until the question of whose rights were more divine would be contested. Once the king wins out, the priest becomes his servant. Once an evil king is able to subvert his priesthood to his personal use, it becomes a corrupt priesthood. The church and state have operated with interdependence but, at the same time, at each other's throats in all places, during all times, in all religions.

Knowing a strong king would sublimate the priesthood, Samuel wanted to keep it out of the vortex of a power struggle. He admonished the elders and told them that only God could rule the people. The elders retorted that only a king could save them from the Philistines. Faced with the bread-and-butter pragmatism of the day, Samuel finally had to yield. The man who least wanted the monarchy was forced to initiate it.

Samuel became the last of the judges, the first of the prophets, the most influential character since Moses, possibly author of the Books of Judges, Ruth and parts of the Books of Samuel. When he set forth to find a king it was apparent that anyone he anointed was predestined to a collision course with him. This is the unfortunate fate that befell Saul.

THE MAD KING

"Tragic" is the word synonymous with every description of Saul. Bursts of psychopathic behavior have made him suspect of a range of insanities from paranoia to schizophrenia. In the beginning he was an ordinary farmer from the town of Gibeah in the tribe of Benjamin. He was large in stature and equally large in his religious zeal.

The Bible is divided against itself on how this ill-fated pair met, with versions written several hundred years apart. Since both stories leave Saul's anointment as king purely up to chance they can be discounted. Considering Samuel's position on the monarchy, the high priest wasn't about to crown some unknown.

Samuel wanted a fellow Benjaminite, someone he knew intimately and someone he felt he could control. Saul obviously had a track record as both a warrior and a leader. The tribe of Benjamin and the Philistines were constantly at war, and although nothing is specifically recorded, Saul must have gained a huge reputation in battle. His prowess was certainly known nationwide because he was called upon to deal with a situation with the Ammonites and for the first time in history an Israelite army had been collected from every tribe. As a farmer turned soldier, Saul followed in the tradition of Joshua and Gideon and was followed in that tradition by David.

Insofar as his reign is concerned, Saul seemed more like one of the judges, a military hero, than a king. Excavations in Gibeah show that Saul's capital was without royal pretensions and his personal citadel was one of modest simplicity.

With his son Jonathan as one of his commanders, he was able to forge a formidable army and system of ready reserves; he won some and lost some against the Philistines. Because Philistine chariots did not function well in the hill country, Saul was able to develop neutralizing tactics.

His major problems started and ended with Samuel. Organizing a campaign against the Philistines, Saul waited for the high priest to perform the traditional sacrifices before battle. When Samuel failed to show up, Saul simply could not delay the war and made the reasonable decision to perform the ritual himself. When Samuel did arrive days late he went into a rage that Saul had usurped his powers and laid the curse of God on the poor man. Of course the entire incident was Samuel's fault and one must deduce that he deliberately set Saul up in order to rebuke him publicly and show him who the boss was.

Saul became utterly confused. His son Jonathan carried the day against the Philistines but had unknowingly broken a religious fast before the battle. Although Jonathan was completely innocent of wrongdoing Saul was ready to kill him. We see here evidence of both his fanaticism and his mental disturbance. Jonathan escaped death by a thread at the hands of his own father.

Saul's twenty-year reign was one bloody war after another. After Saul had cleaned up the Transjordan kingdoms Samuel called for him to engage in a holy war against the Amalekites. In finally destroying their ancient nemesis, Saul showed a tinge of mercy by sparing some of the women and children and saving the best of their cattle for sacrifice. He also took the Amalekite king as his personal prize of war. In doing so he had compromised Samuel's edict of total destruction of the enemy. The old high priest demonstrated his displeasure by hacking the Amalekite king to pieces before Saul's eyes. Samuel then came down on Saul again, condemning him as unworthy of the crown and invoking God's wrath for a second time. The terrified king cringed at the prophet's feet, clutched his robe, wept and screamed for forgiveness. Virtually spitting on the cowering Saul, the old man stomped off to his home in Ramah never to see him again. With the curse of God ringing in Saul's ears for a second time, this man of deep religious fears had the seeds of madness firmly implanted in him.

As a final act of vindictiveness Samuel secretly anointed a new king. David, a shepherd of Bethlehem from the tribe of Judah, was a beautiful man. He possessed the soul of one of the greatest poets who ever lived, and physical charm and grace to match. The secret of his anointing had eyes and ears. From the outset Saul suspected David's role. As the pretender sat at the king's table, loved the king's daughter, commanded the king's troops and gained greater fame in battle...the king went slowly insane.

THE GREATEST LOVE-HATE STORY EVER TOLD

In a vale whose name has long been forgotten there came to pass the original one-on-one showdown. The forces of Saul and the forces of the Philistines were at a standstill, separated by a deep ravine. An attack by either side meant exposure on open and uphill ground and more casualties than could be absorbed. It was custom that such stalemates could be settled in single combat by a champion from each side. The Philistines had theirs, a human tank named Goliath. No doubt tales of his size have been exaggerated, but the man, his armor and his weapons scaled well over five hundred pounds. As he paraded before the Israelite lines, taunting them, he found no takers for the proverbial "forty days." And then a shepherd boy bringing food to his brothers on the battlefront happened on the scene.

Aside from raw courage, David had some other things going for him. The sheer bulk of Goliath was bound to limit his mobility. As mountain warriors, the Israelites had developed the guerrilla tactics to contend with heavier arms. Aside from swiftness afoot, David had the secret weapon of heritage. As a shepherd he had contended with wild animals to protect his father's flock. He and his fellow Israelites could be as deadly and accurate with the sling, the shepherd's weapon, as the enemy with spear and sword. The Israelite armies had included cadres of slingmen for centuries. David was as good as any. The shot he planted between Goliath's eyes was neither accident nor luck. Thus began the strange, awful, tragic relationship of the king and the man who would become king.

David fared well in Saul's court as a soul mate of the king and his family, as a commander, and he blossomed as a poet of unparalleled genius. Singing often at the feet of the tormented Saul, he soothed the king's troubled hours. What emanated from David's soul and harp became the most magnificent praise that man has ever been able to offer God. The psalms of David went beyond mere mortality, they were the hallelujah choruses that transcended space, matter and time. This man David was able to reach out in an exaltation that no man would be able to approach again.

As friends, no two men shared deeper love than David and Jonathan, the king's son. It was an infinite relationship between men of valor. As a soldier, David's renown grew with each battle.

There was never a valid reason to doubt David's loyalty to the king and the king's family. But Saul was starcrossed and his own love for David was soon invaded by the demons which eventually consumed him. As the acid in Saul's brain soured, his creeping suspicions flared into sudden fits of madness. Saul hurled his deadly warrior's spear at David point-blank but in the final instant he deliberately missed his startled victim. Even in the throes of mania he could not kill David but his love was filled with poison.

When the king's daughter, Michal, was coveted by David, Saul used the love as a ploy to get rid of his rival by demanding from David a hundred Philistine dead as her bridal price. David returned with two hundred foreskins of the enemy. Now David was Saul's son-in-law, held unbreakable bonds of friendship with Jonathan and was a warrior who had surpassed the king's fame. As Saul became more and more isolated in his paranoia, David's sweet music and soul-filled litanies no longer calmed his anguish. The years of war, the burden of the crown, real or imagined threat of David and, mostly, the

curses of Samuel all took their toll of a man who had only
sketchy balance to begin with. David inevitably became a
marked man.

With the help of Michal and Jonathan, David fled to
Samuel. Jonathan was not only unable to bring about a
reconciliation but Saul magnified his hatred of David by
ordering the execution of eighty-five priests suspected of
giving him sanctuary. This act, from a man of religious
conviction, surely proved the king's mind had become
unthreaded.

The shores of the Dead Sea and the area to its south
hold a labyrinth of caves secluded in near impassable cliffs
and mountains. For centuries this terrain had been a
sanctuary of fugitives and a base for outlaws. It was to
this place that David fled and gathered a renegade band
about him.

Saul gave pursuit with hordes of soldiers scouring the
caves. About halfway down the shoreline of the Dead Sea
there is the sudden oasis of Ein-Gedi, named after the
wild goats which water there to this day. But it was the
hunted, David, who caught the hunter, Saul, alone and
within the range of his sword. Despite Saul's hounding
hostility and death threats, David was unable to apply the
coup. He allowed the king to escape unharmed and in a
moment of clarity Saul realized it was he who was the
guilty party and condemned himself. Now Saul had an
additional factor of guilt to contend with.

David was soon to learn that his wife Michal had been
married off by Saul to someone else. Living on the run
and prowl, he had to feign insanity at one point to save
himself from certain execution. But his forces grew hard
and wily. His nephew Joab rose as a brilliant commander,
as a Joshua to a Moses. At last the encampment they had
created grew so large that it included wives and children.
Some sort of settlement out of Saul's reach became
imperative.

At this juncture David seemingly made a pact with the
devil. The Philistine King of Gath liked the situation of
rival forces splitting the Israelites. As pretender to the
throne of Israel, the Philistine reckoned, David could
function favorably as an ally and a thorn in Saul's side.
The King of Gath, believing David was willing to war on
· his own people because of his banishment, installed him

and his band in the outpost city of Ziklag. He gained the King of Gath's trust by beating off desert raiders and falsifying reports that he had gone into battle against fellow Israelites.

Saul's continued success against them caused the Philistines to form a five-city alliance and head for a showdown battle. The Philistine force moved north to challenge the Via Maris junction with David's band among their number. It will never be known whether David would have actually gone into battle against Saul, but the other kings were not as sure of David's loyalty as was the King of Gath and at the last moment he was excused from battle, much to his relief.

Israel deployed on the slopes of Mount Gilboa to neutralize the Philistine chariots. Saul sensed disaster. With blackness closing in on his mind, he broke his religious bond and sought out an illegal soothsayer. Deep night found him at Endor, in the foothills of Mount Tabor across the way from Gilboa. It was on this very ground that Deborah and Barak had defeated the Canaanites centuries earlier when a downpour bogged their chariots in the mud. In a dripping-wet candlelit cave, a snaggled-toothed witch wailed for a spirit from the beyond. And the voice of Samuel was heard. From out of the grave he performed the final vilification of the maddened Saul with a prediction of his demise and the fall of his army.

And so the battle went. Jonathan and two of his brothers were slain. Doomed from the very beginning by fates beyond his control, Saul's twenty-year nightmare came to an end as he plunged on his own sword.

When the news reached David he tore at his hair and his garments and writhed in an agony so profound that no man's sorrow was able to record such an awful depth again, in his lament, and how the mighty have fallen.

Days of Glory

❦

THE BEGINNINGS OF JERUSALEM

The first intimation that there was to be a Jerusalem dates from around three thousand years before Jesus and a thousand years before Abraham. Leavings of stone-age flints and arrowheads furnished proof that nomadic tribesmen were drawn to a lush, if sporadic, source of water to be known as the Gihon Spring. This is the fountainhead of Jerusalem and a constant factor in its history and development. The spring became the place of anointment of Israelite kings and the site of a major Christian miracle.

When the great floods receded, around 3000 B.C. an Amorite wave of immigration spread throughout Canaan from Mesopotamia. Jerusalem was one of their settlements. The name of the city appears to have originated from that of an Amorite god and evolved through transliterations to its accepted meaning, "City of Peace."

First written mention of Jerusalem appeared on Egyptian clay pottery known as the Execration Texts around 1850 B.C. It was the first known enemies' list, a hit list of unconquered Canaanite cities. Jerusalem, like most of Canaan, fell vassal to Egypt or to the dominating Mesopotamian power. Their garrisons, governors and tax collectors ran the ship in collaboration with local kings.

Abraham's wanderings took place around 1800 B.C. The Bible records two visits by him to Jerusalem. Abraham's confrontation with the Lord regarding the sacrifice of Isaac happened in a place called Moriah. History and legend have combined to place Mount Moriah squarely in Jerusalem.

A three-and-a-half-century gap preceded the next written evidence of Jerusalem. Around the turn of the last century archaeologists unearthed the site of the royal Egyptian archives at Tell el-Amarna and hit a windfall in the form of hundreds of cuneiform letters on clay tablets from Canaanite vassal kings to the Pharaoh.

Seven or eight of these el-Amarna letters were attributed to the King of Jerusalem, who decried the loss of the Egyptian garrison and of alliances which were out to get him. He went on to predict that woe would befall Pharaoh at the hands of his uncouth vassals. Dated around 1370 B.C., the letters coincided with the end of the Israelite period of slavery and the beginning of the Exodus.

When Israel entered Canaan the tribe of Benjamin was ceded the territory that included Jerusalem; the city was then under rule of a people known as Jebusites. Their history is veiled but one can assume they were a mixture of northern Semites and other Canaanite blood stocks. It is believed that Jerusalem fell to Joshua's forces around 1250 B.C. but they were unable to retain it, probably owing to their lack of urban sophistication. All during the time of Joshua and the judges the city was to remain a Jebusite enclave surrounded by Israelite settlement.

A GEOGRAPHIC ODDITY

The Judean mountains run north and south as a spine down the land of Israel, reaching heights of three thousand feet. On the western slope the mountains flow down to foothills and onto plains ending at the Mediterranean Sea some thirty miles from its peaks. On the eastern slope the drop is a more abrupt one, down to the Dead Sea, the lowest point on earth, only a dozen miles from the top of the ridges. This Jordan Rift runs parallel to the mountains along the eastern side for sixty miles from the Sea of Galilee to the Dead Sea. Across the Jordan River on the east bank are the sands of the great Arabian Desert. The

Judean mountains serve as a watershed, with the sea being one terminal and the Jordan River the other. The range stands as a barrier against the blistering winds off the desert.

Jerusalem sits midway on the north/south mountain axis, nestled down inside a set of higher peaks that allow water to run off down into the city. This water collects at the Gihon Spring and that was the place where Jerusalem was founded. Natural rainfall lines virtually stop in Jerusalem at the city's suburbs. Traveling toward the Dead Sea, the land turns dramatically from green to an arid brown in a few miles.

The Gihon Spring sits midway on a hill which runs up to a plateau called the Ophel or City Hill. This was the hub and heart of Jerusalem. The extended plateau of approximately a square mile is bounded on the west by the Valley of Hinnom (where the Canaanites sacrificed children) and on the east by the Valley of Kidron. These two extremely deep ravines come together like an arrowhead below the Gihon Spring with their slopes forming a natural defensive barrier. The original prehistoric settlement began around the Gihon Spring and ran down to the junction of the valleys, a matter of several hundred yards, at the Pool of Siloam.

The northern side of the Ophel is exposed and most invasions came from this direction. A trench line and earthworks were dug along this side, probably around the time of Abraham. Later they were replaced by the first of many defensive walls.

Sitting as it did, somewhat buried in remote mountains and occupying a mere dozen acres, Jerusalem seemed predestined for obscurity. Few if any great cities ever emerged which were not on a major body of water, a crossroads or terminal, along a trade route, or offered a special product. Jerusalem had none of these prerequisites. She was removed from both major trade routes, the King's Highway along the Jordan Rift and the Via Maris on the coast. Her hills contained neither gold nor valuable export and she had no outstanding commercial importance. Jerusalem remained rather inconspicuous for two centuries, surrounded by the tribe of Benjamin and near the border of the tribe of Judah.

The Israelites had found the tough Judean hills to their

liking. These were eminently defensible against the Philistine chariots. Those marvelous farmers and shepherds lined the deep ravines with incredible terraces which supported life for several hundred thousand people. Vines and olives. Sheep and goats. Honey and grain. Obviously the Israelites and the Jebusites inside Jerusalem reached an early detente. There is no record of discord or violence for two hundred years.

With all its geographic obscurity, it contained a geographic reality that greatly attracted David. As an alien enclave, Jerusalem was neutral in that it belonged to no single Israelite tribe. In distance it was dead-centered between the tribes of the north and south. It literally called out to become the missing link to unite Israel. But David had even more in mind than the capital of a nation. He envisioned it as the center of the earth, a unique and sacred place . . . the link between man and God.

THE CITY OF DAVID

The death of Saul at Gilboa predictably opened a bloody chapter of maneuvering for the united throne. There were four major players, two kings and their generals. On the one side, David and his nephew/general Joab. Not yet thirty years of age, David had run the gamut from shepherd to war hero to king's confidant to immortal poet to outlaw to commander of an enemy city. He and his band left their Philistine sanctuary and entered Hebron, seat of the mighty tribe of Judah, where he was elected king of the south. The Philistines believed that David was still in league with them.

On the other side Saul's youngest son, a weak character named Ish-Baal, had been proclaimed king of the northern tribes. His shaky throne was really the handiwork of Abner, uncle and general of the late King Saul. Their capital was set up on the east bank of the Jordan out of reach of the Philistines.

After two years of intermittent civil war Abner sensed he was riding a loser. By bedding down with one of the late Saul's concubines, Abner indicated his own ambitions.

Although Ish-Baal rebuked him for the act, Abner felt his man scarcely had the stomach for this game of kings and he made secret contact with David, offering to jump sides.

David, on the other hand, had plenty of guts for royal shenanigans and countered shrewdly. His acceptance of Abner's support was conditioned on the return of his first wife, Michal, who was Saul's daughter. The move not only appeased his vanity but strengthened his claim to the united throne. With her returned, Abner supported David's claim before the elders of the north, then traveled to Hebron to cement the alliance.

Joab correctly sensed that Abner was after his job as commander of David's forces. After the festivities Abner was lured back to Hebron's gates where Joab's dagger dispatched him from the scene permanently. Abner's sudden demise put David in the predicament of offending the northern tribes. The old general was buried with honors and a period of mourning was proclaimed during which David publicly vilified Joab. David did not, however, do anything so foolish as to remove his commander from his position.

Shortly thereafter the final obstacle was cleared when Ish-Baal was assassinated. The elders came to Hebron to make a covenant with David and anoint him king of all Israel. Moving rapidly to cement unity, David cast his eye toward Jerusalem.

The Bible gives us a very colorful account of the fall of Jerusalem to David. It is written that the blind, crippled and otherwise afflicted were put on the walls by the Jebusites either in mockery or superstition or somehow to psych David and his army. The city, it is said, fell by some sort of back-door entry.

In light of the hard facts, this tale seems scarcely likely. The Jebusites had lived in peace among tens of thousands of their neighbors for two hundred years. They had no hinterland of tribesmen to come to their defense. The Israelites undoubtedly had intimate daily contact inside the city and in the event of siege knew their water source was outside the walls. Finally, David's prowess and the size of his forces were just too much to contend with.

What most likely happened was that David knocked on the city gates, had a friendly feast with the Jebusite king, and advised him that his proprietorship of Jerusalem had been terminated. In support of this theory we know that the Jebusites continued to remain in Jerusalem because at a later time David purchased the ground which became the Temple Mount from one of them. There is no record of assault, massacre or expulsion. The Jebusites had obviously known how to perform the necessary administrative and mercantile services and were needed for the immediate future. The kind of compact made was entirely in keeping with David's diplomacy. One of his major strengths was his ability to bring many non-Israelites into his government.

If the Jebusites submitted quietly, the Philistines didn't. They took grave umbrage at what they felt was a double-cross by David. He was not only not their ally but as the head of a united Israel constituted a most serious threat. Two expeditions were launched against Jerusalem but the Judean hills were not the stuff of the coastal plains. The Philistines were out of their turf. After some initial penetration, their chariots were sitting ducks in the slim passes and ravines and became easy prey for the mountain warriors. Getting no farther than Bethlehem, their invasions collapsed.

The genius of the young king soon made itself apparent as he constructed the house of David on three indestructible pillars.

Control of the military under Joab combined with loyalty of the tribe of Judah as a personal army placed forces at his disposal hitherto unknown. His military vision, combined with a personal love of battle, brilliant generalship and comradery with fighting men, widened new horizons on what might be conquered in order to gain complete control of the region. In a very practical and astute maneuver to protect his flanks from coups and assassinations he installed a royal guard made up of foreign, gentile mercenaries with Philistines among them.

David's political pillar was centered upon giving his people a new capital on ground untainted by past tribal squabbles. He declared Jerusalem his personal city, David's City, a name it has borne ever since. This act secured the succession to the throne within his family.

The most important pillar was religious. By making the political and religious capital one and the same he assumed personal or royal guardianship over the religious life of the people. This was precisely what Samuel had feared. David established the institutions of court priest with Nathan and court prophet with Gad and was able to dominate his holy advisers.

David's greatest decision and one of the most important ever made for mankind was to bring the Ark to Jerusalem. The moment of its arrival was equaled only by Moses' giving the law in Sinai. The Ark had been bandied about since Sinai without a permanent home. When David brought it up to Jerusalem the national holiday saw people hurrying into their new capital followed by an outpouring of unabashed joy such as they had never known. Wild and exalted dancing has always been part of the Jewish religious experience. During that day and all that night cries of "Hallelujah" and tongue-clucking shrills of pure rapture intermingled with shouts and songs to the glory of the Almighty behind the jubilant wail of oriental flutes and the pulsating banging of drums. The celebration rose to a physical and spiritual frenzy that befitted their own climax of a thousand years of turmoil.

As the Levites inched up to the fortress of Zion, the people leapt and swirled by firelight around the most sacred of all objects. They danced like madmen, they fainted with joy, they wept with total abandonment.

And David the king was the most violently, hilariously crazed of them all. The Bible says David danced with all his might and he was the mightiest of Israel. The depth of this man's ability to reach inward and beseech God in ultimate measure was now matched by a physical explosion beyond that of any other man. On this night David was a wild man. He was in a trance, and he cried out to God of the glory that was wrought.

Among the beholders only his poor first wife, Michal, was infuriated. Torn from her second husband, she had been reduced to a cipher in David's harem for political easons. As he unleashed his delirious ecstasy the royal jewels hung out for all to behold. Michal vented her anger at such unkinglike behavior, as his titillating the handmaids. David didn't give a damn. He was not like other men, other kings, and alas, Michal was never to be loved by him again.

A proper temple to house the Ark was in order but Nathan, his most constant and intimate adviser, told him to let things stand, for there were other pressing priorities. He did, however, select the site, the threshing floor of a Jebusite farmer on a flat area just beyond the walls. For the balance of the forty years of his reign the Ark remained under a nomad's tent as it had in the Sinai, next to his palace.

From the center of the land purchased for the temple there protruded a large rock, the legendary location of Mount Moriah and Abraham's altar. This was destined to become the Holiest of Holies when the temple was built. As the centerpiece of Jerusalem, this awesome bit of stone was to become the most sacred place on earth.

Conversion of the people's loyalty from the tribe to the monarchy was never really accomplished by Saul. From the outset David was a king's king, able to conquer by charm and diplomacy as well as by the sword. Dispensing hard justice here and soft justice there, as the occasion required, he displayed a range from magnanimity to ruthlessness. The Gibeonites, traditional allies of Israel, had been treated shabbily by Saul and demanded retribution by David. Two of Saul's sons by his concubine and five grandsons were served up and slaughtered by the Gibeonites. It was a convenient way to eliminate the house of Saul from any claim to the throne. On the other hand, David cherished and protected the lone son of Jonathan.

Nothing succeeds more than a string of military victories and David provided a cornucopia of these. Organization of the country was so astute, the reserve system is the basis of a similar one used by today's Israel Defense Forces. In those glory days she could put many hundred thousand men on the field. Joab was peerless in his generalship and he struck without mercy at any shadow that crossed David's path. David's inner corps of fabled loyal men stemmed from those who had served with him as an outlaw and now included the foreign mercenaries and his personal guard of Philistines.

For generations the Philistines and Israelites had been like a pair of sluggers whacking away at one another viciously without a clear-cut decision. After Philistine failure in two attempts on Jerusalem, David's army wheeled down from the hills and captured their major stronghold of Gath. Israel was clearly on the rise while the Philistines had peaked and the initiative passed from one to the other. The Philistines were suddenly exhausted and squeezed back into an area approximating today's Gaza Strip, never to threaten Israel again. With this nightmare over and Jerusalem holding the Ark, David rode on a crest of a national popularity so that his more questionable behavior was looked upon benevolently by a people who wilted at his smile.

Israel spilled out of the hills onto the Plains of Sharon. They strung out along the coast and held the Via Maris clear up the Phoenician border to Tyre, where they made a lasting alliance with King Hiram. It was Hiram who provided the materials and know-how to build David's palace.

Inside Israel, the Canaanites were taken over completely, and outside, Edom and Moab were rolled up as vassal states. What was left of the Amalekites was finished forever.

Only the Ammonites on the east bank were cheeky enough to challenge David and they did this, unwisely, by humiliating David's ambassadors. The Ammonites had strong allies in the north, making Israel's conquest a bloody affair requiring several years. When David took the final stronghold and wore the crown of Ammon, his garrison was installed as overlords of Damascus and the Aram-Damascus region as well. For the moment no power, north or south, was strong enough to challenge David's Israel, which had carved an empire from the Euphrates to the Red Sea.

The Ammonite war provided the backdrop for David's infamous act of lust. From the vantage point of the roof of his royal chambers he looked upon a naked woman bathing and was overcome with desire. She was Bathsheba, wife of Uriah, a Hittite captain in his service, who was conveniently at the battlefront. Dispelling any notions of decency or restraint, he seduced her. Shortly thereafter, Bathsheba whispered in the king's ear that she was pregnant. Even David was not immune from such a scandal but the cover-up went the way of most cover-ups.

Uriah was called home from battle to unwittingly bed down with his wife in order to make it appear that he was the father instead of David. However, Uriah was one of those dedicated bricks who remained in the barracks in order not to break his warrior's code. By the oddity of not making love to his wife, he signed his own death warrant. When Uriah was returned to battle, the venerable Joab was ordered to see to it he got permanently dispatched in the line of duty.

David's sin was discovered and denounced by Nathan and the life of Uriah was repaid by the death of the child. Nonetheless, David's feelings toward Bathsheba were not frivolous. She became the favorite of his wives and their second child was Solomon.

The Jebusite city of Jerusalem has been characterized as a sun-baked, filthy pesthole. As Israel's national capital, religious center and hub of a small empire it underwent natural changes and expansion. Generally, it followed the lines of the Jebusite boundaries, running uphill on a triangular spur about a thousand feet in length and no wider than four hundred feet.

Jerusalem lacked any grandeur in the imperial sense in David's time. Royal trappings simply didn't enter his shepherd's mind. His own palace was an unassuming affair at the northern or upper end of the hill with the Ark and its covering tent nearby. A barracks was built to house the Philistine guard; there were other necessary buildings to carry on the function of government. Tomb sites, a royal prerogative within the city walls, were selected. Jerusalem was a working capital and not a showplace.

Because there was no original Hebrew architecture, they borrowed ideas from their Phoenician trading partners or the Egyptians, whose influence dominated the region. Houses were small, square, of native stone, functional and totally unspectacular, a characteristic of the area.

Defensive walls were enhanced, particularly on the vulnerable northern side. Jerusalem was a well-protected city, its safety further insured by a string of fortress outposts and walled towns on the hilly approaches. There have been numerous archaeological digs along the ridge of the original settlement, but most of David's city has completely disappeared. A 1980 dig appears to have located either David's or Solomon's palace.

By setting up a royal court with prophets, scribes and a central governing body, the Israelites now had records and archives. From this point onward much of the Old Testament is less fuzzy and in some places extremely accurate because of on-the-scene reportage.

Although physically Jerusalem was something less than spectacular, the forty years ascribed to David's reign remain unmatched by any other era. Until this day the spirit of David haunts and permeates the city. David the man not only dominated his times but made incredible inroads in Jewish life everywhere, without exception, for all times. Oddly, it was David the man who even overshadowed David the king in the final analysis. If his armies, his conquests and his unifying efforts followed orderly patterns, his personal life was a shambles and this, in turn, eventually threw his reign into chaos.

His first son, Amnon, an underhanded little scum, set off a spiral of tragedy. Lusting for his half sister Tamar, Amnon raped her through trickery, took her virginity and cast her out, bolting the door behind her. Tamar put ashes on her head in a display of grief, tore her garment and wept hysterically. Absalom, who was Tamar's full brother, took vengeance by murdering her attacker. Absalom's action seemed normal, even honorable. But it was a male society and the murder of a son was held far more important than the rape of a daughter. Absalom was forced to flee. David, who had been an outlaw, had now outlawed his own son unjustly.

For years David grieved over the affair until Joab convinced him to allow Absalom to return to Jerusalem. When he did come back David refused to receive him for another long period. When the two finally met, the damage was done. Absalom's abuse at the hand of his father formed an unhealed scar. He became the errant son, a wild one who took pleasure in public humiliation of his father.

David's early popularity unraveled as his tenure wore on, spurred by the unfortunate Jewish curse of family feuding. The tribe of Benjamin, for example, never totally forgave him for destroying the house of Saul. The elders of the northern tribes never completely adjusted to his central authority, which weakened their own, a particularly bitter pill for the ruler from the omnipotent rival tribe of Judah. Even David's own, the Judeans, harbored lasting resentment of his removal of the capital from Hebron to Jerusalem.

Absalom exploited this growing disenchantment and openly announced his succession, although the line of succession was far from clear cut. Absalom was a charmer in his own right and as he conspired he found lots of company. David, a doting father, seemed to have no end of patience and toleration until he was suddenly faced with a rebellion.

Forced to flee Jerusalem, David found loyal ground on the east bank and regrouped. Absalom tore into his father's palace and performed the ultimate debasement by having intercourse with ten of David's concubines, the symbolic act of destruction of an enemy.

The old king was too cagey to be dethroned. He had planted a competent spy in Absalom's ranks who passed back information of rebel plans. Later, the spy fed Absalom false information giving David time to organize the counterrebellion and to thwart Absalom's plans.

This is the first known planting of a spy in the high councils of the enemy to pass out incorrect intelligence or "disinformation." It is a technique used recently with great skill by the Soviet Union.

With it all, David carried the full cup of guilt over his treatment of Absalom, and when battle became inevitable the old king implored Joab to spare the boy. The showdown went disastrously for Absalom, who fled the battlefield on a mule and somehow got his long hair twisted around the branch of a tree, which left him dangling helplessly in the wind. Despite David's plea, Joab killed Absalom personally. Upon learning of Absalom's death,

David went into a fit of anguish, weeping out his immortal "My son, my son!"

Joab had to shake David out of his hysterics and berate him for mourning a traitor while his own loyal troops, who had saved him, went without his praise. For his latest murder Joab was removed from command. As his replacement later went forth to snuff out another rebellion, Joab assassinated him as well, put down the insurrection and was reinstated as head of the army.

The end of David's story is one of excess. More rebellion and an outsized harem, each woman plotting to be the mother of his successor . . . and senility. Toward the end, the aged monarch was given a young girl to serve him and give him warmth as he constantly complained of being cold. Anti-sex apologists are very quick to point out that David did not "know" her. David never slept with any woman he didn't make love to. He had simply become inoperative, not moral. As he faltered, yet another son, Adonijah, hailed himself as the new king.

Nathan, the court prophet and a major force in David's council, came full cycle. He had once roundly rebuked the king for his sordid affair with Bathsheba. Later he raised Solomon personally and fostered his succession to the throne. The prophet conspired with Bathsheba to have Adonijah's anointment annulled. Bathsheba, who had always been David's favorite, persuaded the tottering king to appoint their child, Solomon.

Unfortunately, the old general Joab, who had served for almost a half century, had lined up with Adonijah. In one of his last acts, David warned Solomon that Joab was dangerous.

Thus the pattern was established for royal intrigue, conspiracy, assassination, corruption, rebellion and maniacal blind ambition that would plague the monarchy and become standard operational hell in kings' courts everywhere.

David has been written of in superlatives as a man for all seasons like no other. He is firmly entrenched with Moses as one of the two most important figures of the Old Testament. The tributes declare he was able to reach higher and fall lower than any other human being. The catalogue of his glory is an endless string of adjectives:

heroic, brilliant, inspiring, romantic, courageous, handsome . . . in fact the very inventor of charisma.

Yet what was it that really made David different from all other people? I believe that two distinct minds operated within a single man. Had they operated in disharmony, David would have been a madman like Saul. But the ingredients within him were controlled and operated in harmony, creating an exquisite and unique person.

One side of him was smitten with royal ambition and all the drive, cunning and daring that go with that. His sexual appetite was apparently boundless to the point of consuming his own high sense of decency. His squashing of Edom and Moab were done with extreme cruelty. The deliberate handing over of Saul's heirs to a predestined lynching was an act of savagery. Add to this plain old oriental despotism. If this were the end of the list there would be a portrait of a seamy, dangerous character.

The human David, however, overcame David the ruler, as his conscience and his sense of duty stumbled over each other all his life. He was a sensitive and humble man able to prostrate himself before God in a manner that has never been duplicated. He was a writer of immortal dimension, a scholar who never ceased to study and learn, a devout practitioner and protector of the religion. He was a man capable of unmatched loyalty, even to his enemies. His devotion to Saul was epic. His toleration of Absalom was unparalleled. His love for Jonathan was so profound, it certainly infers a relationship open to speculation. He was able to take harsh words from Nathan with grace and understanding.

He was, all told, a king who gloried in being a king. Yet kingship may have been too brutal and gory for him. He operated in an age when annihilation of one's enemy was standard. Yet he spared the Philistine nation and the Jebusites from certain extinction. He reveled in personal combat because, as a king, he knew that success in battle was a necessary means to accomplish his objectives. There is no evidence he was bloodthirsty. On the contrary, mercy was ingrained in his soul. His final act of forgiveness was to Adonijah, who would have certainly had his head whacked off by another father.

David's story shows the dilemma of all leaders. Perhaps he didn't realize in the beginning what he would have to do in order to become and remain a king. The burden of the throne eventually sapped him as it generally does all kings and all presidents. His deeds were always there for him to ponder.

And ponder he did, as no man ever has.

In the fifty-first psalm we see him caught in a backlash of guilt. He knew he had sinned grievously and begged to be purged and redeemed. Unquestionably his powerful sense of right and wrong qualified and damned every evil deed he perpetrated. A part of his soul and spirit could not and did not tolerate what his lust and ambition had driven him to.

In the twenty-third psalm David soared to sublime heights, even for him, in an expression of faith in God that makes it stand alone both as a human expression and as one of the most magnificent poems ever written. Is it not obvious that a man capable of such intense humility and sensitivity had to continually question many of the acts it was necessary for him to perform in order to remain at the head of his nation?

Evil can be rationalized, even justified, if it stands in the path of burning ambition. David never did. He looked his own foul deeds squarely in the eye. With the courage of unvarnished introspection he saw clearly a portrait of an idealistic young shepherd gone awry. It surely explains the love-hate affair with his general, Joab, who served him unfalteringly for five decades. In the end, Joab came to represent his own blood-soaked right arm. In abhorring Joab, he had come to abhor himself.

It was David's concept that evil must be recognized and fought within one's own soul and conscience. He was the first and perhaps the most profound inner-man who ever lived. He knew that God offered no ready cure-alls for man's transgressions and that each man must suffer and pay for his own sins right here on earth. One cannot cop out by mumbling a prayer or lighting a candle. This is the great gift of David and the central canon of Judaism. One must continually judge one's own values, review one's own deeds. One cannot pass off one's sins to a surrogate. It is a terribly demanding ethic, a lonely place, only man, God, and his conscience with no outside help.

The spirit of David has remained the most powerful inspirational force of the Jewish people for almost three thousand years.

SOLOMON

When Solomon rode to the Gihon Spring on his father's mule to be anointed king, it was probably the first and last act of humility of his life. As the first prince born into royal succession, Solomon presented a radical departure from the roughhewn tradition of the farmer/warrior/leader. Aside from small elitist groups in the priesthood and maybe the military, the Hebrews had maintained an egalitarian society. Solomon changed all that, introducing a class system and superimposing a culture shock of grand elegance on a simple folk.

His first necessary act was to take dead aim at the clique which endangered his throne. Adonijah, his brother, who had laid earlier claim, to be reprieved by David, was the most obvious threat. Either stupidly or arrogantly, Adonijah asked for marriage to Abishag, the young lady who had kept old David warm in his declining days. The act of taking a former king's concubine had all sorts of undertones of an underhanded claimant to the throne. Solomon had him slain.

Next in line for disposal was Joab, who had definitely outlived his usefulness by supporting Adonijah. The old warrior must have been in his mid- or late seventies and should have known enough to retire from court politics gracefully. He didn't and when the die was cast Joab sought out sanctuary by rushing to the altar of God and seizing the bull's horns. It did him no good. He was assassinated by the dagger of his successor. Rather an inglorious end but certainly not without poetic justice for one who had committed an unknown number of assassi-

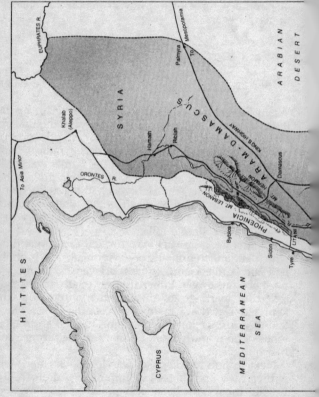

THE KINGDOMS OF DAVID AND SOLOMON

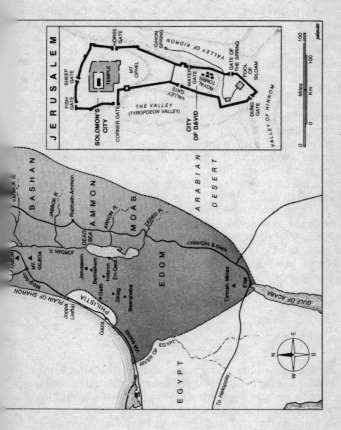

nations himself. Although history tends to treat him rudely, Joab was incredibly loyal to Israel's greatest king; he was the military architect of a united nation at its zenith and Israel's greatest general, whose battlefield accomplishments outshone even those of Joshua.

Solomon served notice that he was made of the stuff to rule. With the nasty bit of business out of the way, Solomon was able to hold the reins so firmly that his forty-year rule was free of further palace intrigue; no small accomplishment.

Solomon was scarcely in his twenties when he inherited a stabilized empire at peace with a minimum of internal and external jeopardy. This placed him in a unique situation never enjoyed by a previous leader. David, Saul and all those before them had the primary task of survival, were compelled to live by reaction, to constantly counter moves of enemy armies, thwart internal disorder or foray out to secure their borders.

Solomon had the advantage of being able to rule through creative action, in control of his and the nation's destiny. He had the unmatched will power, personal vainglory, shrewdness and ruthlessness to propel the nation in an undreamed-of direction that transformed it from a provincial backwater kingdom to one of international stature. Solomon, in a word, was the ultimate master craftsman in kingsmanship.

At the core of his many fabled abilities must have been an uncanny judgment of people. Behind his own unrevealing facade he was a genius at seeing a man's intentions. By separation of the devoted from the ambitious, the clean from the dirty, the dangerous from the innocent... like a calculator... he maneuvered and manipulated people into his scheme of things. No one kissed Solomon's hand with the intention of stabbing him in the back, for he was very ahead of the game. He had finessed his way through a childhood of treacherous court machinations, using cunning rather than force. A personal aloofness of royal birth put people on the defensive around him. His charm, quick wit and bottomless knowledge operated inside a steel-trap mind and had everyone awed, frightened or convinced.

Solomon was able to gain renown in the role of judge not only because of his education and inborn talents but because of a detachment from common people. The thousands of songs and proverbs attributed to Solomon were like rich, full, juicy, tart grapes of wisdom. The catalogue of wisdom found in Proverbs covered the entire behavioral skein of family and faith, of the commendable human traits of work, charity, honesty, fidelity, humility and the damnable traits of womanizing, drinking, cheating, thieving and the like.

Solomon lived outside the creed of decency he had mandated for others, for he invoked a divine vision of himself. As judge, king and author, he was a far cry from the advice he had written. The unimportance of wealth and self-indulgence he prescribed for the common man is the antithesis of a king who makes today's oil princes pale in the shadow of his despotism. Nonetheless, as a moral philosopher, his words have an unchanged value in today's world and give a people of three thousand years ago and their problems and desires a strangely contemporary look.

He understood that the use of warfare was risky, with limited and diminishing returns on a high investment, so he avoided it. His extended empire sat astride all the major trade routes, north and south from Egypt to Mesopotamia and east and west from the Arabian Desert to the sea. By building fortress cities on key junctions he was able to extract enormous tolls.

He was the first known great horse trader, bringing in herds from Anatolia, an area relative to modern Turkey, and selling them off to Egypt at a great profit. From Egypt he obtained the long-sought-after chariots.

The alliance his father had made with King Hiram of Tyre was greatly enhanced. A joint venture was undertaken to build a merchant fleet on the Gulf of Aqaba near today's Eilat which sent trading expeditions down the Red Sea. Nearby, at Timna, copper mines were developed which are still in operation today. The trade voyages took up to three years and reached down the Arabian Peninsula, East Africa and perhaps as far away as India. Many of

Solomon's trading colonies in remote places throughout
the Orient survived and were the bases of Jewish communities which have existed intact for thousands of years.

Solomon replaced military force with an ultimate use of
diplomacy to cement his foreign relations: he married one
and all. Princesses from foreign courts made up a harem
of infinite variety and number. The prize catch was an
Egyptian princess, a singular recognition of his great
stature. As her dowry, the city of Gezer, one of the last
Canaanite vassals of Egypt, was given to him. Some say
Solomon had seven hundred wives but dozens is more
likely, with a few hundred concubines thrown in for good
measure.

He was indulgent of his scores of foreign wives, allowing
them to bring their pagan altars, rituals and priests to
Jerusalem, which alarmed his own priesthood to no avail.
He figured it was better to keep the ladies happy, his
treaties and his legend in the outside world intact, than to
have them write letters of misery back home.

The most famous of Solomon's encounters with the
opposite sex was the journey of the Queen of Sheba to
Jerusalem. She is said to have traveled fifteen hundred
miles with a caravan filled with rare gifts. There is much
speculation of the location of Sheba. It is reasonable to
believe that Ethiopia was the place, for her visit has since
been an integral part of the folklore of that country.
Among the Emperor of Ethiopia's many titles, "Lion of
Judah" has passed down through the centuries. The legend claims that the Ethiopian dynasty was founded by a
son who came of the union of Solomon and Sheba. Black
Jews numbering tens of thousands called Falashas have
existed in northern Ethiopia since time immemorial and
claim their origin from the fabled visit.

The verses in Song of Songs describing the beauty of a
black woman seem firmly linked to her. The matter of
their bedding down seems academic, for the sealing of
treaties in the bedroom was standard Solomonic procedure.

His shrewdness as a trader and statesman was matched by an internal building binge of pharaonic dimensions. In order to implement his ambitious program he made tyrannic political decisions. The Canaanite population was thrown into bondage.

Solomon gerrymandered traditional tribal boundaries, slicing across them and combining them in the creation of twelve new national districts. This was calculated to impose his central authority over traditional tribal self-rule and to render the tribes politically impotent. Each district was directly supervised by a representative of the throne from Jerusalem and not by tribal elders.

Each district had to supply the royal establishment with a quota of food and supplies for one month each year. Solomon's requirements were ponderous. The harem, guard and other royal institutions were horrendously bloated and the king did not skimp when it came to himself. This taxation, amounting to nearly ten per cent of their output, was an enormous burden just to mantain the king's household. It was the fulfillment of Samuel's dire prophecies about the cost of monarchy.

The kicker in this system was Solomon exempting his own tribe of Judah from the twelve districts and their awesome taxation. The Judeans were the largest and most powerful and in the past had been instrumental in crushing revolts of the northern tribes. While his maneuver assured the loyalty of Judah, it set them up as enforcers over the other tribes.

Solomon was a megalomaniac who required immortality and he knew the shortest route to it was to build the Temple. The Temple was intended not only for the glory of God but for the glory of Solomon. The drive to achieve immortality was so insatiable, he was willing to risk alienation of most of the population. Surely he realized he had planted seeds of discontent by exempting Judah from taxation. Surely he knew that after his own reign the chances of continuing a united Israel had been greatly reduced. It did not matter. What mattered was that Solomon have his name eternally linked to the Temple.

The royal cities of Megiddo, Hazor, Gezer and the others held reserve forces of chariots and huge armories, intended not only to guard the trade routes and protect the approaches to Jerusalem but to control the country internally. Solomon had the nation in an iron grip: a slave force of Canaanites and an obscene tax demand laid on eleven of the twelve tribes. In the fourth year of his reign he went forward with building the Temple.

The know-how and exotic materials came from the Phoenicians, who were paid mainly with agricultural produce, further indebting his overtaxed citizens. He eventually went so deeply into the hole that he had to cede Hiram of Tyre a strip of territory containing twenty-odd towns.

Under Solomon Jerusalem changed incredibly. There was a labor force of thousands in and about, all sorts of wealth of kinds never seen before. Splendiferous buildings transformed Jerusalem into a cosmopolitan center filled with foreigners and their pagan shrines, priests, courtiers, scholars and the military. It doubled in size, spilling up the original hill, encompassed the Ophel and Moriah, which became the Temple Mount.

He was obviously enamored of things foreign and constantly mirrored foreign influence. His palace was a magnificent ramble of great courts, terraces, special apartments for important and favorite wives, a mini-palace for his Egyptian wife, servants' quarters, stores, offices, banquet halls, apartments for officials and guard buildings. The House of the Forest of Lebanon, the public hall for festive gatherings, probably led to a Judgment Hall with its great gold and ivory throne. All told, this complex took thirteen years to complete, nearly twice as long as the construction of the Temple itself.

THE TEMPLE

The will of Solomon came to pass mightily. A hundred and fifty thousand Canaanite slaves augmented by thirty thousand Israelites in forced labor bent their backs under the eyes of three thousand supervisors. They cut the cedars of Lebanon and quarried the Judean stone and transported it torturously up to Jerusalem to the threshing floor on Mount Moriah adjacent to the royal palace. Designed and engineered by the Phoenicians and executed

1 detail by their master artisans and masons, it rose over
period of seven and a half years. It followed a basic
pattern of earlier pagan sanctuaries unearthed in the region.
Mount Moriah had to be topped, leveled and recontoured
to hold the massive plateau and plaza.

A three-story outer wall, rectangular in shape, encompassed several acres of ground. This contained the chambers of the priests and a great deal of priestly paraphernalia and, perhaps, some of the national treasury.

Within this wall two great open-air courtyards, one for
women and one for men, served as the national assembly
grounds. This lofty expanse of space was the general area
of worship for the masses. The Temple was not a general
house of prayer like a synagogue, but a home for the Ark,
an altar on which to render sacrifices and a royal chapel.
The open courts were surrounded by a double row of
cedar pillars, ornately carved, with paneled walls and
floors of cypress, cedar and olive wood.

The Temple itself stood at one end of the courtyard, its
outer walls a hundred and sixty feet in length and half as
wide. This building was accessible only to the priestly
Levites and Cohens and royalty. Its interior contained
three rooms or halls diminishing in size like smaller boxes
placed inside larger ones.

The outer walls of the Temple included storage rooms
housing a treasury of vessels, priestly robes, spices of
incense, pure oil and other implements of worship and a
trove of riches from conquests, taxes and tributes.

The outer hall of the Temple was known as the Court of
the Priests and held the mighty four-horned bronze altar
where the wealthy offered bulls, goats and sheep for
burnt offerings and the poor brought doves and grain.
This was the central prayer room of the priests. The hall
had ten ornate basins on wheels presumably for cleansing
rituals. A mysterious object called "The Brazen Sea," a
vessel capable of holding thousands of gallons of water,
was borne on the backs of a dozen bronze bulls. Two
free-standing pillars, overlaid with bronze, gifts of Hiram,

called Jachin and Boaz, stood guard before the inner-
sanctum rooms.

A porch made of cedar and gold holding an incense
altar stood before Devir, the inner room, the Holiest of
Holies. This final room, square and dark, was built over
the rock of Abraham's altar. Here rested the Ark of the
Covenant, the staff of Moses, and a jar of manna. The Ark
was guarded by a pair of fifteen-foot gold-inlaid angels.
This place was considered so sacred it was entered only
once a year by the high priest on the Day of Atonement.

The trappings of the Temple, a choir of ornate objects,
matched the elegance of the structure itself. Copper from
the mines of Timna, silver from David's conquests, an
inordinate amount of gold, carvings of cherubim, sphinxes,
lions, snakes and winged figures. A vast and precious
display of lamps, basins, braziers, incense holders, cups
and candlesticks all magnificently carved and gold-overlaid
symbols of earth, fire, heaven and rites that walked a
borderline between the pagan and the monotheistic.

The consecration of the Temple was done in classical
Solomonic splendor. A weeklong national holiday saw a
great ingathering of elders, tribal heads, notables and
ordinary people from Dan to Beersheba. Twenty-two thousand oxen and a hundred and twenty thousand sheep
were said to be offered in sacrifice. Zadok was named
high priest of the Temple, a post that was to remain in his
family for centuries. Solomon did not carry on as his
father had done when the Ark was taken from its tent and
moved into the Holiest of Holies, for he was a controlled
man. He donned priestly garments, intoned the prayers
properly, firm in the knowledge that he had kept his
rendezvous with immortality. Thenceforth the Temple became the nation's heart, an academy of debate and
discussion, a seat of scholarly endeavor, a center of religious instruction and decision, as well as the national
treasury.

The three main holidays became occasions of national
pilgrimage. To the sound of flute, lyre and tambour and
cymbal tens of thousands of chanting Israelites poured up
the Judean hills into the Fortress of Zion, up the broad
steps to the Temple Mount. They filled the courtyard with
sacrifices of animals and food, they intoned the ancient
prayers, all decked out in ritual attire and bearing symbol-

fruits and grains. These glorious events were based on
agan agricultural feasts: the spring planting after the
ains, the first fruits and the harvest. The Hebrews at-
ched a Mosaic connotation to each holiday and these
ecame the Passover, in celebration of the sparing of the
ews in Egypt when the angel passed over their homes,
havuoth, celebrating the giving of the law, and Succoth,
n memory of the bitter ordeal of living in the desert.

The consecration of the Temple was, in fact, the conse-
ration of the nation and of the religion. It was the last of
hree great events in ancient Jewish history along with
giving the law and bringing the Ark to Jerusalem.

Glory days always flee too soon. Solomon's forty years
were done. The man was extravagant beyond the nation's
means, an unmatched hedonist, a man with an ego factor
that defies normal definition, an oriental despot. He did
little that was motivated by noble thought or compassion.
He set personal vanity over national unity, for no sooner
had his bones gone cold than the kingdom was split
forever. He did all this to link his name to a building
erected on the backs of slaves. Solomon's Temple did not
endure. Not a single stone from it has ever been found.

Yet what if there had been no Solomon and no Temple?
The Jews, predestined to eternal wandering and suffering,
needed to recall their ancient glory as their heartstone of
strength in the struggle to survive. Had they not been
able to focus on this as the centerpiece of their longings,
they might have faded into dusts of history during their
exile. It was the drive to return to Jerusalem, to rebuild
the Temple, that kept them going as a people. Had the
Jews faded and disappeared there would have been no
Jesus, no Christianity, no Islam.

Any balance sheet must look upon Solomon as an
incredible man whose singular will magnified, glorified
and threw open to the world the notion of one God. The
pages of history afford us no similar examples of back-to-
back leaders of the magnitude and historic importance of

David and Solomon. Under Solomon Jerusalem became the center of the earth for the first time. Many times after in its tragic history it was almost eclipsed through decay and the neglect of others. Yet today, nearly three thousand years after the Temple, this different mountain city with little visible means of proper support other than the soul of a people remains the center of the earth.

Division, Decline and Dispersion

There was no way that a lesser man than Solomon could have kept the kingdom united. His eldest son and successor, Rehoboam, whose mother was an Ammonite princess, was certainly a lesser man than his father.

Solomon's discrimination against the northern tribes had wrought havoc on them. Rehoboam immediately rejected a plea of the northern elders for equity and this brought on the split. His poor judgment, lack of political acumen and cruel and arrogant nature ultimately led to a half century of fratricidal civil war. The once powerful nation forged by Saul, David and Solomon would be in some sort of disarray forever after.

In the year 928 B.C. the house of David became a mini-kingdom consisting of the tribes of Judah, Benjamin and Simeon. Though the new kingdom of Judea had Jerusalem, the economic and military consequences of the split were disastrous. Judea possessed the less fertile land, it lost the strangle hold on the trade routes, it lost many of the foreign connections politically, as well as their artisans and craftsmen, it lost the vital city of Jericho among others, it lost its outlet to the Red Sea and the Timna copper mines, and its cultural establishment was thrown into chaos. Judean military power was decimated, exposing her to foreign invasion.

The war drums, which had been dormant for a century, heated up at both ends of the Fertile Crescent. Egypt, which dared not attack the united kingdom under Solomon, was now in the hands of a Libyan pharaoh who promptly overran Judea. Destruction of Jerusalem was headed off by emptying the Temple treasury to buy off the enemy. Yet, with all the calamities that befell them in this period, Judea was able to retain a certain political stability through an unbroken succession to the throne by the house of David. Central to the matter was Jerusalem, which emerged as the heartstone of the Jewish people both north and south.

In the north, the nine remaining tribes established a new kingdom of Israel. Theirs was a better land, with a number of fertile valleys about the Galilee and in the Transjordan area, and with access to the sea. Israel's proximity to foreign nations and her trade capabilities skimmed off the flow of material wealth that had once gone to Jerusalem. However, at the same time this proximity exposed Israel to alien pressures, both religious and military. The first threats came from the rising Syrians, whose empire of Aram-Damascus was directly to Israel's north. Politically, Israel had a terrible time stabilizing herself. The way to the throne was hacked out in bloody coups by a parade of generals turned king.

With the Temple gone, religious life in the north was heavily assaulted by pagan cults. Jeroboam, who had successfully carried out the split, was named the first King of Israel. He established two shrines at either end of the kingdom, at Dan and Bethel, both crowned with golden calves. The Levites were removed from the priesthood and Canaanite festivals were reintroduced.

During Solomon's reign Jerusalem had been thrown open to all sorts of pagan cults to mollify his foreign wives and sport the sophistication of an international city. A multitude of idolatrous shrines and altars lingered on until Asa, Rehoboam's grandson, commenced his forty-year reign with a fit of reforming and commanded a return to the exclusive worship of God. Starting in his own household, Asa removed a hideous idol belonging to his mother, took it to the Valley of Kidron and burned it, then cleaned up the idolatrous sanctuaries within and outside of the city. The treasury of the Temple was restocked from its Egyptian looting. Asa's purge made the Temple the focal point of the religion again and tempted many northerners to return to its altar.

Israel defeated Judea on the battlefield, rolling her armies up to the very gates of Jerusalem. Desperate to save his kingdom, Asa dug into the Temple's cache of wealth and bribed the Syrian King of Aram-Damascus into an alliance. This marked the first time that one faction of Hebrews used a foreign ally against their own brethren.

During Asa's reign, 908–867 B.C., in Judea, an extremely strong and able general gained the throne of Israel. Omri, "the David of the North," established the first dynasty and quelled the internal havoc and cutthroat competition for the throne. He made close ties with the Phoenicians which were sealed by the marriage of his son Ahab to the daughter of the Phoenician monarch. Omri developed a new capital in Ephraim, the dominant northern tribe, on a hilltop overlooking a lush valley. The city was named Samaria and as a rival to Jerusalem it was richer, more beautiful and strongly fortified.

But Jerusalem was yet the "City of David" and still commanded all the sentiment that went along with that. Despite Samaria's prosperity and stature it never gained equal footing with Jerusalem in the hearts of the people.

While Judea progressed philosophically, the northern kingdom continued to jerk and twist convulsively. The king's Phoenician princess, a nasty lady named Jezebel, had become Queen of Israel and was bent on enforcing Baal worship which shaped up a monumental battle between good and evil.

OF PROPHETS AND QUEENS

Although the Prophet Elijah had little to do with the development of Jerusalem directly, no story of the Jewish people can be writ without him. Elijah sounded the trumpet for the coming of Christianity and is believed by Christians to have been reincarnated as John the Baptist. His prophecy of the coming of a messiah is held by

THE DUAL KINGDOMS OF ISRAEL AND JUDEA

Christians to have been fulfilled by the birth of Jesus. Elijah's miracles and those of his disciple Elisha were forerunners of those attributed to Jesus: raising the dead, filling the empty plates, healing the leper and constantly being convoyed by angels.

In Jewish life, Elijah commands a position to this day. A chair is set aside for him at every circumcision and a cup is on the table for him at every Passover seder. Tradition has it that when Elijah drinks from the cup the messiah will descend to earth. Elijah was a spiritual giant obsessed with a single idea: that the people could not march to the tune of two almighties and had to choose between Baal and God. A hell-fire, no-nonsense missionary, he proved an uncompromising zealot against indecent wealth and high-placed despotism. Elijah stood with the people as their champion and defender. He was endowed by God, it is said, to perform all sorts of miracles and, in bringing down paganism in the northern kingdom, he left us with one of the wildest episodes in the Bible.

Ahab, a rather decent chap, who sat on the throne of Israel in Samaria, copied Solomon in many ways. He brought outside wealth into the nation through acutely honed political alliances while his key connection was with the Phoenicians. This was cemented by his marriage to a Phoenician, thereby reaping enormous commercial benefits. Politically, the alliance did much to reduce the Syrian threat of Aram-Damascus. Also like Solomon, Ahab was tolerant of pagan cultism, namely the Baal worship practiced by his wife Jezebel, although Ahab was a devout Jew. However, the Baal worship of Jezebel's native Tyre had elements that utterly degraded the Hebrew God. The priests of Baal indulged in revolting public displays of sadism and masochism, there was sanctification of "holy" prostitution and orgies and some of their rites included the sacrifice of children.

The prophets of Israel objected mightily to the spread of Baal; their brotherhood was strong and had the support and protection of most of the people. As the war between Jezebel and the prophets warmed up, she ordered that the prophets be killed. Forewarned, the prophets were able to disappear into the Judean landscape.

It was during this period that Elijah, a hoary old holy man from Gilead, emerged. Divining God's messages,

Elijah traveled the road to Samaria to warn King Ahab that a drought would soon consume the land as this was the price to be paid for continued Baal worship. Having said this, Elijah then fled, performed a rash of miracles, and sure enough, a devastating drought brought Israel to its knees. Returning again to Samaria, Elijah challenged all the priests of Baal to a showdown on Mount Carmel. In the confrontation that followed Elijah won a mythical contest against eight hundred and fifty pagan priests with the direct intercession of God. Then he had the Baal priests slain to a man.

Obviously this didn't sit well with Jezebel and Elijah fled for a second time, this journey strictly out of Moses, into the wilderness. All along he was provided with food and drink by escorting angels. At the foot of Mount Sinai where Moses had received or written the Covenant, God heralded his appearance in a manner befitting himself . . . by a series of violent upheavals of fire, storm and earthquake. The Lord's voice spoke to Elijah and wrote the script for the prophet to return north and finish off the villains. The Mosaic parallels abound throughout the story of Elijah, including a future parting of the waters. On his return to Israel, Elijah was joined by Elisha, who had been designated as his disciple and heir. A series of bloody prophecies against the enemy were fulfilled. When his work was done the old prophet was spirited off to heaven without the formality of having to die, a distinction shared only by Enoch.

Today Elijah awaits the worthy at the crossroads of paradise where he is a sort of official greeter for God and, when not welcoming the righteous, spends his time weaving garlands for the Lord out of prayers of the pious.

Elisha, a softer-spoken, gentler man, concluded the task of ridding the land of Baal. He secretly anointed a new king, inspired a revolution and eventually brought the house of Omri down. Jezebel met her just deserts, being hurled from the palace window to be devoured alive by wild dogs in fulfillment of a prophecy made by Elijah. What followed was a purge of Baal, its priests and followers that constituted the bloodiest series of acts initiated in the northern kingdom.

In Judea, 842 B.C., the throne was seized by Queen Athalia when her son died. She was the daughter of

Jezebel and a chip off the old block in name and in spirit. Her first move was to order all members of her husband's family put to death to eliminate any threat from the house of David, and she nearly succeeded. One lone member, Joash, escaped and was hidden and raised by Jehoiada, high priest of the Temple.

A Phoenician like her mother, Athalia reintroduced Baal worship to Jerusalem. She was astute enough not to tamper with the Temple and to allow the religions to coexist. Her paganism aside, Athalia shored up the commercial and cultural life of the city and once again it simmered with foreign flavor. Ultimately she went down in a coup led by the high priest, who restored the house of David to the throne. Thus the first century of the divided kingdoms closed with paganism being routed at both ends of the land.

THE FALL OF SAMARIA

The revolution against the house of Omri, around 875 B.C., was inspired by the prophets. The carnage that followed in purging Baal from Israel drained the nation of its blood and stamina. She fell easy prey to an Assyrian invasion, submitted timidly and watched her king grovel at the feet of the conqueror.

Next the Syrians of Aram-Damascus invaded and ravaged the land in a most terrible orgy of destruction. The starvation that followed the Syrian devastation was so great that cannibalism bcame a way of life. When the Syrians finished their handiwork all that remained of the kingdom of Israel was a few miles around the capital of Samaria. Assyria and Aram-Damascus continued to suck the meatless bones of the crippled vassal state until a miraculous turn of events allowed them the time and space to crawl to their feet and rebuild. Assyria was suddenly in a brutal conflict with a rebellious Syria, and in the ensuing war the Syrians were permanently cleaved. Assyria had put down the rising at terrible cost and limped off into a period of quiescence to regroup.

Israel used this time to gather herself up and filled the

power vacuum in the region, regaining most of her territory from the decimated Syrians. Israel not only turned back an invasion from Judea but ended the campaign in Jerusalem and in time-honored fashion looted the Temple. The era of peace that followed found Judea completely under Israel's domination.

However, the social conditions of Israel were so deplorable that her inner erosion spread like a cancer. The poor of Israel were dirt-poor, simplistic peasants impoverished by obscene landlordism, taxation and a raft of ills and privations. The classes were inalterably split and the fabric of national life was shredded. The cities of Israel had become imitations of the great centers of Babylon and Nineveh and Egypt, filled with perfumed and bejeweled ladies, haughtily attired in silk and lace, surrounded and pampered by slaves and handmaids. Wealth garnered by a corrupt clergy, businessmen, the military and politicians was flaunted in inlaid and overlaid mini-palaces, private parks and stables, while the poor lived in utter squalor as social injustice raged.

AMOS

Amos was a shepherd from a little town in Judea who first traveled to the northern kingdom to peddle his wool at festival times. His juices boiled over at the treatment of the poor. Overcoming a speech impediment, he traveled throughout Israel railing against the despotism. Amos contended that people who truly believed in God could not sustain such a distressed society.

He represented a dramatic new element in Hebrew thought in that he saw God as a social reformer. God, he contended, demanded justice for all people. He saw formal Temple attendance as a sham unless the practitioner practiced humanity in his daily life. Israel's society had become so decadent that its house was bound to fall. In abandoning decency toward its fellowman it had abandoned a God who demanded decency.

The true temples and altars to God exist within man's

mind, not in the walls of a stone and wooden edifice. This was the faith of David, that man was accountable for his own deeds. Man, Amos said, owns the power of decision and must not follow blindly. Man must be responsible for his own actions, make just decisions and practice virtue because that is what God demands of him.

The parables of Amos are chillingly contemporary. He attacked corruption in high places, protested the failure of leadership, demanded human dignity as a basic element for man's survival. He deplored the lack of a national conscience and national purpose.

Amos' rebuke of the luxuries, hypocrisy and aping of foreigners brought him into conflict with the establishment, both north and south. It is not clear if he was murdered but he was silenced. His message did not die with him. Amos founded another tradition that insured his immortality in that he wrote his teachings down to be passed along for all generations, thus beginning the doctrine of written prophecy.

HOSEA

While Amos saw God as demanding justice, the prophet Hosea saw God as merciful and loving. The details of Hosea's birth are unknown but he is believed to have been from the northern tribe of Issachar.

The man's personal life was molded by a tragedy which not only brought him great suffering but gave him a deep range of compassion and humility. After rearing three children in their marriage, Hosea's wife left him for another man and bore two children afterward. Years later she appeared on the block of a slave market. Hosea forgave her, purchased her back and brought her to live again in his home. This ordeal endowed him with the vision of a parallel to God's love and patience for Israel. Mercy, he preached, must be part of the religious and social ethic of man.

Although forgiveness was central to his theme, he warned the wealthy that if they did not understand their faith and pursue God meaningfully the alternative would be the fall of the nation and the exile of her people. "For they have sown the wind, and they shall reap the whirlwind."

It is held that Hosea died in the ruins of Samaria when the city fell in fulfillment of his prophecy.

It was clear that these prophets were not heeded seriously by the powers that were. During one stretch of fourteen years Israel saw six kings, four of whom were murdered. The shadow of death fell over Israel as Assyria girded to conquer its immediate world. The city of Samaria defended herself courageously against a foregone conclusion. As Assyrian battering rams finally broke down the walls after a three-year siege, thousands of Hebrews were deported and their land given over for settlement by foreigners from throughout their empire. This followed the Assyrian policy of removing the leadership of a defeated people to prevent future rebellion. Those Israelites who did not flee to Judea were assimilated by the newcomers. The two-century debacle of the kingdom of Israel was done. What can be written on her tombstone? She was a greedy little nation, corrupt and cruel to her own people. Her rolls were filled with blood-soaked men consumed with royal ambition who destroyed her vitality and purpose. She was a nation which dangerously flirted with a paganism that was supported from the throne. She was a nation which continually refused to recognize her evil ways or to correct them.

If anything justified the kingdom of Israel's short existence it was her prophets: Elijah and Elisha in their classic struggle of good against evil and Amos and Hosea for adding significant dimensions to human morality and for having the sense to write them down. These were the forerunners of democratic thought, the first to espouse love, justice and dignity as God-given rights. Indeed, they saw human rights as an undeniable part of God's system of universal moral order. In their writings, perhaps, the reason for the nation's existence was made worth while.

THE KINGDOM OF JUDEA

The high priest Jehoiada had hidden and raised Joash, the last prince of the house of David, from the purge of Queen Athalia, the pagan daughter of Jezebel. In the year 837 B.C. Jehoiada led a successful Temple revolt and placed young Joash on the throne.

So long as the old high priest remained alive, Joash faithfully tended the religion. Baal sanctuaries were dismantled and a desperately needed restoration of the Temple was commenced. In the past monies for repairs had been artfully skimmed off by crooked priests. The king put his own people in the countinghouse, allowing the work to go forward.

When Jehoiada died, Joash reverted to a paganism of the revolting sort practiced in Tyre. This prompted another Temple revolt which the palace put down severely. When Joash paid off a second Syrian invasion out of Temple funds, a conspiracy against him led to his assassination.

Judea finally came into its own with stability, trade, a strong military and regional eminence under the fruitful reign of Uzziah, 783–742 B.C. Much of it was possible because of the peace policy of neighboring Israel.

The Judeans under Uzziah subjugated the Philistines, exacted tribute from Ammon, defeated the Arabs in the desert and reopened the trade routes to the Red Sea. The combined kingdoms knew an instant of glory together, holding territory and vassal states, comparable to that during the heyday of King David.

Uzziah's contributions to the nation's welfare and the city of Jerusalem compared favorably to Solomon's without the backbreaking taxation. While Amos and Hosea ranted against the exploitation of the poor in Israel, Judea managed to spread her wealth more evenly and justly. With the new flow of commerce, wealth found its way into Jerusalem where Uzziah embarked on an enormous building program. Using the latest known military engineering methods, he beefed up the defense walls and installed archery towers and advanced stone-throwing engines. The city itself probably stretched to encompass Mount Zion and to today's Jaffa Gate in what was known as the "Upper City."

Alas, Uzziah was as vain as he was good and great and he managed to antagonize the priesthood by taking some of their powers for himself. His reign ended abruptly when he was stricken by leprosy and forced to turn the throne over to his son as regent while he awaited his inevitable fate.

Uzziah's death brought Judea into a web of alliances and counteralliances in which she was unable to shape her own destiny or to defend herself against the combination of powers without outside help. When Judea's future suddenly turned bleak, another giant came to the fore, the prophet Isaiah.

ISAIAH

Unlike most men of his calling, the prophet Isaiah was born to aristocratic wealth and was perhaps of royal lineage. He was, above all, a Jerusalemite deeply involved in its history. An urbane man of wit and sophistication, Isaiah was a brilliant thinker, writer and orator who was not above showmanship to put his message across. Like Amos, he raged against ill-gotten and greed-motivated fortune, showered love on the poor and downtrodden and fostered human justice and charity. He decried the ills of the society, the sham of bribery in the priesthood and in the dispensation of justice, the shabby treatment of the orphan, the bastard and the widow, the hypocrisy of false religious morality, land evictions on bloated estates, and, of course, paganism. Isaiah's most original contribution was that he was the world's first true man of peace who understood the futility, destructiveness, human costs and Godlessness of war. "For they shall beat their swords into plowshares and practice war no more."

His was no voice of a barefooted wanderer with prophet's crook in hand. Isaiah was a prophet of the Temple itself, an adviser of three and perhaps four Judean kings, a statesman who greatly guided the fortunes of the people and the city. He received his call to prophesy at almost the same hour as that of King Uzziah's death, a moment in history when Assyria under Tiglath-Pileser III mounted an expedition with the goal of annexing everything from Armenia to Egypt. Assyria, which is relative to today's Iraq, fielded an army noted for its cruelty and total destructive capacities.

The Assyrian peril dictated a coalition. Aram-Damascus joined Israel along with the Philistine cities of Ashkelon, Gaza and an army under an Arab queen. When the Judeans under King Ahaz declined to join them, the coalition invaded with the intention of putting a friendly collaborator on the Judean throne.

Within the walls of the besieged Jerusalem, Isaiah preached that Zion had a special relationship to God and would be saved by Him. The prophet challenged King Ahaz to seek out a sign from God on the matter. The king feared Isaiah's advice was not practical in the situation and even more he feared testing the Lord. Instead he sent a message of desperation to the Assyrians along with a magnificent tribute from the Temple treasury and implored their intervention.

The Assyrians accepted the bribe and invaded Israel, reduced Israel's territory and put their man on the throne in Samaria. With this done, the Assyrians' irresistible war machine turned on Damascus. The remaining members of the ill-fated coalition were ravaged and their populations deported.

Judea had survived but the price was vassalage. King Ahaz became completely Assyrianized. Enfeebled, indebted to and enamored of the fearsome Assyrian power, he went so far as to copy their principal altar and install it in the Temple. Ahaz marched to Assyria's tune, introducing its worship of the constellations and the sun god, which totally vulgarized the Hebrew religion.

In a last hurrah, the pint-sized Israelite kingdom entered into an ill-fated alliance against Assyria. In the end the dominant tribe of Ephraim ceased to exist. The population went into exile and never returned, giving birth to the legend of the "Ten Lost Tribes of Israel." Outsiders, along with the remaining Jews, eventually became a hybrid people, the hated Samaritans.

When Hezekiah ascended the throne of Judea the

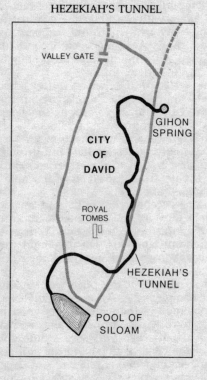

HEZEKIAH'S TUNNEL

VALLEY GATE

CITY
OF
DAVID

ROYAL
TOMBS

GIHON
SPRING

HEZEKIAH'S
TUNNEL

POOL OF
SILOAM

Assyrians sat twenty miles from Jerusalem. Judea paid them tribute and Assyrian idols adorned their Temple. Under Isaiah's tutelage the new king carefully instituted religious reform so as not to start a rumble with the Assyrians. Yet he always kept an eye out for a chance to break away from them.

As Isaiah worked Jerusalem, the prophet Micah preached in the Judean hills. Without the enormous skills of Isaiah, he championed the peasants and the otherwise exploited. Micah proclaimed, "Do justly, love mercy and walk humbly with God." This utterly simple but incredible passage, like no other, expressed the twin goals of the perfection of man and man's commission in life.

These two prophets envisioned a utopian state presided over by God. This belief in a coming kingdom, also prophesied by Elijah, John the Baptist and Jesus, certainly set the stage for the advent of Christianity.

While King Hezekiah instituted a number of important religious reforms, he remained careful not to stir up the Assyrian giant at his gates. In a great renewal Hezekiah declared a Passover celebration that was nationally attended and lasted for a joyous fortnight. God once again ruled supreme throughout the land and Jerusalem once again was the centerpiece of the experience.

In addition to the religious surge, Hezekiah immortalized himself as one of the great builders. No achievement of his reign was more stunning than the carving of a tunnel into solid rock beneath the city to connect the water source of Gihon Spring to its terminal at the Pool of Siloam. The Gihon Spring was outside the city walls, so the city's water supply became extremely vulnerable when it was under siege. The Pool of Siloam was inside the city walls, so connecting the two assured a continuous flow of water. Once the tunnel had been built, the site of the Gihon Spring was so ingeniously camouflaged that it could not be discovered by a besieging army.

Engineers started the project at both ends. The route was some eighteen hundred feet and required several turns. It had to be chipped out of solid rock. When the teams met successfully in the middle of the route and connected, an ancient engineering miracle had been accomplished. This tunnel stands in mint condition to this day and still distributes water evenly through its twisting course.

Despite Isaiah's counseling that Judea should not join any alliances except with God, the anti-Assyrian party within the palace won Hezekiah's ear. The Egyptians to the south were continually brewing toward insurrection against Assyria. In an attempt to dissuade the Judeans from joining the pending rebellion, Isaiah walked through the streets of Jerusalem for months dressed only in a loincloth to symbolize the dress of slaves and the fate that was bound to befall them. When Babylon joined the anti-Assyrian coalition, the region was ready to explode.

But Assyria struck first and went for the head of the snake in Babylon. After crushing the Babylonians, the Assyrian forces rolled down the Phoenician coast and into Philistine country. After an Egyptian army had been smashed, Ammon, Edom and Moab quickly sued for peace. The kingdom of Judea stood naked and alone.

Isaiah warned Hezekiah that God alone ruled the nation and God alone would save them from the Assyrians. As the Assyrian army toppled one Judean stronghold after another, with Jerusalem entering their sights, Hezekiah scrambled to make peace at any price and sent out an enormous tribute. After pocketing the bribe, the Assyrian king demanded the surrender of Jerusalem.

Panic and chaos gripped the city. With all other options closed, Hezekiah went to the prophet and implored him to intercede with God. Isaiah calmly assured him that Assyria would never enter Jerusalem.

And a miracle came to pass. A sudden murderous plague ripped through Assyrian ranks and reduced them to impotency. With news of a new Egyptian relief force entering Palestine, the Assyrians abruptly called off the campaign and retired from the area.

THE LENGTHENING SHADOW AND
THE PROPHET OF DOOM

The passing of Hezekiah brought his twelve-year-old son Manasseh to the throne to commence a fifty-six-year reign (698–642 B.C.) of infamy. Not only were the reforms of his father nullified, the religion was all but demolished. Isaiah retired from the Temple to work among his disciples as Assyria returned to being the power that was. Egypt, now under the rule of an Ethiopian pharaoh, continued to brew insurrection in the region which brought the Assyrians down on them full bore. With Egypt flattened, Manasseh meekly and pragmatically submitted Judea to vassalage.

In total abandonment of the Jewish faith, Manasseh's brutal suppression set him down as the most hated ruler in Hebrew history. Prophets, priests and ordinary followers of Judaism were eliminated in a bloody purge and the sacred books were destroyed. Legend has it that Isaiah was hounded down and murdered by being sawed in half. In a complete reversion to paganism, Manasseh offered his sons in sacrifice in a Canaanite fire ritual in the Valley of Hinnom. An idol of the Assyrian "queen of heaven" was erected in the Holy of Holies in the Temple and sanctioned whores fornicated within its walls. The earnings of the prostitutes and their offspring went to the Temple guardians and all sorts of debauchery were practiced as every trace of Judaism was eliminated.

Only the prophets, working in secret and depending on oral continuity of the laws, stood between this evil man and the demise of the religion. By the time of his death Judaism was but a memory to most of the people. Despite the horror of Manasseh's reign, the people remained enamored of the house of David and placed Josiah, his grandson, on the throne. Conversely, Josiah was to go down as one of the most righteous of the Hebrew kings.

As decades of pagan bilge were removed during the restoration of the Temple, a copy of the Torah was discovered. It was believed to have been a hybrid of ancient writings but also included more recent work of prophets and priests, who had hidden it in the Temple, hopeful it would be discovered later. This was the Book of Deuteronomy and it covered a total spectrum of law in regard to social, political and religious life. It was undoubtedly the most important single legal text ever written.

Josiah saw this amazing discovery as divine revelation. He took it to Huldah, a prophetess of Jerusalem, who confirmed his conclusions. Huldah considered that it was written by Moses, which gave it even more power and credibility, but that was not possible, for it contained the works of many more recent writers. However, with the sanction of this holy woman, Josiah was prepared to declare it the new law of the land.

He called an enormous national assemblage which was answered by priests, rabbis, scholars, scribes and just plain people. In a packed Temple court the king read the code and a loud amen resounded throughout Judea. The idols of Assyria were dismantled and pagan worshipers were sent packing. Again a national Passover feast was decreed and the ancient Covenant reconsecrated.

But Judea remained a land bridge as in the days of Canaan and strange new alliances were in the offing. Little Judea was drawn into war against Egypt, and Josiah was killed in battle in 609 B.C. at Megiddo, that war ground of the ages and the future Armageddon of the New Testament.

W hen the body of Josiah was returned to Jerusalem the nation was breathing its last breaths of free air. In the city there stalked a man cursed in life to carry the terrible burden of prophesying the destruction of the Temple, the holy city and the Jewish nation. Jeremiah, whose personal tragedy was equal to Saul's, spent his life figuratively treading on hot coals and bringing on vicious reactions against himself by those who could not bear to hear his truths. His suffering was epic. Doomed himself to speak of doom, he was morally unable to shrink from the task despite the spittle spat on him, the beatings, the tortures, the imprisonment that caused him to rue the day he was born. Tragedy and debasement dogged his every word and act. Like all great writers, Jeremiah was driven, by inner demons beyond his ability to control, to lay bare his soul and torment for all to see. He gives us the deepest personal insight into any character in the Bible.

From a priestly family of a village near Jerusalem, Jeremiah answered his calling at a young age, perhaps thirteen. After working in the countryside he came to Jerusalem during Josiah's reformation and concurred with the king's good works. Unmarried and childless, he bore his task as a loner with the exception of his lifelong relationship with his scribe. Baruch was a priest and prophet in his own right and the two of them created a literature beyond that which has been attributed to them.

Sensitive and incredibly introspective, Jeremiah was incapable of preaching false prophecies of illusions that the king and the people wanted to hear in order to shut out the perils and impending disaster. He stood alone and damned his people for bringing themselves to destruction. Horsewhipped, imprisoned, on trial for his life, barred from the Temple, Jeremiah would not be stilled.

When Baruch read Jeremiah's oracles at the Temple and then read them to the king, they were shredded and burned, for they foretold the demise of Judea. A second dictation of the scroll by Jeremiah to Baruch became the basis of the mighty Book of Jeremiah. It is strongly considered by many scholars that the two of them edited and rewrote many of the earlier books of the Old Testament as we know them today. Their style, cadence and philosophical content ring of Jeremiah although his authorship will never really be proved.

Judea had gone from Egyptian vassalage to Babylonian vassalage as Babylon's power peaked and her brief moment of glory was at hand. A stalemated battle between Babylonian and Egyptian armies was incorrectly interpreted in Judea as a sign of Babylonian weakness. As the proud little Judeans seized upon the information as a cause to rebel, Jeremiah implored the king not to revolt because that would only hasten their destruction. This advice went contrary to the court and the Temple prophets, who were singing songs of revolution. The priests declared that Jerusalem was under God's personal protection and therefore invulnerable.

Jeremiah pounced upon this notion. In decrying the hypocritical interpretations of Deuteronomy, Jeremiah took the opposing view and warned that God would indeed destroy Jerusalem and disperse its people, who were desecrating his law. Be peaceful, Jeremiah warned, stay out of treacherous alliances, practice the law of the Lord truthfully. God, he proclaimed, did not invest in nations but in men's souls! The crowd, from king to commoner, detested him. They were afraid to kill this man as they had lesser prophets for preaching the same message. But abuse him they did.

When in 597 B.C. the anti-Babylonian party seduced the king into revolt, Nebuchadnezzar, the Babylonian monarch, was swift to react. In came the Babylonian war machine and reduced fortress after fortress. The ill-advised king was assassinated and quickly replaced by his brother, whose first and only royal act was to surrender Jerusalem. He and eight thousand of the cream of the nation were taken off to exile in Babylon, the Temple was looted, and Zedekiah, the son of Josiah, was installed on the throne as a figurehead. Zedekiah was to carry the dubious distinction of being the final king from the house of David.

Even as twilight dimmed the Judean hills, the royal court remained split. Pagan worship had returned, sponsored by the two major outside forces. Those favoring the Egyptians formed a cult that worshiped sacred animals. The pro-Babylonians embraced Ishtar, a goddess of love, renowned for her wild sexual practices. The latter, with sanctioned debauchery as a ritual, gained great popularity, particularly among the women.

In Babylon the exiles were stirred up by prophets among them who predicted the collapse of Babylonian power. They wrote back to Judea pleading for rescue and otherwise fanned revolt. In explaining the realities of the day, Jeremiah dashed the exiles' hopes in his famous message to them. Babylon, he wrote, was not going to suddenly fade. The exiles were told to adapt to their captivity, build homes, remain peaceful, fortify morally by a massive return to God and in turn, in God's good time, they would be allowed to return to Zion.

At court Jeremiah continued to argue peace to Zedekiah. But the king was a terminal weakling and others were influencing the Judean court. Ambassadors from Edom, Ammon, Moab, Tyre and Sidon sought Judea out as an ally in rebellion. Likewise, Egyptian mischief always lurked in the background. As the war fever mounted, Jeremiah took to the streets of Jerusalem wearing a yoke about his neck to demonstrate the wages of rebellion just as Isaiah had walked naked a century earlier. Jeremiah was denounced as a lunatic.

Against his will, Zedekiah was sucked into an ill-fated action along the coast to reinforce an Egyptian expedition and this act slammed the lid and sealed the fate of the Hebrew nation. As the Babylonian punitive army neared Jerusalem, Jeremiah called for the city's surrender. This latest act caused him to be thrown into a dungeon and branded as a traitor and a coward.

As Babylon encircled the city with a rampart, the terrified king sent for the prophet. Jeremiah held his ground and warned that Jerusalem was doomed to fall if it did not surrender. Zedekiah was too fearful of the prophet's courage and powers to put him to death and actually sent him to a more decent prison. Even from the cell, Jeremiah continued to call for surrender. The Judean princes, many of whom had tolerated and even defended the strange prophet, now demanded his death. Wary to the last, Zedekiah had him lowered into a cistern and left to perish but did not actually consummate the act. The prophet was saved by an Ethiopian eunuch.

As month after month of siege passed, starvation began to flow into every corner of the city and water, always a problem, became desperately scarce. The cisterns which were part of every home went bone dry. Death stalked on the heels of hunger, disease and dreaded thirst. Soon its stench could be smelled beyond the walls by the invaders as they erected their breaching engines opposite the vulnerable northern battlements.

When the breach occurred, Zedekiah fled with his family but was overtaken at Jericho, bound in chains and dragged before Nebuchadnezzar. Zedekiah's sons were butchered before his eyes, after which he was blinded by a hot branding sword and carried off as a trophy to be displayed in Babylon as a message to the dissident Hebrew exiles. Tisha b'Av, the ninth day of the Hebrew month of Av, has been mourned by the Jewish people since the year 587 B.C. as the date of the destruction of the Temple. Nebuchadnezzar, making certain there would be no more Judean problems, and that the city would never be used again as a fortified post, ordered it put to the torch. As the flames consumed the Temple of Solomon, the palace and the rest, the walls were torn down and the royal family along with anyone of consequence were exiled. Judea was now a Babylonian province.

Jeremiah, considered by Nebuchadnezzar to be an ally, was given a choice of remaining or going into exile. He chose to live among the ashes.

A short-lived autonomous Jewish community turned on its governor and, fearing Babylonian reprisal, fled en masse to Egypt. Jeremiah and his scribe, Baruch, were carried away with them, against their will. He continued to preach among the scattered Jewish remnants in Egypt against the return to paganism. Aged but unbowed, this unrepentant tower of righteousness now demanded the faith be kept in exile. It is said that the noble and tragic Jeremiah met his end by being stoned to death by his own people.

Thus began the Jewish Odyssey. Could a people, a small and relatively obscure and powerless people, survive without its nation, particularly in light of the fact that they alone had proclaimed a God and a religion contrary to the rest of the world around them? If God, indeed, intended a continued presence among men on earth, the survival of the Jewish people was absolutely mandatory. The odds seemed infinitesimal that they could remain and not pass into history among the forgotten.

Jeremiah, so maligned in life, was granted ultimate honor and status after death. From beyond the grave, his writings became the Jewish canons of survival. Jeremiah said that Jews would remain Jews so long as they maintained the religion. God required neither sacrifice nor prayer nor altar nor Temple nor holy city nor nation, so long as he lived in the hearts and minds of the people. If such a faith could be sustained through all future adversity, they would ultimately be rewarded by a return to Jerusalem. The indomitable spirit of Jeremiah sounded a battle cry of the ages. His personal tragedy was to be mirrored by Jewish tragedy. His unyielding faith has surely been reflected by the faith of the Jewish people.

The first cycle of history thus closed on the Hebrews, who not only presented God to man but who formulated the first great ideals in law, religion, democracy, philosophy and literature. Their ideas will remain a cornerstone of Western life.

Among the unique features of the Jewish religion and its nation was the demand for constant moral reappraisal and personal introspection, as a nation and as individuals.

Paganism was no simple matter to chuck off. It claimed to provide easy answers to complex, often desperate problems. The cultist in the throes of a Baalish ritual is capable of entering an entranced stage of ecstasy, one in which the mind can levitate from the body as it seeks out a union with the idol, be it an animal god or some sort of human or semi-human configuration. In its most frenzied form the ritual seeks real or simulated or surrogate union by human sacrifice, sexual orgy or actually tearing of one's own flesh and eating the animal of sacrifice and drinking its blood.

God is keenly aware that human beings are dancing an eternal dance to drive the devils out of their souls . . . or to embrace them. The frenzy of the pagan ritual was a release from crushing earthly problems, a desperate disguised cry for freedom.

When such crowd hysteria is molded into something other than a religious experience, it leans in the direction of modern Baal worship, such as a rock concert, a voodoo rite, peyote or mushroom cults or even political mobs run amuck in the streets. Mass ecstasy has been practiced everywhere in acceptable form and in bad form since the first heartbeat of history, in primitive and in highly developed societies. From the frenzied cultists of the "Rocky Horror Show" to the "anything goes" discos, man writhes for a moment of escape and spiritual liberation. Our predecessors were doing it on firelit mountaintops in Canaan five thousand years ago.

This sort of spiritual detachment was enormously attractive to the ancient Hebrews, who lived in a sea of it while they alone had the counter-ideologies to combat it. And they swung back and forth, back and forth. Somehow, God always had the potency to win out. Early on the

Jewish religion allowed for great latitude for individual interpretation uncluttered by dogma. In allowing the human mind to explore, to question, to take responsibility, to be free, Judaism was able to replace cult ritualism for human spiritual flight.

Jeremiah was reviled because some people didn't want to be reminded of God's demands. As the citizens of Jerusalem turned on Jeremiah, so have entire nations turned on the Jews, who have been both cursed and privileged to keep God's laws. Their religion was to accompany the Jewish people into dispersion like an albatross, and when a nation wished to revert to paganism, as the German people did in the Nazi era, the destruction of the Jews became mandatory in their eyes.

With the end of statehood, the Jews embarked on a story of perpetual wandering, suffering, humiliation, slaughter and a final conquest of the human spirit which finds no parallel in man's history.

BY THE WATERS OF BABYLON

"Vast as the sea is thy ruin," spoke the Book of Lamentations. After Nebuchadnezzar's Babylonian destruction Jerusalem was a heap, a corpse of stone. Judea may have held a few hundred thousand people when the end came. The denuded land was watched over by the keepers of the ashes, impoverished shepherds and peasants, who alone, now vulturized by ancient enemies, picked whatever fruit there was on the barren trees of the destroyed nation.

It was in Babylon that a most incredible revival blossomed as the Jews discovered that God was yet in and with them. Those many thousands of exiles had been the cream of the fallen country and were transplanted into the most stupendous cosmopolitan colossus of the ancient world. Babylon's very name implies splendor. Nebuchadnezzar was in total command of his precincts and permitted the Hebrew colony religious freedom so long as it didn't make trouble. A number of the families prospered, achieved high social status, and many integrated and were never heard from again.

A die-hard nucleus retained the old religion, finding it workable without a homeland, and constantly added new dimensions. The tradition of the local prayer house, the "synagogue," to replace the Temple started in Babylon. As the uniqueness of their religion became apparent to them, their inner strength solidified. And it was learned that the magnetics of Jerusalem pulled from anywhere. The dead city never stopped beckoning and exiles' intensity for it became boundless.

"If I forget thee, O Jerusalem," was first heard there in what was to become a lament of the ages to be moaned from dark and desperate places.

The prophet Ezekiel, himself an exile, was the chief motivator in Babylon along with the preachings of the late Jeremiah. Ezekiel told the Hebrews that their nation had been denied them as punishment for playing footloose with God. He conjured up visions of the holy city and prophecies of a glorious return which turned this remnant into a possessed people.

With the death of Nebuchadnezzar mighty Babylon trembled. From the deeper reaches of Asia, a genius named Cyrus was on the rise with a small but brilliant army of Persian peasants which was soon to create an empire from India to Greece. Babylon was the major obstacle to be removed.

As the great city came under Persian siege, an unknown prophet who has been called the "Second Isaiah" predicted the end of the Babylonian society, which was shallow and spiritless because it had been created upon materialism. The glory of Babylon had been as empty as the glory of Egypt before it. The lesson of this brilliant, anonymous prophet was that all empires with materialism as their foundation were doomed to crumble. Only a people sanctified by morality had the ability to survive. In the end, Babylon fell ignobly to internal treachery.

Cyrus the Persian was distinctive beyond his times. He felt that the way to win the foreigners' loyalty was to allow and even encourage the various peoples of his empire to pursue their own beliefs. An edict of emancipation in 538 B.C. not only permitted the Jews to return to

Jerusalem but offered assistance in rebuilding their fallen land.

THE RETURN

A half century in exile had drained much of the nationalistic fervor from the Jewish community of Babylon, which had grown fat and content. When the trumpet of the return was sounded, it was answered by a hard core of the devout. A few thousand under Sheshbazzar, a surviving prince of the house of David, led the band of redeemers on the six-hundred-mile journey in 538 B.C.

What they came upon shattered dreamy visions. The desolation of Jerusalem was an overgrown rock pile of thorn and weed. The impoverished Judean peasants who had remained had become apostates wallowing in misery. They feared the returning exiles would snatch what was left of their meager holdings. Old enemies on Judea's borders perched like vultures ready to emasculate any attempt to rebuild the country.

The idealism of the returnees faded in the light of devastating privation, lack of funds, extreme weather and unabated harassment. Work among the ruins proceeded at a turtle's pace.

The prophets Haggai and Zechariah were unlike the earlier prophets. Social injustice took a distant second place to the need to rebuild the Temple. They verbally flogged the people to commence work, for its restoration was to be the consummate symbol of the resurrection of the religion.

In the year 516 B.C., almost two decades after the exiles' return, the Second Temple was completed. It was as large as Solomon's but simpler, without the luxurious materials and other trappings of grandeur. It was also an odd affair, for it rose on a rubble pile without city walls, fortifications, the former palaces, government buildings and very few homes. It stood alone on its hot dusty plateau and whispered out to a desolate land and a lethargic people.

No sooner was the Temple in operation than it was taken over by a corrupt priesthood who forced the Levites

out, condoned the horrendous social injustices and played
loose with the Temple offices. Tobias, an anti-Judean Ammonite and member of an influential Gilead family, gained
great power under the Persians and had himself installed
in the Temple. He keynoted a general religious slump as
the Sabbath was desecrated, funds squandered and despotism practiced until Artaxerxes I took the Persian throne.

T he man required by the hour was named Ezra. From
his Babylonian exile he petitioned the new Persian king to
allow him to return to Jerusalem with a missionary legion
of the pious. Eighteen hundred answered Ezra's call. The
balance of the Babylonian Jewish community, mostly affluent,
backed the venture with heavy donations, establishing a
tradition of self-help and charity.

Armed with sweeping powers, Ezra set out to put the
religion back on course. The population of Judea had
dwindled to under fifty thousand, with but three thousand pawing among the ruins of the holy city. Not only
were physical walls needed around Jerusalem but an
anti-apostate wall was required around the entire province.
Intermarriage had diluted the faith to the point of extinction.
In a drastic action Ezra nullified all mixed marriages,
which outraged Judea's neighbors and intensified their
efforts to keep her from rebuilding.

A bombardment of complaints from the Samaritans in
the north to the Arabs in the desert plus the internal
transgressions of Tobias in the Temple caused the Persians
to order the work stopped again. Judea stumbled along
beset by misery. Its plight reached Jewish ears in Persia,
where, fortunately, some of their number carried weight
with the king. One of them, Nehemiah, was a close
confidant of Artaxerxes I and begged to be allowed to
journey to Jerusalem and complete the work. Granted
only temporary leave from the Persian court, Nehemiah
arrived in 445 B.C. and at once became the dynamic force
needed to rebuild city and state, and to restore the
people's confidence and dignity. Debts were canceled in a

sweeping edict and land was restored to the poor. Tobias was thrown out of the Temple. Nehemiah's clean sweep lifted the pall of degradation and allowed new air and new spirit to fill the hills.

The walls had been down for nearly a hundred and fifty years. Work now commenced on them with a fury, following the lines of the earlier city in most sectors. The basic outline of the wall was laid down in a mere fifty-two days, although the completed work with fortifications and gates took two and a half years.

Nehemiah personally stood in the center of the activity with a bugler at hand to signal impending raids from the Samaritans and other bitter opponents. To combat the constant harassment, one half of the building crews worked while the second half guarded them.

By use of stick and carrot, Nehemiah coerced ten thousand Judeans to live in the city, set up tithes to operate the Temple and otherwise redignified Jerusalem with proper buildings, pools, towers and renewed waterworks. Shrunken but potent, the new Jerusalem rose from its ashes, enveloped by first-rate fortifications and eight entrances. It encompassed the original city of David, the Temple Mount and Ophel and the Pool of Siloam.

The description of renewed life is given in vivid detail in the Book of Nehemiah and in somewhat mystical form in the Book of Ezra. Once again Arab traders peddled the wares of the Levant outside the northern walls and within the city with a jangle of burdened asses bringing and taking wares. The sheep gate where Temple sacrifices were prepared was in the same area as today's colorful Arab sheep market. And there were fishmonger gates and horse gates all bubbling with activity.

As the city throbbed to life, Ezra joined forces with the good and great Nehemiah to complete the moral wall. Ezra read and interpreted the Torah, which was again declared the law of the land. The people united behind these two fabulous men, vowed to return with proper offerings, keep the Torah, quit the debilitating intermarrying and altogether salvage their torn relationship with God. The oracles of Ezra became the very cornerstone of the practice of Judaism, which gave it a clarity and definition. Today's Orthodox Jews worship almost strictly according to Ezra's dictates.

To celebrate the religious rededication Nehemiah called for a national festival of Succoth, a feast which had been abandoned for centuries. Booths or shacks, called "succahs," of branches and leaves were built in every home and courtyard to commemorate the privations of Moses in the desert, while the fruits of the harvest were offered at the Temple. This was the actual moment when Judaism set down the rules and practices of the religion that were to endure.

Of all the men who have contributed to the greatness of Jerusalem, none stand on higher steps than Ezra and Nehemiah, whose singular wills resurrected the holy city.

Judea continued to flourish under Persian rule, particularly the institution of the scribes. These men, different in commission from both the priests and the prophets, wrote interpretations of the Torah and refined the earlier works of the Old Testament. They expanded the understanding of the Deuteronomic law, truly encoding the religion and breaking open the restrictions. The visions and damnations of the prophets were overpowering in the strictness of their demands to the point of being histrionic. They had channeled the religion into dogma. On the other hand, the scribes wrote books of protest, books of allegory, books of interpretation, books of controversy. Ruth and Jonah and the others opened up the religion onto its parallel track, one which gives the individual room to seek and ponder and breathe. It was an era during which all the history and teaching fell into place and gathered its legs for Judaism's long run through the ages.

THE GREEK ERA

Left to their own devices during the Persian era, the Jews defined, encoded and expanded all aspects of the religion through the continued scholarship of wise men and scribes. As the generations of prophecy finally took root in the minds of the people, the need for its continuation disappeared. Prophecy had prepared the people to invest in God and the Torah. The religion was now practiced so that it emerged as the most important element of the national character. The outpouring of brilliant commentary from the compiling of wisdom made Judea the Lord's sanctuary unintimidated by the pagan world beyond its borders. All of the learning was solidified by the dialogues of great convocations, called synagogues or assemblies, in which scholars and holy men discussed, digested, divulged and reinforced the hold of the Torah.

Although Judea's territory had shrunk to little more than an extended district, it was an autonomous ministate with its own language, religion, educational system and internal rule. The Temple was the de facto capital of the state, whose precincts held both the theological and educational facilities. Its high priest was the de facto state ruler and the Torah its constitution and law.

The fortunes of the people were still largely dictated by the often desperate realities of hard-rock farming done by primitive methods, low land yields and recurrent drought, pestilence and famine. Yet this tiny mountain nation lived with a fulfilled sense of destiny. It was not the glory of conquest but the glory of the prophets and piety to God. In the year 334 B.C. one of the glamor figures of all history, the young Macedonian military genius Alexander the Great, embarked on the campaign that ended Persian domination and Hellenized the civilized world.

Alexander was looked upon as a liberator by the Jews in Egypt, who allied with him and helped him found Alexandria, which was to rival Babylon as the great Jewish community in exile. Alexander rewarded them with privilege. The man who had created the world's greatest empire, from India to the gates of Rome, died in his thirty-third year, a burned-out case.

In the inevitable split of the empire, Seleucus, commander of the fearsome Macedonian heavy infantry phalanx, assumed rule over the eastern regions.

The general Ptolemy, meanwhile, established his dynasty in Egypt. The strip of land that included Judea and Palestine was, as always, the object of contention. The imperial ambitions of both factions made conflict inevitable. In the beginning, Ptolemy won out and Judea fell under governorship of the Alexandrian Greeks.

A wave of Greek humanism swept in behind their armies. They fashioned a string of new cities and Hellenized old ones. The Greek love of beauty and art, the physical pursuits and body-worship cults, the philosophical giants and democratic ideas penetrated and eventually consumed nearly every society where they established a presence. Judea was no exception. The Hellenization of the country was broadly accepted. But they were water and oil that would not mix. Strict followers of Judaism were offended by a whole spectrum of Greek practices and they stiffened in opposition. The moral demands of the omnipotent Hebrew God were bound to clash with the Greek aesthetics, philosophies and free-wheeling paganism. The Jews, it is said, believed in the beauty of godliness, and the Greeks believed in the godliness of beauty.

Despite the penetration of Hellenism, the Jews of the Diaspora continued to practice Judaism. They turned toward Jerusalem when uttering their prayers, and tithing to support the Temple became a way of life. On holy days pilgrims from Antioch to Carthage ascended to the holy city in reaffirmation of the faith. The Jews of the Diaspora adopted a liberal attitude toward Hellenism. In Alexandria, where the strongest of these communities lived, the Jews no longer spoke the Semitic language of Judea and were unable to read and write Hebrew, the language of the Bible. At one point seventy-two elders traveled from Jerusalem to Alexandria to translate the Torah into Greek.

In Judea itself, Hellenism won great favor among the privileged class. This sector, which co-operated with the new rulers, was generally entranced with the sophistication and cosmopolitanism of the Greeks. What emerged in this class was the practice of a quasi-Judaism heavily laced with Greek influence.

In opposition, the priests and general masses of the people saw Hellenism as an assault on and a perversion of Judaism. As the two opposing forces polarized and the rift between them widened, a collision of ideologies seemed inevitable.

In the year 198 B.C. the Egyptian-based Ptolemists were defeated and Judea passed to control by the Seleucids, based in Syria. An era of treachery and counter-treachery for control of the Temple's wealth and political life became a roll call of perfidy with a cast of infamous characters that plunged Judea to the pits.

Antiochus IV, the Seleucid ruler, saw himself as a god whose birthday was to be celebrated monthly. He took the name Epiphanes, a godhead connotation, and was the Hellenizer of Hellenizers, a builder of outsized statues to himself, a worshiper of the body culture, a participant in drunken orgies and lewd reveling that represented the swill pit of the Greek culture.

The Hellenization of Jerusalem was overseen by a succession of licentious high priests who promoted everything Greek from fashions to debauchery for personal profit. Jason was originally installed on his promise to wring more taxes out of the Temple. He wasn't bad enough, however, and was soon replaced by Menelaus, the vilest man ever to set foot in the holy sanctuary. As the worst of the Greek ethic was imposed upon Jerusalem, the taxation and tribute for the dubious distinction of becoming "citizens of Antioch" became backbreaking. A gymnasium was erected where Hebrew lads played pseudo-Greek games in the nude and it was only a matter of time until the Greek gods were knocking at the Temple door. Even the liberal pro-Hellenist Jews were aghast at the all-devouring philosophy of Antiochus Epiphanes. Today, in modern Israel, the attempt to build a sports stadium in the vicinity of an ultra-Orthodox neighborhood has brought on cries of "Hellenism!"

Antiochus Epiphanes went into battle against the Ptolemies and, although he was defeated, incorrect information filtered back to Jerusalem that he had been killed. This led to an eruption by the priests and Hasidim, who purged the city of Hellenism. But alas, Antiochus Epiphanes was alive and well, though steeped in humiliation over his defeat.

His wrath fell on the hapless Judeans. Antiochus Epiphanes' punitive army fell on the city on the Sabbath and the pillaging, rape and butchery were as horrendous as Jerusalem had ever endured. While the walls were being torn down and thousands taken off into slavery, a decree ending the practice of Judaism was issued.

Judea was compelled to bow down to Grecian idols and all remnants of Judaism were destroyed. In the year 167 B.C. the Temple was rededicated to Zeus while other outsized sanctuaries went up to Apollo and the range of Greek deities. The Temple grounds were converted into a place of orgies where the blood of pigs profaned the altar.

Torah scrolls went up in flames. Mothers of circumcised

children were publicly humiliated before they were murdered and those who refused to comply were simply destroyed. The Hellenist Hebrews whimpered feebly but did not protest, while the Hasidim chose martyrdom. In 169 B.C., Antiochus Epiphanes built a citadel called the Akra which overlooked the Temple grounds and in which he installed a force of several thousand troops.

The darkness of this hour was reflected in the defiant Book of Daniel, one of the last works of the Old Testament, which foresaw the ultimate triumph of those believing in God, although walking through the fires of hell would have to be the price of victory.

THE MACCABEES

An elderly priest had abandoned Jerusalem to live in a nearby village in order to continue the worship of God. He was Mattathias of the house of Hasmon. When the Greek troops fell upon the village, rounded up the population and demanded the oath to their idols, Mattathias became enraged and chopped down the first Jew who obeyed, struck down the Greek general and destroyed the Greek altar. With the chilling call to arms, "He who is with God, follow me!" Mattathias fled into the hills with his five sons and the revolution was on. Upon the death of the old man, the command passed down to his son Judah, who was soon to be known as the "Hammer" or the "Maccabee."

Hit-and-run raids, theft of enemy weapons and supplies, harassment of enemy movements, destruction of enemy outposts all displayed the generalship of this guerrilla master. As the band grew to a small national force, Judah Maccabee was able to gain control of the approaches to the holy city, making it extremely difficult for the Seleucids to keep a firm grip on the area.

The Seleucids put together a retaliation force from Samaria intent on reinforcing their garrison in Jerusalem, unclogging her arteries and establishing more power around the city than the Maccabees could cope with. Judah's personal courage and leadership and the wild fighting abilities of his people utterly crushed the Seleucid army and sent them reeling back to Samaria. The Seleucids mounted a second and larger force. This too was crushed. Now taking the Maccabees seriously, the Seleucids put together a massive field army certain to break them, and when this failed a fourth attempt was made. Again they were beaten.

With the hills around Jerusalem solidly in Maccabee hands, history took a turn in their favor. The Seleucids were having troubles elsewhere and could pour no more resources into Judea. When they moved eastward into battle Judah Maccabee brazenly moved his band into Jerusalem, surrounded the enemy garrison in the Akra and held them to a stalemate.

Judah then went up to the Temple Mount and bore the tragic sight of four years of neglect and Greek desecration. After restoring the Temple to God, the Maccabees called for an eight-day celebration. The year was 164 B.C., the day, the twenty-fifth of Kislev, exactly four years after the Temple's destruction. Hanukkah, always a feast of rededication, honors this high-water mark in man's struggle for his rights.

The Maccabees held the Temple Mount and most of Jerusalem's approaches while the Seleucids were buttoned up in the Akra directly opposite them. The two armies stood eyeball to eyeball for over twenty years with neither side able to dislodge the other.

When the abominable Antiochus Epiphanes died, his empire faltered and it became more and more difficult for the Seleucids to control the troublesome Judean province. In one attempt to break through, the Seleucids sent in a terrifying corps of Indian war elephants backed by tens of thousands of foot troops.

Rome now reared its head and boned up its ambitions, causing all in the civilized world to re-evaluate their alliances. Initially, the rise of Rome came as a blessing to Judea, who befriended the Romans and used them to capitalize against the declining Seleucids.

On the other hand, the Maccabees were extended by a series of conflicts with their neighbors all around. The skirmishes and mini-wars never ceased. Judah Maccabee fell in battle as did his brothers Yohanan and Eleazer. The Maccabee command eventually went to the youngest of the brothers, Jonathan. He wove a skillful military and political course between Seleucia and Rome.

Demetrius I, the Seleucid monarch, was beset on several fronts and desperately needed a stabilized Judea as an ally. Jonathan used this need to wring vast concessions. The Maccabees now returned to Jerusalem with Jonathan as the legitimate governor of the province as well as the high priest. The only condition Demetrius I demanded was that he should retain his outpost in the Akra fortress.

Once again the rebuilding of Jerusalem took place under the tender loving hands of the Jews. Jonathan was able to ward off fresh Seleucid pressures, then brought his armies down out of the Judean hills and annexed some Philistine ports, giving the land-locked nation a much-needed access to the sea. The resulting trade routes greatly enhanced prosperity. A region of Samaria was taken to secure the northern approaches to Jerusalem, and when all seemed to be getting healthy Jonathan's reign was abruptly halted when he was assassinated by a Seleucid officer.

The last of the Maccabee brothers, Simon, assumed command. He was to prove the most capable of the lot. Although he established himself as the undisputed ruler and high priest he never claimed the title of king. He gained for Judea recognition of its independence from the Senate of Rome, a brilliant and far-reaching political step. After a number of assaults, the Akra finally surrendered, freeing Judea of foreign troops for the first time in centuries. Simon was able to complete his political victories by gaining similar recognition of independence from the Seleucids.

Extending Judean hold on the coastal plain, Simon installed his son John Hyrcanus in the vital fortress city of Gezer. A Seleucid thrust to regain this coastal area was turned back by a Judean army which had been honed tough by the Maccabee experience. The nation was a hard military nut, self-sustaining and independent. The Judeans were held in world esteem, its citizens admired for their stamina and ability to liberate themselves. From Antioch to Alexandria to Athens to Rome, Jewish communities and their scholars had gained respect and position. The best of Judaic law and the Covenant merged with the best of the Greek philosophies in a marriage that influenced the direction of Western culture.

In the year 140 B.C. a Great Assembly convened in Jerusalem which resulted in charging the Maccabeean house of Hasmon with the deliverance of Israel. Simon and his successors were endowed with the dual responsibilities of monarch and high priest, thus founding the Hasmonean dynasty.

But even as Judea climbed in esteem, a new cycle of court intrigue, as dastardly as any in the past, started with the birth of the dynasty. Simon and two of his sons were treacherously murdered by his son-in-law, the governor of Jericho, in an attempt to seize power. The coup was thwarted by Simon's remaining son, John Hyrcanus, in an affair which saw his mother held hostage and slain. With the last of the five original Maccabee brothers dead, all through violence, a new era of royal cutthroat politics was begun.

THE HASMONEANS

In the beginning John Hyrcanus came to terms with the Seleucids but with the passing of their last major king, Antiochus VII, the Hebrew monarch succumbed to delusions of grandeur. Blatantly looting the tomb of King David of its riches, he used the proceeds to hire an army of foreign mercenaries and carved out a mini-empire from Seleucid territory. Samaria was crushed and its rival temple in their capital of Shechem was destroyed.

Judaism, as an ethic, has almost never sought conversion by either sword or persuasion. Neither proselytization nor heavy-handed evangelism was practiced, nor are they now. John Hyrcanus perverted this legacy when he defeated the Idumeans, the nation formerly known as Edom, and forced them to accept Judaism or face exile.

In order to justify his war policies and give them a measure of sanction, John Hyrcanus installed a council of elders called the Sanhedrin. This group was endowed with political, judicial and religious powers. It was composed of a right-wing, reactionary element of priests, landowners, the military and aristocrats—those who stood to benefit most by expansion. Their party was called the Sadducees. By selecting them exclusively for the Sanhedrin, the Hasmonean monarchy was able to perpetuate its own ambitions. The Sadducees controlled the Temple as its power base, but when one examines the history of the Temple, corruption, money and power have always made inroads. The Sadducees failed to protest Hellenism.

An opposition faction, the Pharisees, began to divide the Jews among themselves during the reign of John Hyrcanus. The Pharisees came from a broad base of the people and, although deeply religious, they held that Judaism did not begin and end with sacrifices at the Temple. Oral law, liberalism, and constant re-evaluation and the ability to progress by changing the religion was deemed the true way to interpret the Torah. The Pharisees represented a living and evolving religion while the Sadducees represented dogma.

The successors of the house of Hasmon were to prove a far different lot than their Maccabee ancestors. John Hyrcanus' son Aristobulus was married to an intriguing lady, Salome Alexandra, who was to be queen in three separate circumstances. Her husband died after a year on the throne. It was traditional that the eldest unmarried son wed his brother's widow. The groom designate, Alexander Yannai, was a reprehensible character who had been hated by his father and imprisoned by his brother. Striking a sordid deal, Salome Alexandra married the imprisoned Yannai, who was elevated from prison cell to throne with the position of high priest thrown in.

Alexander Yannai opened his reign (103–76 B.C.) by snatching control of the entire Palestinian coast from Mount Carmel, site of present-day Haifa, clear down to the Egyptian border. Gaza was annexed and the Transjordan further penetrated.

In short order Alexander Yannai alienated himself from the people just as he had alienated himself from his father and brothers. During a Succoth festival he deliberately profaned the altar and caused a riot. The pious in the Temple court pelted him with citrons, the traditional limelike fruit used in the festival. He answered this insult by launching massive persecutions which ended in the execution of six thousand Pharisees, who had objected to his joint posts as king and high priest.

Discontent over this king plunged the country into a civil war of Pharisee against Sadducee. In the next six years fifty thousand people were killed, mostly Pharisees who fought in the name of religious purity. As their slaughter reached monumental proportions, the Pharisees petitioned their ancient enemy, the Seleucids, to intercede in their behalf. Forming an alliance, they defeated Alexander Yannai near Shechem in 89 B.C. Only after the victory did the Pharisees reconsider their action, do a complete turnabout and then go on to rally behind their errant king and stop further Seleucid advance. Legend, probably exaggerated, has it that once the Seleucid danger passed, Alexander Yannai ordered the roundup of eight hundred Pharisee leaders and their families. At Golgotha, site of other noted crucifixions, he had all eight hundred men nailed to eight hundred crosses. As the life oozed from them Alexander Yannai ordered the dying men's families beneath their crosses. The last sight these men were to witness was their wives and children having their throats slit. It is recorded that Alexander Yannai watched all this while he banqueted with his harem. He died in a drunken stupor during the siege of a Transjordanian fortress.

On his deathbed in a final irony he named his wife, Salome Alexandra, as his successor. The Pharisees, however, saw this as a way to end the civil war and restore unity and made a magnificent gesture by giving this rotten brute a grand funeral in Jerusalem.

Salome Alexandra, thrice queen of the Jews, immediately set the stage for future strife by splitting the two remaining high positions between her sons. Hyrcanus II, the elder, was appointed high priest while Aristobulus II was placed in command of the army. For a time each had standoff power against the other. Reversing her husband's vicious anti-Pharisee policy, the queen nominated a number of them to the Sanhedrin.

Unhealed division between Sadducee and Pharisee began to gurgle ominously as each of her sons sided with one of the factions. At the instant of her death in 67 B.C., Hyrcanus II grabbed the throne with Pharisee backing.

Aristobulus II marched against his brother, forcing him

to flee. History had created a golden moment for a clever opportunist to step in. The man's name was Antipater, an Idumean, a converted half Jew who governed a small border area. Antipater sized up Hyrcanus II as a weakling and calculated that the deposed monarch could best serve his own ambitions.

Rome was operating in the region after quieting an Armenian insurrection. Pompey, the Roman general, swung down into Syria and took Damascus. In Jerusalem, both sides of the warring Hasmoneans petitioned the Roman commander to intervene on their behalf, making the situation irresistible for Roman exploitation. Choosing as his ally Aristobulus II, who was locked up with his forces in the Temple compound, Pompey dispatched a legion toward Jerusalem. At the last instant Aristobulus II renounced his summons for Roman help, cut the connecting bridge between the Temple and the Upper City and vowed to fight it out to the end.

In Jerusalem proper, Hyrcanus II was being advised in quite the opposite vein by the wily Antipater. With Rome at Jerusalem's approaches, resistance would be futile. The Pharisees, wanting to put an end to the fratricide and persecution, were in agreement. Hyrcanus II ordered the city gates opened to Pompey, who promptly laid siege to the Temple Mount, filled the ditch opposite the Temple embattlements and erected breaching towers.

After three months Pompey was able to crack the Temple fortifications on a Sabbath. Faced with an inevitable massacre, and rather than profane the Sabbath, the pious among the Sadducees offered no resistance. Roman broadswords went to work methodically, decapitating and crushing skulls of hordes of Jews who bowed their heads in prayer. In the city, families of known Sadducees were hounded down and butchered remorselessly. As the toll ran over ten thousand, Pompey called off further sport.

Thus Judea was annexed to Rome. Antipater, as the power behind the throne of Hyrcanus II, kept abreast of the Roman generals, who warred among themselves, and managed to come up on the right side. In gaining Roman citizenship for himself he was able to win favorable conditions for Judea and had two of his sons installed as prefects of the two major Judean districts. One of these sons was Herod. Despite his ability to deal with Rome,

Antipater was loathed by the Judeans as a foreign ruler and an apostate. His ambitions came to an abrupt halt during a banquet at which he was poisoned. Herod, with little time or inclination for grief for his father, quickly moved to the side of Hyrcanus II to fill his father's role as a manipulator of the king.

The Parthians, who occupied an area relative to today's Iran and Iraq, constituted Rome's major enemy. At the moment the Roman commander in the east, Mark Antony, was immersed in his love affair with the Egyptian queen, Cleopatra. His legions were mostly tied up in the ongoing civil war between the Roman generals. All of this left the Middle East undermanned. The Parthians capitalized on the situation by successfully invading Syria and Palestine in 39 B.C. and many Jews sided with them. In Jerusalem, Hyrcanus II and Phasael, the brother of Herod, traveled out of the city to make contact with the Parthians, hoping to negotiate a settlement, but they were seized and thrown into prison. Phasael committed suicide. Hyrcanus II was personally mutilated by his nephew, who was on the Parthian side and wanted his throne. His ears were bitten off and he was otherwise permanently incapacitated.

As the Parthians entered Jerusalem and sacked the Temple and installed as king Antigonus, the last of the Hasmoneans, Herod and his family fled. As he left Jerusalem with his guard, the Parthians and their Jewish allies gave hot pursuit. The Hebrews, it appeared, wanted to get their hands on him the most. They hated him as an impostor as they had hated his father. After beating off his pursuers, Herod deposited his family in a Dead Sea fortress called Masada. Herod continued on alone to Alexandria, then proceeded to Rome as the Parthians routed the last of the Romans from Palestine and Judea.

HEROD THE GREAT

Had Herod been a Hebrew, from the house of David, or even a Hasmonean, he would have ranked with David and Solomon as one of the three great kings in Jewish history. Historical judgment regards the man severely, and not without justification. At his worst he was as brutal and despotic as any man who occupies the pages of history. Conversely, he was one of the most brilliant and successful leaders ever to step onto the world stage. He was a political genius, a top-rate military leader and the peer, even the superior, of Solomon as a builder. Yet he is mostly judged at his worst.

From the outset Herod's story was dictated by his relationship with the Jews. He was an Idumean, an Edomite, whose nation had been forced into conversion by John Hyrcanus. He was considered at best a half Jew or something less, as were the Samaritans. He was the son of Antipater, a foreign opportunist, who had woven a slippery path to power among the Jews.

Despite this, the bottom line on both Antipater and Herod showed that they did more good for the nation and the religion than all the Hasmoneans put together, excluding the Maccabees. Even though Herod went to great lengths to win favor among his subjects he was universally hated throughout the thirty-three years of his reign.

It wasn't that the Hebrews were all that intolerant. Their history already reached back two thousand years, during which they alone had embraced monotheism. They had beaten off hundreds of assaults on their religion. Geographic reality had put them in the path of countless invasions by great empires and countless wars with their neighbors. The foreigner always represented a threat to their beliefs. They had undergone centuries of back-to-back nightmares as the giants of Assyria, Babylon, Persia, Greece plundered and oppressed them. Rome, in their eyes, was no less evil and destructive than the others and Roman paganism was no less a threat than Canaanite and Philistine paganism had been.

Herod was an out-and-out extension of Roman policy. He was a Hellenist, and Hellenism represented probably the greatest threat of extinction Judaism had ever encountered. It was not only the horror of an Antiochus Epiphanes but the tremendous psychological and philosophical inroads of Hellenism, which so many Jews had found attractive. It was the most furiously battled of all pagan assaults, on the battlefield, in the Temple, in the home and within the school.

To throw oil on the fire, Herod, as an Edomite, represented the longest-standing enemy of the Hebrews. Descendants of Esau, Moses had prophesied that the Edomites would be the eternal Hebrew foe. In sum, Herod was Rome's boy, a Hellenist, a pagan, and from an enemy tribe.

When Herod made good his escape to Rome in wake of the Parthian invasion, he was greeted beyond all expectations. He had a past history, as prefect of the Galilee, of dealing mercilessly with Rome's enemies. Many of these had been bands of Jewish brigands. His father, Antipater, was remembered well for having served Rome unflaggingly.

Mark Antony was in Rome at the time of Herod's arrival, having effected a truce with his archenemy, Octavius. Both men were in a boil over the Parthian invasion of Palestine and saw in Herod the man to restore Roman rule over Judea. In an unprecedented move, for Herod had no royal blood, the Senate of Rome declared him King of Judea. This act was consecrated by offerings at the Temple of Jupiter, an incongruous act for the man who was to be ruler of the Hebrews, but an act typical of Herod.

He landed in Palestine with his commission and forged an army of two Roman legions, mercenaries, Syrian units and a large force of his fellow Idumeans. As he slowly cleared the region of Parthians, the Jews took up the fight against him, reckoning it was better to have a bad Hasmonean on the throne than a good Idumean.

Herod's war of consolidation sputtered along for three years until Rome was able to release sufficient forces to invade Judea proper. For the final siege of Jerusalem, Rome massed eleven legions with six thousand cavalry, upwards of seventy-five thousand troops. These were fighters of such quality, they have been described as "having been born with their weapons attached to them." Many of the siege machines were constructed on the spot by the engineer corps who maneuvered them up against enemy walls on earthen ramps, which filled in the defensive moats and ditches.

Crossbows hurled six-foot-long wooden flaming darts with a half-mile accuracy while catapults hurled hundred-pound boulders a like distance. The thirty- and forty-foot siege towers contained battering rams which were pulled up against enemy walls and when the breach was made they could disgorge hundreds of troops over a lowered drawbridge.

Sooner or later everything had to fall before the discipline and might of Rome's men and armor. The breach in the walls of Jerusalem came in the fifth month of siege. The Jews continued to fight from the Upper City and the Temple but were isolated and inevitably weakened. As the Jewish defense units were cut into small pockets the legions went on another rampage. Herod vainly tried to stop the carnage. The finale of the bloodbath came when Antigonus, the final Hasmonean king, was beheaded along with all forty-five members of the ruling Sanhedrin council. Small wonder the Hebrews did not take a fancy to Herod.

He was completely beholden to Rome and kept his kingdom in Rome's hands by sword and guile. He remained loyal to Mark Antony until Octavius emerged the victor in their struggle. Herod was able to jump over to the new ruler just as his father had been able to flip from one Roman Caesar to the next. At a meeting in Rhodes, Herod convinced Octavius fully of his continued usefulness.

Herod extended Judea's borders as the nation became a fortress ringed with powerful outposts and Jerusalem itself a city under the observation of internal towers and battlements. He ruthlessly destroyed real or imagined pretenders, particularly from the house of Hasmon, squashed all political opposition and completely Hellenized his court. Celtic mercenaries from Germany and the Balkans manned his fortresses and guarded his palace halls while Greeks advised him and tutored his sons. Greco-Roman games and cultural events dominated the city's life.

To shore up his court against internal intrigue a high council made up almost exclusively of foreigners supplanted the Sanhedrin, which was reconstituted and stripped of its powers. The new Sanhedrin had members chosen of weaker stock and was converted into a glorified debating society. The high priests and general run of priesthood were appointed from middling sorts to neutralize the Temple as a possible rallying point or place of conspiracy.

The underlying theme through Herod's reign was a fruitless attempt to win favor with the Jews. It is said that on a number of occasions he showed compassion for the people, giving up personal wealth to help the hungry in times of famine, and he otherwise protected his subjects and tried to see to their well-being.

Midway through his reign, Herod made his most determined effort to gain affection as well as to secure his own immortality by launching his greatest achievement, the renovation of the Temple. Yet, when this incredible edifice was ready for dedication at the end of ten years' work, he managed to incense everyone by placing a Roman eagle over the main entrance. Creeping paranoia eventually rotted his mind and dimmed whatever legacy of magnificence was due him. He could not, in the end, come to terms with his subjects and that was his undoing.

HEROD THE BUILDER

Herod had at his command Roman legionnaires, mercenaries from Gaul and Thrace, comparable to today's France and Balkans, as well as Celts from Germany. Inside and outside Jerusalem he interlocked the city and nation into defensive zones designed to thwart internal dissension and outside invasion.

A series of desert fortifications on both sides of the Jordan kept an eye on every movement. Two of these, Herodion and Masada, warrant special mention as marvels.

Some ten miles south of Jerusalem there stands an inverted cone or breast-shaped lone mountain rising to a height of two thousand feet. Herod converted the hill to serve as both a fortress and a sort of weekend retreat. At the base of the hill a support town included a pool, a hippodrome and lovely areas for gardens. The Herodion spectacular was in the hollowed-out mountaintop where he built a petite palace near the main barracks. The craterlike inside was topped by a tower of some ten to twelve stories which rose over the edge and afforded a three-hundred-and-sixty-degree observation post, a protective citadel and a place of respite from the often debilitating desert winds. Herodion was his choice for his burial. The funeral is fully documented with all the pomp one would expect but the actual site of the tomb has never been unearthed.

Even more smashing than Herodion was the fortress Masada, farther south along the Dead Sea, another lone mountain rising on sheer-walled cliffs thirteen hundred feet over the desert floor. Its flat top covered an area approximately three hundred by five hundred yards, afforded a spectacular view to Moab over the sea, and northward to Ein-Gedi. It stands in the midst of a wonderland of muted and ever changing desert tones. Masada had been used previously as an outpost by an unknown person or persons for centuries. Herod had deposited his family there for safekeeping when he continued on to Rome to claim the crown.

In converting Masada to a near impregnable redoubt Herod had a twofold purpose which had to do with his sense of paranoia. He envisioned Masada as a refuge against the internal threat of his Jewish subjects, whom he rightfully feared.

Externally, Cleopatra, the Greek queen on the Egyptian throne, was enormously ambitious to annex Palestine and Judea. Her influence on Mark Antony gave Herod a number of sleepless nights. Despite the fabled intensity of their affair, Mark Antony never submitted to her on this issue but Herod saw Masada as a refuge from possible Egyptian invasion.

Recent excavations carried out by Israel's pre-eminent archaeologist, Yigael Yadin, proved that Masada was a royal citadel in which Herod intended to suffer no loss of comfort despite its arid, scorching, lonely location. The mesa atop Masada was walled and turreted, immense storehouses were built for grain and other supplies, arsenals and barracks and everything else were put in place for defense against a long siege. The water system was one of incredible ingenuity. In this water-sparse area, Herod took advantage of the periodic winter flash floods by a delicate channeling of canals and aqueducts which caught the rampaging waters out of the wadi beds. These were dammed up at intervals and their overspill flowed into a series of cisterns. The cisterns, of monstrous proportions, were lime-coated to prevent leakage and still retain water to this day. The captured water was then carried to the top of Masada by slaves or beasts of burden along a snaking path which is still in existence. This water was poured into other huge cisterns atop Masada which had been hewn from solid rock. The main cistern held 140,000 cubic feet of water.

Even the genius of the waterworks took second place to Herod's Masada palace. This three-tiered masterwork dangled off a sheer precipice on the northern side of the mountain and was so uniquely integrated into it that it was not discovered until 1950.

The builders had to work on sketchy platforms which dangled into space a thousand feet over the ground. The palace was mainly for relaxation and entertainment with its spectacular mid-cliff colonnaded view, time-muted Roman-type paintings, lush mosaic floors and a Scheherazade-like banquet and lounging area. Above the palace on the plateau stood a Roman bath of kingly proportions with hot, cold and lukewarm running water.

Throughout the rest of Judea, Herod's bastion mentality resulted in an integrated system of fortresses, military colonies and new cities. His greatest single achievement outside Jerusalem was the conversion of a small coastal village into a Romanesque deep-water port renamed Caesarea in honor of Rome's rulers. The town became so important that it supplanted Jerusalem as the administrative capital of the state.

Under Herod, Jerusalem became a Romanized jewel. Within its thick new walls were numerous palaces, Hasmonean, the high priest's, Herod's and others. Soaring towers, magnificent fortresses, large public pools, aqueducts, cisterns, monuments and tombs of past kings and Jewish immortals, a broad avenue with gardens and ornate fountains, a hippodrome for Roman games and an amphitheater for their plays. There were some five hundred synagogues in addition to the Temple. In the old City of David thrived a world of tanners, fullers, oil factories, pottery works. In the Hellenistic Upper City colonnaded market stalls were hawked goods from the entire world. Single, double and, in some places, three-deep walls defied outside attack.

The walls also discouraged insurrection from within. Herod internalized Jerusalem as he had internalized the nation from real or imagined enemies. Across the city from the Temple, Herod's palace on the northwest boundary was built on the highest hill. A pair of lofty palace towers soared a hundred and fifty feet and served as barracks and arsenals for his Celtic guard. From here they could observe movement within the city. A third tower, half the height, named for his wife, Mariamne, contained the most sumptuous of the royal apartments. The palace was a rambling affair of columned walkways, terraces, gardens and pools and the richest appointments the world could offer. A hundred Roman-style couches were in each of the two main rooms for food and entertainment and another hundred rooms were available for guests.

The second internal grip Herod held on Jerusalem was a self-contained fortress called the Antonia, after his patron, Mark Antony. From its towers the Roman garrison was able to look directly down into the Temple courtyards and a secret tunnel connected the two, affording the Romans swift access, particularly at festival times when the Jews were apt to stir up trouble.

About halfway through his reign, Herod determined to win over his subjects, as well as to identify himself with Jerusalem's most important establishment. The reconstruction of the Second Temple, or Herod's Temple, was undertaken with typical Herodian largesse. Ten thousand workmen were turned to the task. A thousand of these were priests who were trained in the building arts to construct the most sacred inner parts of the sanctuary. The Temple structure was enlarged and the decorations about its massive white stones were plated in gold. According to one description, it appeared in the sunlight like a snow-covered mountain.

The outer buildings, courts and colonnades were some eight years in construction. The original mount was increased in size by reconstructing the entire hillock with an enormous amount of fill to create a gigantic platform. Herodian stones of ponderous proportions, some weighing a hundred tons or more, formed the retaining walls of this three-hundred- by four-hundred-yard plaza. One of these walls, the Western or Wailing Wall, which became the last remnant of Herod's Temple, has passed down as the most sacred place of Jewry.

A series of courtyards, an outer one for foreigners, one for women, one for Israelite men and one for priests, were terraced, making giant steps up to the sanctuary. This was no Temple to be compared favorably or unfavorably with others of the region, as had been done in Solomon's time.

Herod's Temple was equal to the great temples of Greece and Rome. With its completion he was endeared to the Jewish communities flung about the Roman Empire. Among the Hebrews of Judea, he was loathed.

HEROD THE FAMILY MAN

The Roman emperor Octavius remarked, "It is better to be Herod's pig than his son." On Herod's way to the Judean throne his father had been poisoned at a banquet and his brother committed suicide in Parthian captivity.

When Herod besieged Jerusalem during his quest for the throne, he took a Hasmonean princess as his wife in a maneuver to win both favor and legitimacy in the eyes of his future subjects. Mariamne, however, was not a nice Jewish girl. Her relationship with her husband was as rancid and stormy as Herod's later relationship with the Jews. Yet he loved her with boundless passion and consumed her with oriental possessiveness. For it all, he earned her unabashed hatred. The Hasmoneans were the heirs and successors of the Maccabees, the most beloved of Jewish heroes, and the direct rivals to Herod's monarchy. He had married his menace, a woman whose primary interest was Hasmonean succession. He was to reign for over three decades listening to Hasmonean footsteps behind him.

Trouble was not long in coming. Unable to take the role of high priest for himself, Herod chose a weak Egyptian Jew for the job, one whom he could absolutely control. In so doing, he bypassed the legitimate heir, who was Mariamne's younger brother.

Mariamne and her mother had weight with the Egyptian court and after an appeal to Cleopatra the Egyptian was withdrawn and replaced by her brother. The new high priest was but a teen-ager but he became extremely popular with the people. As a Hasmonean he posed the kind of threat Herod dreaded. At a swimming party in Jericho, during the fun and games, the young man was drowned.

The next Hasmonean to fall was poor old Hyrcanus II. When Octavius won out over Herod's patron Mark Antony,

Herod hastened to Rhodes to plead for his throne. In order to remove an alternative choice, the old man, harmless, mutilated and in his eighties, was charged with conspiracy and executed.

The twin murders of Mariamne's brother and uncle did not augur well with her. Her leverage lay in Herod's obsessed love for her and her two sons by him. Unfortunately for Herod's sons, they had Hasmonean blood in their veins.

When Herod returned from Rhodes with his throne secured, he was to receive charges of Mariamne's infidelity during his absence as well as an alleged plot to assassinate him. Herod turned into a raving maniac, utterly consumed with jealousy. During his frothing hysteria he dragged her before a family court which convicted her and he then had her put to death. What he did unhinged him forever. He became sick with guilt and remorse, took heavily to the jug and staggered about his palace wailing her name; he was ravaged by grief. From that moment on, Herod felt betrayed by the Jews and his paranoia flared into full-fledged insanity.

Next to be fed to the executioner was Mariamne's mother, who had sought vengeance and led an aborted revolt. He sent his sons by Mariamne to Rome to be educated in the hopes that they would take to his Roman ways. Herod's reality was Rome. Without Rome he felt the Jews would be living in the kind of anarchy they had been afforded under the Hasmonean dynasty. Moreover, Rome alone protected the Judeans from constant warfare with their neighbors and their religion as well.

The Romanization of his sons completely failed. They did not quibble or hide their hatred of their father, who had murdered their mother, their grandmother, their uncle and their great-uncle. The Judeans remembered these two boys as Hasmoneans and bestowed upon them all the warmth and popularity that went with that.

Court intrigue became licentious. The mad Herod's ears twitched at the whispers. His sister had allied herself with another of his wives, Doris, a Nabatean. Doris' son Antipater was the instrument of their conspiracy. This ill-begotten trio spread the necessary muck about Mariamne's sons so that Herod's suspicions raged out of control. He brought them before his high council, who convicted them of

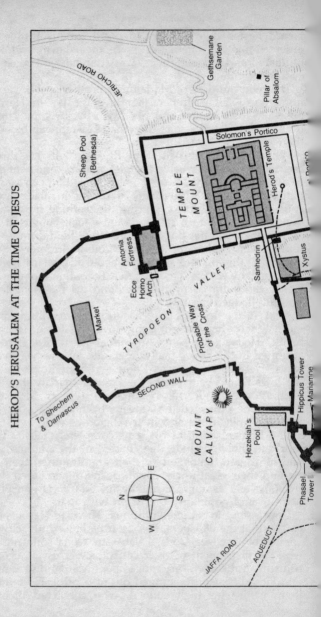

HEROD'S JERUSALEM AT THE TIME OF JESUS

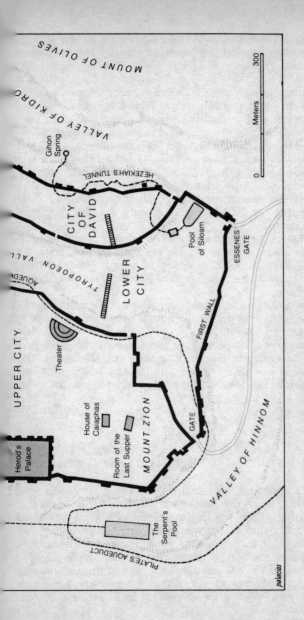

MOUNT OF OLIVES

VALLEY OF KIDRON

Gihon Spring

HEZEKIAH'S TUNNEL

CITY OF DAVID

LOWER CITY

TYROPOEON VALLEY

Pool of Siloam

ESSENES GATE

FIRST WALL

VALLEY OF HINNOM

UPPER CITY

AQUEDUCT

Theater

Herod's Palace

House of Caiaphas

Room of the Last Supper

MOUNT ZION

GATE

The Serpent's Pool

PILATE'S AQUEDUCT

palacios

Meters

0   300

plotting his overthrow. As the succession of the Judean throne was a matter for Rome to decide, Herod sought Octavius' permission to execute them. Octavius did not let his loyal servant down. Herod then ordered his sons put to death. The plot of the women failed when Octavius refused to endorse Antipater as Herod's successor.

Antipater was enraged. To worsen matters, there was the incredible business of Herod doting on his grandsons, the children of the fathers he had murdered. As Herod aged, Antipater conspired to kill his father. Herod, now a mad, guilt-ridden drunk, was dying of stomach cancer. He spent his days in Jericho seeking relief from the excruciating pain at the nearby thermal springs. A few days before his demise Herod ordered his son Antipater put to death.

As the life gurgled out of this hideous creature, word of Herod's impending death reached Jerusalem. Led by a pair of fervent rabbis, a group of young Pharisees tore down the Roman eagle from the Temple gate and hacked it to pieces.

Herod lay invalided, wracked with pain, his mind aflame, his constant companions the ghosts of his murdered wife and sons. In this state he received his final rebuke. His three-decade attempt to win the favor of the Jews had ended in crushing failure. The forty-odd Pharisees and their rabbi instigators were rounded up, taken in chains before Herod in Jericho and burned alive before his eyes.

THE PROCURATORS
AND THE LAST JEWISH KING

Herod's kingdom was split among three surviving sons who had somehow managed to avoid his meat ax. Archelaus, a son by Herod's Samaritan wife, inherited Judea and Samaria. He was immediately confronted with a demand for vengeance for the forty Jews his father had incinerated for tearing down the Roman eagle. Deeper problems of the tax burden and general oppression surfaced immediately in the form of brush-fire uprisings. Archelaus answered the discontent by ordering the annihilation of three thousand Passover pilgrims to the Temple court, then made off to Rome to have his throne sanctioned by the Senate.

A second revolt followed immediately. The principal province and headquarters of Rome's eastern empire was in Syria, which was drawn into the unrest in Judea. An army was dispatched which quelled the revolt and a large force remained to assure peace in Jerusalem.

Archelaus returned from Rome with a reduced rank, somewhat less than that of a king, and the balance of his ten-year rule was marked with continued outbreaks, tension and increased oppression. The Jews and Samaritans hated Archelaus even more than they hated each other and combined in an appeal to Rome to have him removed. It was in Rome's interests at the moment to keep a lid on things and in A.D. 6 Rome commenced direct rule by a series of imperial governors. Archelaus was given his walking papers and lived out his miserable days in exile in Gaul.

These governors, later named procurators, set up Caesarea as their administrative capital. A large Syrian civil and military contingent in the city quarreled constantly with the Hebrew minority, which eventually turned Caesarea into a flashpoint. The governors traveled regularly up to Jerusalem on government business and for such perfunctory occasions as Jewish festivals. The governors were a mediocre corps, not necessarily Romans, from various parts of the empire. They had virtually no understanding or feeling for the Jews. In the beginning they were under orders not to aggravate the Hebrews in their religious affairs and Rome even allowed the Sanhedrin to control theological matters. This body, made up mostly of priestly families of the Sadducees, arbitrated the religion for the Diaspora as well as Judea. Rome's attempts at moderation were short-lived. Sabinus, first of the imperial governors, set the tone of despotism, corruption, tyranny and Roman cruelty that was ultimately to enfrenzy the Jewish people into a series of self-destructive revolts.

Apocalyptic literature had replaced prophecy with books of doomsday writings of a people whose backs had been broken too many times, who had been squashed under one international power after another for century upon century. These writings enforced prophecy, particularly in the longings for deliverance by a savior. One would-be messiah after another came forward to claim the role. The worse things became, the further the Jews were driven into what became a messianic fanaticism. The more these hopes were galvanized, the fiercer their resistance to Rome became.

Sabinus put down a new revolt with typical Roman barbarism which ended in a traditional plunder of the Temple. Rome then called for a hated census in order to jack up the already topheavy tax rolls. The inevitable happened.

Judah the Galilean rallied the Jews under a messianic banner into a band who called themselves the Zealots and who went on a rampage against the Romans in the north. The fire was put out only after the Roman governor in Syria rushed two legions, supported by Arabs, into the Galilee and destroyed the main rebel city of Sepphoris near Nazareth. Two thousand rebels were crucified and the balance of the city's population was sold into slavery.

When Tiberius became emperor the campaign of tyranny was heightened with his appointment of Pontius Pilate as procurator. He squandered Temple funds, fostered the return of pagan symbolism to Jerusalem and had uncounted thousands of Jews nailed to the cross, including Jesus. The worst of a bad lot, Pontius Pilate proved too severe, even for Rome, who eventually recalled him and forced him to stand trial, mainly on the charge of failing to dispense justice properly.

In Rome, a young ne'er-do-well named Agrippa, the grandson of Herod and Mariamne, buddied around in the jet set, running up large debts as a high liver. Out of deference to the Herod family's services to Rome, the Emperor Tiberius canceled Agrippa's debts but he eventually ended up in prison. When one of his pals, Caligula, became emperor, Agrippa was appointed governor of a territory in northeast Palestine.

Caligula was a madman and megalomaniac without parallel. Among his more noted pranks was the naming of his horse to the supreme Roman council and changing the statue of Zeus for a statue of his own image in the Temple of Jupiter. In family matters, he committed incest with his mother and impregnated his sister. When he realized the child his sister was bearing could be a threat in the future, he personally slit her belly open and ate the fetus.

In one of the towns under Agrippa's rule the Jews tore down the Roman altar. When word of it reached Rome, the mad emperor ordered a golden image of himself to be placed in the Holy of Holies in the Temple in Jerusalem. Although it was tantamount to suicide to challenge Caligula, Agrippa dared to travel to Rome and succeeded in having the order rescinded. Caligula's assassination ended this touch-and-go situation. Claudius, the new emperor, had been friendly to Agrippa and elevated him to King of Judea and Samaria in A.D. 41.

Agrippa turned around the slide to anarchy for the moment and became a great as well as the last king of the Jews. Adopting Judaism, he rekindled the failing spirits of the people, brought them peace and served their interests. He was everything Herod might have been but was not. His most important piece of work in Jerusalem was to commence the building of a third wall on the weak northern side of the city. Agrippa died unexpectedly in Caesarea after only three years on the throne. Foul play, poisoning, is suspected and his pro-Jewish attitudes were undoubtedly the main cause.

For the next two decades direct rule came from Rome in the form of a procession of procurators, some worse than others. A few attempted some sort of fair-handedness but the body of these men were brutes who drove the people to hysteria and fanaticism. Their lot consisted of a former slave, an apostate Jew, a Greek and several whatnots. The tax collectors who inundated the province were described as flies swarming on open sores. The atrocities ordered by the procurators became a swollen catalogue of horrors.

The road from every village, township and city in Judea was a Golgotha lined with tens, dozens, hundreds and even thousands of crosses bearing crucified men. The dying went on in the anguish of a slow, oozing, excruciatingly pain-filled death. It was a Roman sport to prolong the agony for hours. Not until the crucified's legs were broken at the knees and his full weight sagged from his nailed hands did death come quickly. The torture of the crucified was matched by the torment of wives, children, family and friends who wailed at the feet of their loved ones. At eventide flocks of vultures, grown almost too fat to fly, tightened their overhead circles.

Seeing the futility of continued resistance to Rome, the aristocratic and priestly families of the Sadducees headed up a pro-peace faction looking for ways to co-operate as they had done with the Greeks. But the Zealots had grown larger in numbers, resolution and fury. The Sicarii, a band of extremist Jewish Pharisees, named after their short assassins' daggers, took up the point of revolution. They mingled in crowded narrow streets and dispatched their enemies with a quick twisting thrust of their daggers. Other Sicarii bands nipped off the wealthy and held them for ransom and release of prisoners. In retaliation, Jews were decapitated by Roman soldiers on the slightest pretext, prison cells bulged, crosses toppled to the ground from overuse. All imperial powers had to cope with rebellious peoples but Rome had never seen the likes of the Hebrews.

The Zealots cried out to the tormented land, "No God but God, no tax but to the Temple, no friend but the Zealot." Vengeance wrought vengeance while martyrdom became commonplace in the wake of fanatical Zealot courage. New messiahs stepped forth to proclaim themselves while others ran around the countryside prophesying the end of the world or the coming kingdom of God on earth. Chaos reigned as Rome became utterly perplexed and reacted with heightened butchery. With Judea a bloody mess and war fever raging, the last procurator set the match to the powder keg.

As malevolent as any procurator before him, Florus would find few equals for the sordidness of his reign. After he looted the Temple to pay off personal debts the people mocked him by dressing as beggars and taking up a collection for him. Enraged by the insult, Florus ordered the sacking of the Upper City and hundreds of crucifixions, as fast as the crosses could be raised on Golgotha. With the Romans wading ankle deep in blood and bones, the nation revolted!

Under Menachem the Zealot, the Jews made good a surprise raid on the Dead Sea fortress of Masada, destroyed the Roman garrison, collected their weapons and marched on a Jerusalem inflamed with the rising. Unable to cope out on the streets, the Romans buttoned up in the Antonia fortress. The Zealots cut the bridge between the Antonia and the Temple Mount, then seized the Lower City of David. Florus fled back to Caesarea complaining about his unruly subjects and sent out the alarm for help. In one of the most wanton of all massacres, the Romans and Syrians in Caesarea destroyed the entire Jewish population of that city.

As the Zealots tightened their grip inside Jerusalem, the Roman garrison fled to Herod's palace, then laid down their arms. The Zealots fell upon them and slaughtered the lot and rid the holy city of Rome. Across the land of Judea the Jews erupted and caused the Romans to flee.

A relief column from Syria attempted to break into Jerusalem without success. As they retired they were carefully lured into a gorge where the Zealots pounced on them, wiped out those who did not turn tail and returned to Jerusalem with a cache of Roman weapons which included sophisticated stone catapults and fire-dart throwers. For the moment, no Roman walked the land.

The Emperor Nero clearly understood he had a major confrontation on his hands and chose his most brilliant general, Vespasian, hero of German and British campaigns, to restore order in Palestine. Gathering up the available forces in the region, Vespasian methodically subdued the Galilee and forced the Zealot hero, John of Giscala, to retreat to Jerusalem with the balance of his people.

THE ZEALOTS

Among the last Jewish survivors of Vespasian's Galilee campaign was their general in Judea, a man named Josephus, who was one of the most unusual and far-reaching characters of the era. Of a priestly Pharisee family, he had been raised in Rome and at one time returned to appeal for the release of some imprisoned priests. Although appointed Jewish commander of the Galilee, he was suspected of being a dove by the Zealot leader in the area, John of Giscala.

Josephus managed to outlive a suicide pact he had made with his men when trapped in a fortress near Tiberias. He surrendered to the Romans, talked them into taking him under their wing and in time acquired Roman citizenship and the Roman name Flavius Josephus. Although distrusted by both sides, he became the ultimate historian of the era. His work is recognized as the final word and almost exclusive authority on the period. Traveling with the Roman legions and later with access to their archives, he compiled his work with dazzling accuracy, so much so that archaeologists have used his writings as their bible to locate antiquities. He left as well an incredible set of eyewitness and verbatim accounts of events.

With the Galilee in Roman hands, Titus, son of Vespasian, arrived with three more legions plus thousands of auxiliaries. During the two and a half years of Vespasian's campaign (67–69) in the north, the free Jews in Judea ruled themselves by a revolutionary council and even struck coins bearing the years "one," "two" and "three" to denote their freedom of Rome. But the Jews had fallen prey to their ancient malady of internal disunity and Jerusalem was being torn apart by disparate groups and their leaders. They not only failed to prepare Jerusalem's defenses properly, they often fought openly in the streets. It was in a condition of disunity, of Jew battling Jew, that four Roman legions and thousands of auxiliaries were found to be marching on the city.

By a quirk of history, the Emperor Nero died and his successor was murdered. The Jerusalem campaign was suspended until the political dust settled in Rome. Vespasian was recalled to be named emperor and left his son Titus to finish the job.

The Tenth Roman Legion camped on the eastern side of the city on the Mount of Olives, which afforded a high point from which to observe the Temple Mount. The three remaining legions established positions on the western side, beyond the Hinnom Valley, facing Herod's Palace.

Inside Jerusalem, Zealot forces were under the command of John of Giscala, who held the Temple, the Antonia and adjoining Upper City areas. Simon Bar Giora faced Rome on the western front. The obvious weak spot, the largely uncompleted third wall on the north side, was immediately spotted by Titus and in this area he ordered the construction of platforms and earthen ramps on which to position his mobile towers and battering rams. As Roman construction inched closer to the third wall, both sides unleashed rains of arrows, darts, fire and stones on one another. Time and again the Zealots came out of the city gates to engage in hand-to-hand combat and harass the construction. The construction engineers were shielded by thick lines of infantrymen and the building pressed closer. Now at the wall, Roman battering rams, in the base of their towers, whacked away under cover of bowmen. The third wall finally gave way.

Inside the city, the Jews knew every rooftop and alleyway. Hard, vicious street fighting ensued, with Roman progress measured in inches. At the Antonia, John of Giscala's men stalled the Roman advance by destroying their siege tower. Later, they stopped cold a Roman assault with scaling ladders.

Titus pulled back from the Antonia and concentrated on breaking through the second wall in an area somewhere around the future site of the Church of the Holy Sepulchre. A clanging, vicious, bloodcurdling hand-to-hand battle raged for two weeks before the legionnaires could split off Jewish forces and isolate sectors. This kind of Roman work was carried out with matchless efficiency. On some days up to five hundred men were rounded up and crucified at Golgotha.

Food in the remaining Jewish areas became scarce. Foraging parties were forced to go out at night on raids but the task was made nearly impossible by the quick response of Titus' cavalry. More battering rams and tow-

ers were set afire in Simon Bar Giora's sector by Zealots
who hurled themselves, torches in hand, into the face of a
curtain of flying missiles.

After consolidation of his positions, Titus called his
officers into council and decided that no more assaults
would be made until the Jews were starved into submission.
An earthen siege wall was built around the entire city to
insure the effectiveness of the blockade. Titus had asked
on several occasions for the city to surrender. These calls
were answered with renewed fury by the Zealots, half
starved, half weaponless, who continued to fight with
whatever they had down to bare hands. By night the
Zealots repaired breaches, raided for food and weapons,
struggled for one more day of battle and rested only with
death.

Titus turned once more to the Antonia. Under a roof of
human-held shields which protected the engineers from
the overhead rain of stones, spears and arrows, they
whacked away at the fort's foundations. Still the Antonia
failed to yield to either battering ram, stone artillery or
direct assault. Finally it was fire which forced the fortress
gates and this was followed by some of the fiercest hand-
to-hand combat in Rome's history. Debilitated but with
the will of cornered beasts, the Jews were forced back into
the Temple grounds. It is said that Titus might have
spared the Temple but his soldiers were so enraged by
Jewish resistance, he was unable to prevent the ensuing
slaughter.

On the ninth day of Av, Tisha b'Av, 67, the same date
when about six hundred fifty years earlier the Babylonians
had destroyed Solomon's Temple, the legions of Rome
ripped into the sanctuary, then hacked their way into the
Lower City in a path of carnage.

The two Zealot leaders managed to join their remaining
forces in Herod's Palace where they held out for another
month. The last defenders collapsed of hunger and could
offer no further resistance. Some of those who survived
the final massacre were hauled off to Antioch and Caesarea
to serve as human fodder in the gladiatorial victory games,
pitted against wild animals. Others went into slavery and
certain death in the mines of the desert.

The pick of the litter were saved for Titus' victory
parade in Rome before his father, Vespasian, the emperor.

The treasures of the Temple were a great hit in Rome but the grandest prize was Simon Bar Giora bound in chains. He was taken up to a sacrificial rock and hurled from it to his death. Rome's triumph was commemorated by the construction of the Arch of Titus in the Forum but in the end it served to glorify the people who eventually outlived the Roman Empire.

MASADA

Judea lay in shocked submission. Jerusalem leveled, a city of the dead. Only the towers of Herod's Palace hovered above a kingdom of poking rats, like the chimneys of Auschwitz.

During the last moments of Jerusalem's agony, Eleazer, one of the Zealot commanders, spirited out of the city a group of men and their wives and children. They were of the Sicarii sect, the most zealous of the Zealots, and numbered slightly over nine hundred. Their goal, a torturous forty-mile trek down to the Dead Sea to the bottom of the world, thence south along its salt-caked shores to the table-top mountain fortress of the Masada, which had been wrested from the Romans at the onset of the rebellion.

Years before, Herod had converted the fort into a place of last resort where a king could go out in style. With its vast stores of grain and cisterns filled with water, the Zealots settled in, knowing their time was limited but with the intention of making their deaths meaningful. Masada, by their choice, had become the final outpost of freedom in their vanquished nation. Shunning the Herodian splendors, they set up to live, work and worship modestly and they waited for the foe with infinite calm and purpose. During the daytime the heat blared off the desert floor to wilting heights, but evening brought cool respite and a renewal of magic colors of sky, rock and sea. The calm was deceptive, the stillness a stage for deep meditation. Each day broadened an understanding of their terrible mission and their duty to God. They scanned the horizon during odd moments of the day and in long pensive passages of evening. But Rome did not come.

Rome too had been exhausted in subduing five years of revolt and realized a major effort would have to be mounted to dislodge the Jews from the mountain. For two years Eleazer beefed up the casement wall and defenses. With usual Zealot daring the Sicarii came down under cover of darkness for raids on desert communities and caravans. Soon Masada's continued defiance became an embarrassment to Rome.

In the year A.D. 72 Flavius Silva, the governor of Syria, was charged with the commission to take Masada and bring the Jews off alive. Silva was a general who had been in on the conquest and destruction of Jerusalem and understood both the tenacity of the enemy and the strength of their desert redoubt. He summoned the Tenth Legion to the task and added thousands of auxiliaries and more thousands of slaves. The logistics of moving an army into this deadly hot area, feeding and watering it for months, maybe years, were staggering and bespoke the importance of ending Masada's resistance.

Although the Zealots had conditioned themselves to expect it, when the first clouds of dust appeared on the horizon, their hearts had to skip a beat. It was not the dust of a windstorm but was followed by a terrifying mass moving slowly down the shores of the Dead Sea. They watched helplessly as the mass took recognizable form, as the sun glinted off armor, as the antlike activity of the slaves set up the stone perimeters of the Roman camps . . . and these can be seen from the mountaintop to this day. No man or woman who has gone up to Masada can avoid the clutch that fills his stomach as he looks down on what was the deathly power of Rome. Perhaps their aloneness with God for two years had fortified them. They did not panic. Day after day they watched from the heights as Rome methodically set up the conditions to conquer and capture them alive.

Silva's tactical problem was the sheer cliffs on three sides which ruled out attack. The snakelike path by which Herod had built and supplied Masada was treacherously narrow, steep and too vulnerable to ambush.

Silva reluctantly had to settle for siege, construction and the long and costly haul. A siege wall, thick and high, ran a two-mile course encircling the base of Masada to prevent escape out and smuggling in. Eleazer and his people were aware that Silva wanted his human prizes for the big parade in Rome. Eight guard camps at strategic points sealed the victims' fate. Once satisfied the Jews were bagged, Silva worked out the final details with his engineers. The one soft spot was on the western side of the mountain where the distance between the ground and the mountaintop was a mere three hundred feet. At this point, known as the "white cliff," the slaves built a long, easy sloping ramp upon which he could mass thousands of troops.

Once the ramp was completed and ended opposite Masada's casement wall, Silva rolled up protective towers with battering rams. The Roman breaches, however, were ingeniously neutralized by an inner wall which caused the outer wall to strengthen itself as it was rammed. But the casement defenses contained much flammable material and when this was ascertained by the Romans, fiery darts did their work. As the fire took hold and smoke poured heavenward, the long-prayed-for miracle seemed to occur with a sudden wind shift that spewed the flames down on the Romans. This hope was short-lived. A second wind shift consumed a large section of the defenses and left it unrepairable. With nightfall upon them, Silva called off the final attack until daylight and retired down the ramp to the base of the mountain.

For night upon night, week upon week, month upon month the defenders had watched the campfires of Rome below them, heard the shouts of changing guards and the taskmaster's whip crack the backs of the slaves. This night was different, sorely different. Dawn would bring an angered horde up the ramp, aching for the finale, unstoppable over bridging ladders. The defenders would be hounded down with nets and ropes, shackled and dragged before the citizens of Rome as living proof of the end of the Jewish revolt and the Jewish nation. From then on, death, mutilation, debasement, slavery. Their ultimate fate would be broadcast far and loud to the restless provinces under Roman rule.

In the middle of the night Eleazer gathered his captains about him and told them in part:

"Since we, long ago, my generous friends, resolved never to be servants to the Romans, nor to any other than to God himself ... the time is now come that obliges us to make that resolution true in practice ... We were the very first that revolted from them and we are the last to fight against them; and I cannot but esteem it as a favor that God has granted us, that it is still in our power to die bravely, and in a state of freedom. ... It is very plain that we shall be taken within a day's time; but it is still an eligible thing to die after a glorious manner. . . This is what our enemies themselves cannot hinder, although they be very desirous to take us alive. ...

" ... Let our wives die before they are abused, and our children before they have tasted of slavery; and after we have slain them, let us bestow that glorious benefit upon one another mutually.

" ... and let us spare nothing but our provisions; for they will be testimonial when we are dead that we were not subdued for the want of necessaries, but that ... we have preferred death before slavery. ...

" ... We revolted from the Romans with great pretension to courage; and when, at the very last, they invited us to preserve ourselves, we could not comply with them ... no man will be obliged to hear the voice of his son implore help of his father, when his hands are bound ... our hands are still at liberty, and have a sword in them ... and let us go out of the world, together with our children and our wives, in a state of freedom. This is what our laws command us to do. ...."

Eleazer amazingly spoke at great length of the Far Eastern religions, of the separation of body from soul. And then lots were chosen. Ten men who had drawn the lots were to serve as the executioners of the rest. Each man then retired into a tight family circle and embraced. Each man told his children not to cry out lest it give the enemy comfort. He then held his hands over their eyes and had to witness the horrible moment of their decapitation. When they had fallen headless to the ground, he offered his own neck to his comrade. When each man and his family had been slain, one of the chosen killed the other nine executioners and then fell upon his own sword.

After thirty months, the nine hundred and sixty defenders of Masada granted Rome its pyrrhic victory.

Two old women and five children who had hidden in caves were the sole survivors. Flavius Josephus, the apostate Jewish historian, was in the Roman camp and miraculously preserved Eleazer's immortal words and the incredible scene for posterity. According to tradition the Romans entered the Masada on Tisha b'Av, 73.

Judea had been stilled.

THE JABNEH EXPERIENCE

The focal point of the nation, Jerusalem and the Temple, lay in ruins. Jerusalem was nothing more than a garrison for the Tenth Legion, its encampment in Herod's Palace beneath the remaining towers. The basic fabric of the nation's political and social structure was torn asunder. The province was operated solely by procurators from Caesarea as Rome basically converted Judea into a ranch belonging to the emperor, who leased it back to tenant farmers.

The only group to have retained position among the people were the Pharisees. It fell to them to redirect the religion within the framework of statelessness. The town of Jabneh, midway between Jaffa and Ashkelon near the coast, was established as the new religious and cultural center. A new Sanhedrin and a succession of dynamic rabbis had a definitive influence on Judaism and Jabneh's scholars became the beacon light in this otherwise desolate land.

With the central authority of the Temple and its sacrifices, rituals, national holidays gone, educational and financial functions and all other trappings of nationhood vanquished, new options for the religion had to be considered. There began the considerable task of collecting the vast range of oral law, the two-thousand-year history of Israel, and young people had to be trained as missionaries to go out to the Diaspora.

The functions of Jerusalem's former authority had to be

redefined so that each community could govern itself independently. The commitment to the orphan, the widow, the poor, the beleaguered farmer, the bride's dowry, support of educational and religious institutions now became everyone's responsibility. The Jewish tradition of taking care of their own was cemented, for self-help became a condition of survival in an often hostile world. Charity replaced ritual sacrifice as a sign of holiness.

Jabneh's rabbis went out to the fifty-odd Jewish communities within the Roman Empire and to an equal number beyond it. The Temple, the kings and the glory had departed. Judaism was now to be practiced within the family unit, the community, the synagogue and, mostly, within the minds of its adherents. It would become a lonely, isolated religion bonded only by the believers' love for it. Jewish communities in the Diaspora solidified into a brotherhood whose inspiration still emanated from the wellspring of Israel.

While Jews everywhere had come to accept that they were different and often set apart, Rome made absolutely certain of it by singling out the Jews for a collective guilt tax which went directly into the Roman treasury. Other exclusive acts against the Jews let Jews know they were Jews. They were drawn even more tightly together in the belief that the only one a Jew could depend upon was another Jew.

In Judea, things seemed to be pacified but the undercurrent of hatred of Rome was never far from the surface. The memory of the Zealot debacle was too fresh for much activism, but elsewhere in the empire Jews were only too anxious to join dissident movements.

Sixty years of Jabneh found the state of the religion strong and entrenched. The passivity of those formerly rebellious people in Judea was totally misread by the Romans. So long as Jerusalem lay in ruins and so long as outsiders ruled them, the dry timber was always there waiting for the match to light it.

Rome did not fail to ignite the blaze.

RABBI AKIVA AND THE STAR

The Rabbi Akiva is one of the greatest figures in Jewish history. A theological genius, the main body of his work consisted of gathering and codifying the great masses of oral law. Akiva could discourse on every letter and vowel of the Torah although he exasperated his colleagues with many unorthodox and mystical interpretations. Yet the heart of his message was utterly simple: that the true meaning of the Torah was that one should treat one's neighbor as oneself. As the scholar of his age, a traveler and brilliant preacher, he fortified Judaic ideals as much as any other single man. A good part of his life was spent in the Jewish colonies instilling them with knowledge of heritage. He was universally loved by the people.

The Rabbi Akiva was also an ultranationalist. In the year A.D. 130 the Emperor Hadrian visited his eastern provinces and sensed a mounting unrest and resentment in Judea. Acting with total insensitivity, Hadrian decided to put the Hebrews in their place. A series of oppressive edicts which followed only served to intensify Jewish anger. Two of these decrees blew the lid off. An anti-mutilation law, deliberate or otherwise, included a provision to prevent the Jews from circumcision, their greatest badge of honor since Egyptian slavery. The second edict, equally heinous, was Hadrian's plan to rebuild Jerusalem as a Roman city, with a Roman name, with Roman temples, and to eradicate all memory of its Jewish past.

It was at this juncture that Rabbi Akiva made his shattering revelation. He saw in a young Jewish activist, Simon Cozeba, the fulfillment of messianic prophecy and proclaimed him Bar Kochba, "The Son of the Star," the "savior."

Bar Kochba was the stuff of legends, a Samson/Robin Hood/Elijah figure in an era of grievous injustices and suffering. With the venerated Akiva proclaiming him and serving as his armor-bearer, the nation rose as one, with the exclusion of the small new Christian sect, which fled to Pella in the Transjordan.

The irrepressible Bar Kochba's mission was to rid the

land of the tyrant in preparation for the kingdom of God on earth, a typical apocalyptic vision. Rome was not ready for what happened. The fervor of the Jews for combat toppled one Roman stronghold after another. Roman reinforcements from Syria and Caesarea were death-trapped and chopped to pieces in the Judean hills. Bar Kochba was the consummate guerrilla master of a land and a people who had had a long history of them. The revolt chalked up one stunning success after another until all the approaches to Jerusalem were in his hands. Bar Kochba then turned on the holy city and obliterated the defending Roman Tenth Legion.

Hadrian was forced to call up his top general, Severus, from Britain and personally accompanied him to Judea with an outsized army. Severus was compelled to use the tortuous tactics of an inch-by-inch reconquest. Avoiding open battle, Bar Kochba's men were everywhere and nowhere, using camouflage and terrain as lethal angels of death; they struck, they vanished. The task became equal to any in Rome's long, glory-filled military history. It settled down into a grueling battle of attrition that raged on for three bloody years. But Rome was not Rome because it could not deal with insurrection. Rome finally turned the tide with her overpowering weight of arms but also took a terrible punishment as the Jews extracted a heavy price for every redoubt, cave and village.

Once more history has it that on the fatal ninth of Av, the most dreadful date in Jewish history, the last stronghold of Betar, west of Jerusalem, fell in the year 135. Simon Bar Kochba was put to death and the Rabbi Akiva was to meet his own death in a prison cell by being skinned alive.

It had long been a Roman triumphal tradition for the victorious general to end his campaign bearing a report to the Senate with the words, "I and my army are well." So terrible were Roman casualties, these words were omitted from the report.

And the Jews paid the piper. All fifty fortresses and a thousand villages and cities of Judea were leveled. A half million Jewish fighters were killed, either in the fighting or in the Roman massacres after the fall of Betar. More thousands were put on the blocks of slave markets so that the price for a slave fell to less than that of a horse. More thousands were sent to the gladiatorial arenas. More thousands died of famine while thousands, who could escape, glutted the ports as exiles. Some of these traveled as far as the Rhine and into Gaul.

Jerusalem was leveled to her foundations and rebuilt as Aelia Capitolina, named jointly for the emperor and the patron god of Rome. With the Jewish religion outlawed, no Jew was permitted to live near, much less enter, the holy city. Even the name, Judea, was changed to Palestina. From that day on, the Jews were to be a minority in their own land until they reclaimed their nationhood eighteen hundred years later.

Aelia Capitolina became a quiet Roman outpost town. All that remained of Jerusalem's long, ancient history was that single retaining wall on the western side of the Temple Mount. Yet the Jews refused then, and for nearly two thousand years, to let Jerusalem go. Once a year, on Tisha b'Av, the Jews came to mourn, and bribed or begged their way past Roman sentries. As they stood before the wall and wept, it gained its tragic name...the Wailing Wall. And thus came to an end the first great cycle of Jewish history.

A NOTE OF REFLECTION AT THE END OF THE FIRST JEWISH STATE

When one examines the gory saga of the Bible and the post-biblical revolutions, it comes as some sort of miracle that the Jews outlived their ancient history. By the second century they were already the world's oldest players in the game of survival. The pages of the Old Testament are so bespattered with blood, it leaves us to ponder about the savagery of ancient peoples.

But it becomes even more devastating to reflect on human behavior since, say in the past half century. With all of man's history of inhumanity to man, none has been more constant, brutal or of longer duration than man's history of inhumanity to the Jews. After all the centuries of it, it finally took an advanced, Western, Christian, civilized nation in the twentieth century to culminate everything with the assembly-line murder of six million Jews. When the world learned of it, had modern man at last shocked himself into sensibility? Did the German-manufactured Holocaust finally revolt the human race into screaming, "No more!"? The crematoria had scarcely been replanted with flower-bedded lawns to serve as "memorials" than genocide was on the loose in Biafra, in Bangladesh, in Cambodia and elsewhere. Whether ancient or modern man is the more civilized is a moot question.

The Hebrews were the first light of man. Their concept of the creation is the giant metaphor in which man is singled out as unique among all living things on earth, for he alone was to be gifted with the power to shape his own destiny and to demand his own dignity. Accordingly, the Hebrews held that a single human life was the most significant and miraculous of all creations. This emphasis on the value of life has been constant for four thousand years.

The well-known Jewish persecution complex was not the creation of some sort of mysticism. It is very real for very real reasons. Singling out Jews for punishment, murder and ill-treatment simply for being Jewish was begun long before our times by a succession of ancient pagan powers. Since the first Jewish state was destroyed for this reason in the second century, little since has happened through their wanderings to change this complex. The Holocaust of World War II was but a climax to eighteen hundred years of major and minor holocausts imposed upon them. Every Jew born since the destruction of the Second Temple has learned an early fear and suspicion of gentiles, almost always based on a hostile act against him for the "crime" of being born a Jew.

Yet the Jews, infinitesimal in numbers in the grand scheme, refused to alleviate their own sufferings by the easy outs of conversion and assimilation. In clinging to their idea of God and refusing to have other versions and variations imposed on them, the Jews singled themselves out for punishment by a world that resented them for being different. Only two religions survived the Roman Empire, Judaism and Christianity. Had the Jews been less tenacious, had they even gone under or dissolved themselves among the Canaanites, the Egyptians or the Greeks, neither Christianity nor Islam would have seen the light of day. One can go into all sorts of wild speculation about how the world would have turned out had paganism been the surviving belief of the Roman Empire. For this reason alone, there is a debt to the stubborn Jew that the world scarcely seems to understand. Quite the contrary. The Jewish discovery and concept of God has brought them little but misery among the nations. So long as the Jews lived up to the demands of God they were resented by men and nations who didn't want to live up to these demands. The resentment of the Jewish relationship to God, in my opinion, is the guts of anti-Semitism.

Judaism, like no other faith, recognized human failure. The Old Testament is replete with it. The sinning virtually never stopped. What then did God inspire Moses to mean by the Ten Commandments and the Torah? Were these intended to be the absolute marching orders for the human race? Not so. The very word "Torah" means "instruction." The Torah was given as a set of guidelines, a code of universal moral decency, to lend direction to man's individual search for meaning in life. As holy as the Torah is held to be by the Jews, every line has been haggled over for centuries. The religion's beauty is that it calls for constant change and improvement and grants the believer a wide range of interpretation to find it. Continued curiosity and exploration are deemed far more important than blind acquiescence to a ponderous theology. No message in the Torah is clearer than the conclusion that individual human action is the most significant of man's achievements, for his quality of life and his dignity depend on it. Man was made unique and declared unique so his unique mind could take wing and not be stuffed into a closet of ignorance and fear. In bowing down to dogma, man often dilutes and even surrenders his greatest power when he closes his mind to discovery and improvement.

When Pompey entered the sacred chambers of the

Holiest of Holies in the Temple at the Roman conquest of Jerusalem, he was baffled by the absence of a symbolic creature to represent the God figure. All that was there was the Torah. The Jews have chosen to retain a mysterious and mystical relationship with God. Even when messianic fervor swept over them it was more a manifestation of the desperation of the times. The coming of a messiah was and still remains an allegory. Hope for a deliverer will remain so long as there is suffering, hatred and bloodshed and that apparently will be as long as man exists. "Messiahs" have come and have totally failed to bring peace on earth. Thus failing, the emphasis of the disciples of these "messiahs" then tilted in another direction . . . to prepare the people for the kingdom of heaven, supposedly a far superior place to what is here on earth.

Fear of death has always been the most misunderstood and feared of all human events. In that no one has ever escaped death, the fear of death presented a fertile field for exploitation by ancient as well as subsequent religions. Heaven, likely as not, is a human illusion born out of man's fear of death. So long as there has been no proof of the existence of heaven, heaven is a moot question. This earth, this life, are real and this earth is certainly a part of God's universe.

Redemption, therefore, becomes the most magnificent element of all Jewish thought. In recognizing human failure the Jews contend that man has the duty and the ability to redeem himself here on earth; for, indeed, this earth may be all the heaven there really is.

Moral renewal should not be the result of guilt or fear of one's sins but the ability of the individual to reach inside himself and to see himself. This is what makes him unique and affirms his unique value. The lopsided imposition of guilt for sin has become a warped value based on man's known imperfections and his fear of death, and such guilt has been used as a weapon against him and has squashed his ability to redeem himself.

In other religions man has been taught that judgment of him will be based on divine wrath. For each of his wrongdoings he will lose valuable brownie points needed to get into heaven, such brownie points handed out or taken away by men who consider that they hold the keys to the divine kingdom. The only way to get into heaven, man is told from the beginning, is to accept doctrines of morality without question. Thus, the fear that heaven will be withheld has been converted into a menace. Man's imperfections, his normal capacity for sin and his primal fears have been distorted and played upon.

In Judaism, judgment is not imposed by teaching guilt or by terrorism, but by man's ability to redeem himself. The purpose of judgment is less to determine degrees of guilt than to encourage change here on earth.

The agony and ecstasy of being Jewish impose on one a continual intellectual exercise in order to reach man's full potential for goodness. When the Jews were forced from statehood to the tight communal existence, they were cut adrift in an often hostile world and rendered defenseless by repugnant laws and ghettoization. It should be remembered that no Jew anywhere in the world had equal rights of citizenship in any land from the fall of the Second Temple until passage of the American Bill of Rights near the end of the eighteenth century. They neither sought converts to their faith nor killed others in the name of their faith. Today, outside of the United States and Israel, there are a mere eighteen hundred synagogues worldwide! Continued survival imposed upon the Jew the necessity to practice the God-given gift of individualism through intellect. Individual Jews have contributed thousands of percentages greater than their meager numbers for human betterment, often in the face of hatred.

The Coming of Christianity

The most far-reaching universal event in Jerusalem's history took place on a single day in April around the year A.D. 33 when a twenty-nine-year-old Jewish rabbi out of Nazareth was tried and crucified as a heretic.

When a Jew writes of Jesus, it becomes tiptoe time. Very early in the development of Christianity the Jews were accused of having committed the dual sins of failure to recognize Jesus as the son of God and of condemning him to death. Although neither is true and nothing in the Christian ethic supports a doctrine of eternal collective guilt for an entire race of people, that's precisely what happened. Scapegoatism and hatred of the Jew have been ingrained in word and deed in Christianity from its inception. In the name of the cross and beneath its shadow Jews have been mercilessly subjected to death and degradation from the Crusades to the heinous pogroms of eastern Europe. If these be the book ends of recent history, they hold in place volumes spilling over with accounts of massacres, ghettoization, expulsions, legal thuggery, gang beatings and the Inquisition of an innocent people.

While we cannot embrace the life of Jesus with the zeal of an evangelist, we can say that all Jews of reason cannot and do not hold Jesus personally responsible for what Christians have done in his name. More and more Jewish writers and scholars have come out of the closet to seek truth and clarity in the matter of Jesus and Christianity, a matter which has been confused and muddled by the total splits and endless theological warfare within the various Christian subdivisions.

Jesus, whose Hebrew name was Joshua, was never anything but a pious Jew from birth to death. His conversion to Christianity was made by others long after his mortal departure. Between the actual event of his crucifixion and the emergence of Christianity there is a vast gray area filled with enormous conjecture. For decades after the death of Jesus the new religion depended solely on oral tradition. Christian literature was very slow and tentative in establishing itself. When the written literature finally did emerge, it was long after the fact, highly suspect as to accuracy, and so unreliable in parts, it has confused and embarrassed Christian theologians in all ages. John Paul, the Polish-born Pope, visited Turkey in 1979 with the aim of clarifying the "gospels" with the Eastern Orthodox Church. The word "gospel" infers a sort of absolute truth, yet "gospel" was wrangled over, for centuries in some cases, before it was accepted as gospel. Much of the actual Christian religion was invented long after Jesus' lifetime and much of the writings and rituals were sculptured to conform with the politics, mores and needs of an emerging religion.

As Jews we believe him a genius, a great prophet and teacher, and one of the world's foremost humanitarians, but a mortal. Treating him as a man rather than a deity, we often get contrasting views, for the historical Jesus and the religious Jesus are often wholly different matters.

As the father of a religion Jesus did not found, his road to and from Calvary has been traveled by more writers than any road in history. The details of the events scarcely need another recounting here but comment begs to be made concerning the incongruities that have laid false blame on Jesus' own people.

To understand what happened that day in Jerusalem, one has to review the temper of the times. Over the centuries all the pieces had fallen into place for the arrival of a messiah who was to convert the world into the kingdom of God. The prophets, aroused by eras of outside oppression and inside greed, had long had the prediction of a deliverer on the books. Before and after the advent of Jesus, Jewish history is replete with messianic claimants. Scores of rabbis, holy men, warriors, scholars and scribes stepped forth to claim they were the fulfillment of such prophecy. They had their followers and formed cults but always remained faithful to Judaism and the Torah. Simon Bar Kochba, the most famous of these, was declared the savior by no less than Akiva, the greatest rabbi of the era, and as we know, "The Son of the Star" led the final revolt against Rome. Bar Kochba rates much more note from the historians of those times and he was a hundred years after Jesus. Most of the "messiahs" have gone down in Jewish legend and folklore with great favor. What is important to remember is that messianic fervor was part and parcel of life in the time of Jesus, so he was neither unique nor an exception. These messiahs all came on the heels of oppression and were largely an expression of the aspirations and longings of the people.

During the Greek rule of the Hasmonean era, directly preceding Roman rule, a small sect of ultra-pious Pharisees quit Jerusalem and the world to shrink into a monastic order known as the Essenes. They had the look and style of pre-Christians. The main group of Essenes lived in a cave area along the Dead Sea. They left Jerusalem in disgust over priestly corruption and perversions of the religion. With their rigid structure, seclusion from the outside world, the practice of celibacy, study, prayer, a self-contained communal life, secret rituals, they were remarkably similar to the early Christian monastic sects. The Essenes left a great deal of written literature, some of which was miraculously discovered by archaeology and known to us as the Dead Sea Scrolls. It proved them to have been devout Jews but somewhat ethereal and a bit "off the wall" in mysticism. They were heavily into apocalyptic literature which envisioned the end of the mortal world and the coming kingdom of God. They also practiced baptism, expanding on the ancient Hebrew ritual of the mikva bath, a symbolic act of purification by water.

John the Baptist was an Essene or was greatly influenced by them. He formed his own band of followers who were made righteous for the pending new kingdom through the instrument of baptism. Working out in the desert, which was also Essene country, John the Baptist declared he was there to "make a way in the wilderness for the coming of the Lord."

We are not certain of the exact link between Jesus and the Essenes. We do believe Jesus spent time in the wilderness, most likely in or near the Essene compound, and we know that his baptism by John was the turning point in the young rabbi's life. One senses the strong philosophical continuity and can even speculate on the possibility that Jesus had been an Essene.

Jesus was born the oldest son of a large Jewish working-class family. He had four other brothers. In keeping with the male chauvinism of his day, we do not know the names of his two sisters. The theory of the virgin birth, like many Christian theories, emerged long after Jesus was dead. The family is linked, rather conveniently, to the house of David, a prerequisite for fulfilling the messianic prophecy.

At the age of twelve he traveled to Jerusalem to celebrate a holiday and there is reason to consider he and his family often went up to the holy city for Passover, Rosh Hashanah, Succoth and other national festivals. It was quite simply what an observant family would do and it can be speculated with some degree of certainty that he heard sermons of the great Rabbi Hillel and others and that these influenced his life and thought.

He was eventually drawn to John the Baptist, who performed the ritual on him and set the state and tone for his rabbinate around the theme of the coming kingdom. Jesus preached around the Galilee for only a year or so before his fateful journey to the cross.

He obviously possessed divine gifts as an orator and teacher. His physical appearance and personal charisma were overpowering. His ability to move people created an aura of heavy mysticism. We do not know if Jesus' power to heal was genuinely miraculous or that of faith healing, which was commonly practiced by the rabbis of the time. So profound and magnetic was Jesus' appeal that his followers began seeing in him the fulfillment of the messianic prophesies. Apparently Jesus did nothing to reject the notion. The word that spread around the Galilee was founded on desperate hope mixed with fact and fantasy.

Jesus gathered apostles and preached in synagogues about the most beautiful aspects of Judaism, of the fruit of the wisdom of the prophets, of universal love and, of course, of the thriving apocalyptic yearnings for the kingdom of heaven. Although Jesus was "far out" and deviated from the strict formalities of the Pharisees, he never preached heresy or unacceptable doctrine. He had absolutely no quarrel with Judaism. On the contrary, he felt his main objective was to complete the work of Moses and the prophets.

What he did object to was the rigidity and formality of the Temple and the corruption of the priesthood. The protests of Jesus were exactly the same kinds of protests countless thousands of rabbis had made before him and after him. There had always been room in Judaism for Jesus' liberalism and unorthodox style. Nothing he said or did, nor his growing flock of devout followers, alarmed the establishment for a second. There were, indeed, rabbis similar in message and style to Jesus all over Judea and the Galilee.

Every preacher, priest and rabbi before Jesus and since Jesus has had a messiah complex to some degree. No preacher, priest, prophet or rabbi could or did carry or has carried on his work without a feeling of his special connection to the Almighty. If, indeed, Jesus had a highly developed messiah complex it was probably justified by the adoration heaped upon him. His claim, if he made it, was not unique in those times and had little or no bearing on what happened to him in Jerusalem.

The raw fact is that the deification of Jesus was not even a major point of the early gospels and Christian writings!

THE TRIAL AND CRUCIFIXION

According to the New Testament, Jesus and his followers traveled to Jerusalem for the Passover with the intention of declaring himself the son of God. All previous talk of his being the messiah had been a closely held secret. Did he really come to spill it?

What were the realities of the day as Jesus knew them? He preached in a land where he knew of the cruelty of Rome. It is not possible he could have been insensitive to the tensions and volatility that always surrounded national holidays in Jerusalem. Even if he believed himself the messiah, was he there on a suicide mission or sporting for martyrdom? The gospels seem to point out that Jesus was consumed, overwhelmed with fear, before his ordeal and considered breaking and running. His apostles had abandoned him. His final agonies report he bewailed his abandonment by God. Not a single word gives a clue that he had come into Jerusalem for the purpose of killing himself, nor can one believe he felt an inevitability about death. What then was his purpose in going up to Jerusalem?

Tens of thousands of people poured into the capital for a national holiday. Jesus had done so himself since he was a child. Among the country folks in Jerusalem that day were hundreds of other rabbis and their flocks. One can envision the tent cities and portable synagogues on the Mount of Olives with the Temple in view and more of the same on the western side of the city beyond the Valley of Hinnom. The hillsides were alive with campfires, and singing and dancing and prayer. Donkeys of the poor and horses of the rich added aroma and sound. The tents of the wealthy preparing for the seder were elaborate affairs, and of the shepherds, the basic skins and rugs of poverty. Inside the city walls, there was a half-frenzied holiday mood of last-minute purchases for the Passover seder. Dozens of rabbis were on soapboxes in and about the Temple selling their wisdoms, protesting the Temple cult, arguing and carrying on discussions with other sages. The city was ringing with lively comment.

The Temple grounds were no sacred precinct of hushed worship and sacrifice. They bristled with dissent and vented anger and hoopla. The Jews were a lively bunch, practicing a religion of intellectual gymnastics, not sterility. Messianic claimants on any given national holiday were not unusual. No festival would be complete without a score of them.

Among the thousands of visitors, hundreds of Zealots filtered into the city to rendezvous behind closed doors or slithered through the marketplace crowds, nodding quickly to contacts. All of this added a second brew to the festivity, a brew of high dissent, of spoiling for another round with the Romans, for since the death of Herod the land had undergone one brush-fire revolt after another. The Sicarii had their short daggers concealed and ready for pre-picked targets.

The story of Jesus leads us to believe that it was the only show in town that day. Christian literature has isolated the event and focused a spotlight on it . . . conveniently leaving out the explosion of people, the bustle and, mainly, the hundreds of other groups similar to Jesus' who had made the pilgrimage.

These holidays were headaches for the Romans. The possibility of trouble always increased a hundredfold at Passover and Succoth. Jewish history was filled with such outbreaks during the festivals. The Roman garrison had been beefed up for security reasons and their spies drifted among the pilgrims in the bazaars, in their tent cities, about the Temple grounds. The cohorts were in place in the twin fortresses of the Antonia and Herod's Palace, ready to move in and snuff out the first signs of trouble.

Jesus was in his rookie year as a rabbi and was undoubtedly making his first pilgrimage with his followers in tow. He had been buoyed up by the success he had had in Galilee and undoubtedly attempted to win new supporters, to register the standard complaints against an ultra-conservative control of the Temple and to air his beefs about the abuses of the religion. Countless prophets and rabbis had sought to redress grievances of this nature for centuries before Jesus and many were doing so on the very same day. This was the early-day Hyde Park Corner, utterly common to tradition and an integral part of Judaism's liberal practices.

What is completely false is the notion that Jesus and his followers had come to Jerusalem with any intention of starting a new religion. They were good Jews, all of them, and whatever protest they intended to register had time-honored Jewish precedent.

The reported events at best are filled with conjecture. Verbatim conversations later written in the gospels were absolutely impossible to know. What has been claimed seems to run contrary to the history of the moment. Again, Christian literature did not evolve for decades and was accepted only after bitter theological tugging and hauling, some of which is still contested by different Christian denominations to this day.

There was an enormous and highly emotional crowd. As Jesus agitated, he may well have drawn derision from the Temple priests and the aristocrats, who didn't hold high opinions of poor, countryside rabbis. He may have gotten into a heated argument with another rabbi. Some of his followers could have gotten into a shoving match.

He may have declared himself the messiah. This was cause for neither alarm nor punishment. It was happening all the time.

From Rome's point of view, the situation was being watched very closely. Galilee was known to be filled with rebels. Perhaps there was a tip-off from an unrecorded "Judas" that Jesus was mixed up in Zealot business. This certainly seems the most logical reason why he would have been hauled up before the Roman procurator. At any rate, Jesus managed to create either enough nuisance or enough suspicion to be taken in.

At this point the account of the trial becomes so far-fetched as to border on the ridiculous. Historical truth brings up all sorts of contradictory facts that belie the so-called pretrial of Jesus by the Jewish leaders of the Sanhedrin. From the time of Herod and particularly during the Zealot rebellions after Herod's death, the Sanhedrin had been virtually stripped of its powers. It had neither the stature nor the standing to deal with matters other than petty religious misdemeanors. It had no power, for example, to convene in a private home. That was against the law. It had no power to gather to try a case at night. That was against the law. It had no power to try a case on or about a national holiday. That was against the law. The law required that eyewitnesses be present at any trial and these were missing from the so-called pretrial of Jesus. Most damningly important was the fact that the Sanhedrin could recommend a death sentence only for the single crime of mentioning the name of God. All other blasphemies were irrelevant. To summarize, Jesus had done nothing punishable in Jewish law so there was nothing for him to be tried for in what was an illegal gathering, according to Roman law.

The second facet of the trial is even more suspect, a real piece of historical revisionism. In the gospels, Pontius Pilate is depicted as a reasonable fellow, even sympathetic, and obviously terribly reluctant to go through with the judgment. Two distinct inferences come out of Pontius Pilate's alleged behavior.

First, we are led to feel that, deep down inside, Pontius Pilate must have felt enough presence of some kind of Almighty to hedge his bet and put the ball in the Jews' court.

Secondly, we have a vividly detailed picture of the trial being held in the presence of mobs of Jews with the sinister members of the Sanhedrin sulking and hissing in the background. The confused Roman procurator flounders, right?

The purpose of these particular exercises in doublethink is to get across the point that poor old Pontius Pilate, decent chap that he was, had come under the spell and influence of the evil Jews. What we have here is a deliberate concoction to take the onus for Jesus' death off the Romans at a time when Christianity was trying to win converts in Rome.

It's long overdue to tell it like it was about Mr. Nice Guy. Pontius Pilate was the cruelest of the cruel in a line of procurators known for cruelty. What is strangely missing from this story is the fact that Pontius Pilate was so savage, he was even too savage for Rome. He was recalled and put on trial himself on the charge of failing to dispense justice, found guilty by a Roman court, and we think he was given the means to kill himself. So much for Pontius Pilate's confusion and "humanism" at the trial.

As for the rest of it, under no circumstances would any Roman procurator allow a public trial, seek the advice of a mob or play word games with a Sanhedrin which he detested and which Rome had castrated. To have done so would have been degrading to his station. Pontius Pilate had nailed up so many Jews, one more didn't matter tuppence to him. He had come up to Jerusalem on that day to show the flag of Rome. The first Jew marched before him on even the vaguest suspicions was destined to be crucified to set an example to a city filled with troublemakers. It was a deliberate measure to send the message that the festival was going to go off without incident. Nailing up Jews was all in a day's work for a Roman procurator, and he was the worst of the lot, who did it to fifty or a hundred Jews on any given day for any given reason. It is absurd to believe that this butcher would engage in a Cecil B. DeMille mob scene to get his instructions.

Yet even Pontius Pilate had enough common sense and political acumen to set aside a pending execution during a holiday. Unless, of course, it was a calculated move to strike a little Roman fear into the Jews and exact respect on the occasion.

Finally, one has to beg the question of why the Jews would have turned on Jesus, if indeed they were ever present at the pretrial and trial. He had committed no crime punishable by death as far as the Jews were concerned. But more than that, the Jews loved Jesus deeply. Moreover, toleration of a messianic claim had been long established within the religion. History gives us no examples of the Jews ever having punished anyone for having made that claim.

The reporting of the event becomes even more suspect because it took a hundred years after the incident to create a written literature from an oral tradition. During that time the nature of Christianity had changed from a small band of followers to a quickly expanding establishment. In the light of this new day, the evangelists desired to make it appealing to prospective converts and the heart of the conversion effort was Rome and Romans. The original Christians were all Jews who continued to practice Judaism with but a few small additions to the old religion, namely, baptism and the last supper. Judaism and Christianity were completely compatible and one could be a Jew and a Christian at the same time. Dozens of splinter Jewish sects all had their little different bits and pieces but continued to operate within basic Judaism.

But the Jews had to go. They were a tiny people and the new religion's growth was stunted so long as the gentiles had to observe the Torah. In order to tap the vast gentile market and make conversion palatable it was necessary for the evangelists to separate Judaism from Christianity. Jesus was deliberately divorced from his Jewish ancestry, as though he were really not one of them, and the blame for his death was shifted to the Jews and away from Rome where the wealth of converts awaited. These revised writings were deliberate and political with the intent of saddling an innocent people with the blame. Although modern Christian theologists, including the Vatican, have "absolved" the Jews of any blame in the death of Jesus, once a tradition is programmed into a religion it is virtually impossible to deprogram it through truth and reason.

The murder of Jesus was a Roman show from beginning to end. The crucifixion itself had been a non-event. It was no big deal to see three men packing crosses in the streets of Jerusalem or any other Judean city. Ordinary Jerusalemites in the crowded prefestival streets probably offered no more than a sorrowful glance at him and a nod of sympathy to the small knot of mourners trailing the procession. Perhaps they cursed Rome beneath their breath in suppressed rage that Pontius Pilate would do this on a holiday, but they knew what Rome was all about.

Calvary has always depicted the agony of those three poor souls. How is it that none of the art shows the dozens of other crosses which surely must have been in the scene? For this was a prime lynching ground of Rome.

Neither Flavius Josephus nor the leading Roman historians give more than passing mention to Jesus and the event. It was long after his death that the messengers of the new church converted this non-event into what has become one of the most important events in man's history. What was written by them to promote the religion and what happened in Jerusalem on that day leaves so terribly much to conjecture...and so much tragedy in its aftermath.

If the Jews did not love Jesus and first see him as the messiah, who did? His entire band was Jewish. All the creators of Christianity were Jews and virtually all the original Christian literature was written by Jews. The New Testament is Jewish in flavor, in content and in authorship. Without the Jews, before, during and after the life of Jesus, Christianity had no possibility of existing. However, without the revisionism of the evangelists, Christianity would have remained an obscure Jewish sect.

Of all the messiahs who graced Jewish history, Jesus was the one destined to take hold. He arrived at a time when the Jewish people had bottomed out and the human race, no longer satisfied by paganism, was groping for fulfillment. Evolution in man's religious thinking was inevitable. Many Eastern religions were gaining support in Rome and the early founders of the Church realized that Christianity was not an absolute but an option. The new religion came at a moment in history when a movement like this could take off, if it was competitive enough.

So long as Christianity was locked into basic Judaism, its appeal and growth were limited. Judaism's practice and demands were simply too stringent for mass acceptance. Paul, in mid-first century, saw quite clearly that for Christianity to flourish it had to win the masses of gentiles who made up the world's population. He was the first to relieve the new converts of having to uphold the Torah. After a while it was time to get rid of the Jews entirely, for they were too few in number and too rigid in practice to have universal appeal. The job was done by pinning a murder rap on the Jewish people and removing the stigma of Roman guilt and otherwise pursuing the tactic of anti-Semitism.

The most crushing blow was Rome's destruction of Jerusalem in A.D. 70, which left Judaism without a base and central authority. A so-called sin of the Jews was not to convert to Christianity en masse, but had they done so they would have invoked the wrath of Jesus himself. Part of the de-Judification of Christianity was the attempt to depict Jesus as someone other than a Jew. Jesus was never a Christian. He was born, lived and died as a pious Jew and was given distance from his own people in order to allow Christianity to thrive. It is infinitely clear that Jesus had no hand in all of this. He would have been revolted by any notion that a religion created in his name would abandon the Torah, nor would he have sanctioned any religion without the Torah as its most sacred doctrine. He would have been appalled that his people were used as sacrificial lambs to promote a religion in his name. Jesus would have denounced it from every synagogue in the Galilee and in the courts of the Temple and he would have done so as a Jewish rabbi.

AELIA CAPITOLINA

The Bar Kochba revolt ended with the fall of Betar in A.D. 135. The Emperor Hadrian was now able to go forward with his plan to build an entirely new city on the site of Jerusalem's devastation. It bore the name Aelia Capitolina.

The Roman wall compares closely to the wall around today's Old City. Under Roman design the original city of David and Mount Zion were left outside the wall in the south and the "third wall" in the north was receded by several hundred yards.

The city plan was a typical Roman square with a major north-south axis running roughly from today's Damascus Gate to Zion Gate. The east-west arterial followed a course from the edge of the Western Wall to today's Jaffa Gate. At the intersection, a four-way arch denoted the town's center. The encampment of the Tenth Legion was set amid the ruins of Herod's Palace beneath the remaining towers, just inside the Jaffa Gate.

The general area of Calvary or Golgotha was inside the new Roman wall. The Romans put the town forum on this location and built a temple to Venus in a deliberate attempt to eradicate the site of Jesus' crucifixion and tomb. On the Temple Mount, Hadrian constructed a pantheon to Jupiter overlorded by an outsized statue of himself. The Ecce Homo Arch of "behold the man" fame, supposedly connected to Pontius Pilate and Jesus, was, in fact, a victory arch to Hadrian.

Only odd bits and pieces of the Roman city have been unearthed: inscriptions on arches, fragments of baths and the like. It was a bland period with little recorded history; a Roman garrison in the middle of nowhere and of minor consequence.

Both Jews and Jewish Christians were forbidden within Aelia Capitolina except on Tisha b'Av, that day of catastrophe and mourning when Jews begged and bribed their way inside the city gates, made to the Western Wall—all that remained of Herod's Temple—and wept. After the death of Hadrian, the anti-Jewish edicts were somewhat relaxed but the general ban on access to Aelia Capitolina lasted for several centuries.

Jerusalem's fate and fortunes now shifted from a thousand years of Jewish occupation and rule to become inexorably tied in with the burgeoning growth of Christianity. As bishops succeeded the apostles and strong churches were established in Antioch, Alexandria, Carthage, Rome and elsewhere, Aelia Capitolina's population grew under a constant influx of Christian scholars and pilgrims.

CONSTANTINE AND HELENA

Second-century Christian churches spread along the Levant, Asia Minor, Egypt and portions of North Africa, with Rome and regions north of Italy as Christianity's western boundary. Inroads into the European continent were to come later. The early Church was compelled to adjust and conform to a variety of local conditions so that unity and doctrine differed. Ignatius of Antioch developed the first system for a structure of authority to be used by bishops as local high priests or caretakers. By A.D. 150 the rule of bishops was in universal use.

Centralization evolved as bishops of various and far-flung and often diverse churches assembled in synods to clarify, codify, gather and interpret writings, establish rules and otherwise develop the new faith. The first synods took place in the Asian provinces around A.D. 160. Strong regional churches arose throughout the empire but the Roman Church and its bishop were destined to emerge above the others. As the see of Paul and Peter and the capital of the empire, the power of the Roman church became dominant. By the year A.D. 185, under the leadership of the Bishop Irenaeus, who established the concept of the trinity, Rome irresistibly became the center of Christianity.

Periodic persecutions of Christians were pursued by various pagan emperors through the second and third centuries. The dawn of the fourth century saw the Roman Empire undergo a series of traumas. By A.D. 300 the empire had become too cumbersome and widespread to control from a single capital. Rome had faded in value as the administrative center and was under a growing threat from the barbarian tribes of central Europe. Accordingly, the empire was divided into eastern and western regions, each ruled over by a separate emperor. New capitals were established in Milan in the west and Nicomedia, in today's Turkey, in the east. During this time Armenia had become the first nation to adopt Christianity, in A.D. 301, and five years later the Edict of Milan gave Christianity legitimacy while affording its followers a series of tolerations as well as human and property rights.

The "big bang" came for Christianity with the emergence of the Emperor Constantine in the early part of the fourth century. Constantine had inherited the eastern region, which he ruled from a city called Byzantium, and thus the name, the "byzantine" Empire. He later renamed the city Constantinople after himself. There was a predictable era of turmoil and complex civil wars after the east-west split. Constantine ultimately won and ruled both the eastern and western regions from Constantinople.

Constantine had converted to Christianity at the urging of his mother, Helena, who had adopted the religion late in life. He credited his military victories to Christianity and embraced the new faith with all the zeal of an apostle. Declaring Christianity the official faith of the Byzantine Empire, Constantine's works on behalf of the religion really got it moving.

At the time there was a great deal of theological tugging and hauling, particularly from the Alexandria church. There was wide variance among the bishops over the concept of the trinity, which ultimately caused a permanent rift among the Christian denominations. At first Constantine urged toleration of different points of view but the schism continued to grow dangerously. In the year A.D. 325 he called the first ecumenical council of some two hundred and twenty bishops throughout the empire to iron out the differences. This assembly took place near Constantinople and had far-reaching side effects on the future of Jerusalem.

Among those in attendance was Bishop Macarius of Aelia Capitolina, who lobbied heavily with Helena regarding the neglect of the holy city. A year later she traveled to Aelia Capitolina in what was ultimately to become the most important Christian happening since the crucifixion: Helena and Bishop Macarius labored to reconstruct the events of the final days of Jesus and to identify the holy

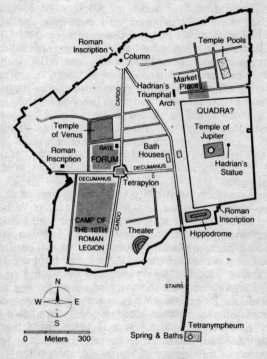

Roman Inscription

Temple Pools

Column

CARDO

Hadrian's Triumphal Arch

Market Place

QUADRA?

Temple of Venus

GATE

FORUM

Bath Houses

Temple of Jupiter

Roman Inscription

DECUMANUS

Hadrian's Statue

DECUMANUS

Tetrapylon

CARDO

Theater

Hippodrome

Roman Inscription

CAMP OF THE 10TH ROMAN LEGION

N
W   E
S

STAIRS

0   Meters   300

Tetranympheum

Spring & Baths

AELIA CAPITOLINA

sites. Together they fixed locations for Calvary or Golgotha,
Gethsemane, the Grotto of the Nativity, the Via Dolorosa,
the room of the Last Supper and other sites.

This event took place three full centuries after Jesus'
death. In the interim Jerusalem had been completely leveled and rebuilt along different lines and within new
walls. One must consider their intention rather than insist
on the question of their accuracy. All sorts of questions
are raised, none of which can truly penetrate the stone
wall of history which obscured the events.

For instance, it is uncertain whether the confrontation
between Jesus and Pontius Pilate took place in the Antonia
fortress or in Herod's Palace, either of which could have
been the headquarters of the procurator. Latin tradition
says it was in the Antonia and thus the Way of the Cross
and its stations could be similar to what is trod by today's
pilgrims. Conversely, the Armenians, who had been in
Jerusalem as long as any Christian denomination, believed the trial was conducted in Herod's Palace and, if
so, the Via Dolorosa would have followed an entirely
different route.

Calvary was beyond the city walls at the time of Jesus.
It is also called Golgotha, which literally means "a bald-
knobbed hillock." There were many bald-knobbed hillocks.
In determining the most sacred of all Christian sites,
Helena and Bishop Macarius subscribed to a theory that
the crucifixion occurred where Hadrian had built the Temple of Venus. Hadrian was violent in his hatred of the
Jews and was bitter over the price of putting down their
final rebellion. By erecting a pagan temple on the spot of
the crucifixion, he seemed determined to eradicate the
memory of both Jesus the Jew and Jesus the father of
Christianity. Again this is all conjecture. Hadrian ordered
construction of the Temple of Venus a century after Jesus'
death and there was no historical reportage which gave
any degree of accuracy in confirmation of these locations.

The discovery of the "true cross" in a cistern near
Calvary leaves even more to the imagination. There may
or may not have been relics of crosses in the vicinity three
centuries after the fact. If there were, Helena surely had
any number to select from, for Jesus was far from being
the only one hung up at Calvary. Different denominations
have their own "true crosses" while other sects such as

the Ethiopian Coptics have an entirely different version of the discovery of the "true cross."

None of these questions diminish the significance of Jerusalem to Christians. Throughout the holy land there are dozens of "traditional" sites in contrast to other dozens of "historical" sites. The Temple Mount and Masada, for example, are historical sites, places of positive identification. Other places, such as the Tomb of the Patriarchs in Hebron and the Room of the Last Supper, are traditional sites or at least it is reasonable to assume that certain events may have taken place there. Jericho is a historical site, the ruins are there for us to see today. The battle of Jericho is traditional and, according to the best archaeological data available, Joshua never conquered the city in quite the way described in the Bible. All three religions connected with Palestine have places of fact and places of conjecture that they hold sacred.

What we do know is that a man named Jesus was put to death on or about the time subscribed to, in or near the city of Jerusalem. Whether he walked left to right or right to left or whether a particular locale was several hundred yards away has little bearing on the outcome. It was impossible for Helena to bestow indisputable accuracy and authenticity on these sites, so a best effort had to do. Christianity, in consecrating its beginnings, fixed these places, albeit arbitrarily, and they have become accepted over the centuries.

What one must always bear in mind about Jerusalem is that it is an incredible mix of fact, fantasy, legend, superstition and conjecture from three religions and dozens of sects representing more dozens of cultures from every corner of the earth, all blended into one enormous euphoric caldron. If the Christians stretch the imagination, some Judaic beliefs bend all credibility and the Islamic fable simply blows out rationality. This tinge of glorious madness is an integral part of the city. While scholarly study, archaeology and historical record have their place, acceptance of mysticism is part of what Jerusalem is all about.

With the designation of the holy sites, Constantine had precommissioned his mother to go forward with erection of suitable churches to sanctify them. Helena was directly responsible for the most important building in Christianity, the Church of the Holy Sepulchre, constructed near Calvary and containing the tomb of Jesus. In addition she was responsible for celebrating the traditional birthplace of Jesus with the Church of the Nativity in Bethlehem.

The original Holy Sepulchre was a circular church, a popular mode of architecture in those times, and featured an enormous rotunda a hundred feet in diameter over the tomb. The great outer dome called the Anastasis was a golden magnificence. The main church body, called the Martyrium, was supported by several rows of thick columns into which prayer niches were tucked. In the center of the church, steps descended to a chapel named after Helena, and a second flight down led to the cistern where the discovery of the "true cross" took place.

Heaps of gold, silver and marble decorated the main basilica, which led to a colonnaded courtyard where the Rock of Calvary stood in a far corner adorned with a bejeweled cross. This grandiose structure was consecrated in A.D. 335 with three hundred bishops in attendance. The original structure remained until a Persian conquest in 614 saw its ruination. The Holy Sepulchre was to undergo a series of destructions and reconstructions until the Crusaders built an enormous rambling and massive building which covered both the tomb and Calvary. Today's church closely follows the Crusader lines with little of the Byzantine building of Helena remaining.

In the Constantinian era a number of Christian developments helped formalize the religion. Although devoutly Christian himself, Constantine appeased the non-Christians in his empire by merging many pagan beliefs into the new religion. The first day of the week, which worshiped the sun, was of pagan origin and converted into the "Lord's Day" or the Christian sabbath. The celebration of Easter was established and Christmas originated when Constantine joined the birth of Jesus with an ancient pagan rite celebrating the origin of the sun. Other basic features, such as the mass and the sanctity of the priesthood were ritualized.

By the middle of the fourth century the city of Rome had abandoned its former imperial pretensions. It had lost its administrative, military and cultural greatness. By the end of the century the city had been downgraded, with the shift of power going directly to Constantinople and the Byzantine Empire of the East.

The Huns of Asia had encroached on Russia and eastern Europe, eventually overran the western Roman Empire from the Balkans in the east to Britain, Spain and Gaul in the west and to Carthage on the northern coast of Africa. Rome, which had been the hub of the world for so long, with its stability, its leadership, its power and its glory, was conquered early in the fifth century by Alaric the Goth. Its fall sent shock waves throughout all civilizations. In the sacking that followed, Alaric spared the churches and their properties, permitting the papacy to continue. Rome's principal function now was to be the universal center of the Latin or Roman Catholic Church.

While Rome declined the Byzantine Empire flourished. Constantinople was a splendid, crashing mixture of East and West where the silken robes of mandarin China walked side by side with Roman togas. The influx of the Roman government and military establishment blended with a potpourri of orientals. Classic Hellenistic architecture, long married to ponderous Roman building, was now embellished with the arches, domes and magnificent mosaics of the Near and Far East. Although Latin was the official language, the spoken tongue was a bastardized Greek, similar to the modern language.

The demise of Rome had sent numerous important aristocratic families and members of the clergy scurrying for safer places. Jerusalem found great popularity, particularly among a series of pious ladies who enriched the city. One of them, Pomenia, was responsible for the building of the Church of the Ascension on the Mount of Olives. Jerusalem blossomed with a cornucopia of Byzantine churches, splendid public buildings and magnificent petite palaces. Likewise shrines, churches and monasteries erupted throughout the holy land, which was now called Syria-Palestina, denoting it as a province of Damascus.

THE ARMENIANS

The Armenians have been identified as a people for five thousand years; their homeland includes the mountainous regions of southern Russia, Turkey and Iran and is said to have held the Garden of Eden. Mount Ararat is the legendary site of Noah's Ark. The Armenians were the first nation to officially adopt Christianity in A.D. 301 but rejection of the concept of the trinity brought them abuse from fellow Christians as well as pagans and Moslems. The Armenian Quarter on the crest of Mount Zion was the first of the Christian quarters, in continuous existence since the tenth century. It occupies three hundred acres or one fifth of the area of the Old City. The Armenians have a chapel in the Holy Sepulchre. Their Jerusalem patrons are the two St. Jameses. James the Greater was an apostle, the brother of John and the first apostolic martyr, killed by Herod Agrippa in A.D. 44 in Jaffa. His head was recovered and is buried in the cathedral. According to legend, his body was moved to Spain, where he is known as Santiago de Compostela. James the Less, the brother of Jesus, was also martyred, and the first bishop of Jerusalem. The cathedral was constructed over the first Christian house in Jerusalem, dating back to the fifth century. The quarter, first used for monks and nuns, was opened to Armenian citizens as a result of persecutions. Between 1894 and 1922, seventy-five per cent of the Armenian nation was slaughtered, climaxing with the murder of two million of them by the Turks in World War I. It is said that world indifference to their genocide paved the way for the Holocaust of the Jews by the Nazis in World War II. The Armenian Quarter today is a self-contained area with its own schools, shops, entertainment, printing presses, patriarch's residence, seminary, monastery and convent. The livelihood of Jerusalem's three thousand Armenians mainly comes from jewel trading, photography and tile making. They are a poetic and passionate people, soul brothers of the Jews. Their diaspora includes thousands in Lebanon and a half million in the United States.

Most prominent of the displaced persons was the Empress Eudocia, who arrived under rather peculiar circumstances. She had lost her position in the court of her husband, the Emperor Theodosius II, owing to the intrigue of her sister-in-law and her Greek origin. As she fled in the wake of an infidelity charge, the enraged emperor dispatched after her party an assassin who managed to kill a number of them, only to be slain by Eudocia's own hand. When the bloodletting was done the emperor opted for an amicable settlement by exiling her permanently to the holy city. She built a palace near today's Damascus Gate and became the leading patroness of innumerable churches and shrines. Eudocia was directly responsible for the Church of St. Stephen, commemorating Christendom's first martyr, and a church to the Virgin located by the Pool of Siloam.

Living virtually as a ruler, the empress ordered the city walls enlarged to encompass Mount Zion and the original City of David in order to permit more Christian sites to be included within a protected area. An important church dedicated to Mary in today's Jewish Quarter and a church next to the Pool of Bethesda were among these. Outside the walls and beyond the Valley of Kidron other sites were marked with buildings at the Garden of Gethsemane and the Tomb of Mary.

It is strange to note in passing that there is no record of any building on the Temple Mount. Jesus had certainly been involved with the Temple, as were the earlier patriarchs and kings of the Old Testament. It was a weird bit of anti-Semitism, and probably part of the de-Judification of Christianity, for this incredibly sacred place eventually became the city garbage dump.

When Eudocia lifted the cruel three-hundred-year ban on the Jews they were scarcely able to recognize the city, for all that remained of its Jewish era was the Western Wall of Herod's Temple.

Christian pilgrims poured in from everywhere, from Armenia, Syria, Egypt, Georgia, Gaul, Britain, India and lands whose names have long been changed and other lands which have long been forgotten. These travelers were enraptured by the dazzling beauty of the Byzantine jewel and permanently venerated it as a place not quite of this mortal world. A most remarkable record was uncovered in the form of a Byzantine mosaic on the floor of a church at Madeba in Jordan. A section of the floor contains a pictorial map of the holy city. This is the earliest known visual record of Jerusalem and confirms its splendor during this period. The city was packed with churches of the far-flung Christian communities, and many of the West, along with Armenia, Ethiopia and Egypt, had rooted establishments.

* * *

Beyond Jerusalem's walls full-blown theological warfare had erupted which subsequent ecumenical councils were unable to resolve. An irreversible direction for Roman Christianity had been established, structured on a pyramid of authority with the papacy resting on pillars of bishops. Rome locked in concepts which became dogma and irrefutable cornerstones of the religion. Dissident bishops who questioned the virgin birth, the resurrection and the trinity were beaten down as Rome demanded absolute obedience of its clergy and of its followers.

An Eastern Church emerged with powerful centers in Antioch, Alexandria and Jerusalem. Constantinople as the capital of the Byzantine Empire was its administrative center, and a growing rival to Rome's authority. The concept of the holy trinity was unacceptable to the Eastern Church and in addition they rejected the supremacy of the papacy. Rome, in turn, rejected Constantinople's jurisdictional powers and so the fabric of Christian unity was torn in half. From A.D. 451 onward this split was never bridged and the centuries to come were marked with bitterness, hatred and bloodshed.

The deification of Jesus has always been a thorny subject among Christian scholars. Recent archaeological discoveries point up the fact that as late as the mid-fourth century the role of Jesus was unclear to one important sect. The Gnostic gospels found near the Nile were Egyptian Coptic Christian writings discussing matters which were squelched by the authorities in forming the early Church. In this early Christian view the resurrection was a concept, not a fact. The actual physical, bodily rising of Jesus came as a miraculous vision flimsily reconstructed and was not accepted in many Christian quarters at the time and not incorporated into the religion until decades later. The Gnostics wrote that a literal view of the resurrection was the "faith of fools." Their interpretation of the event was closer to the religions of the Far East: that of a spiritual divorcement from the physical body. The early shapers of the Church considered the resurrection so vital to the validity of Christianity that all other views were suppressed.

These scriptures likewise question the deification of Jesus, suggesting that he had a twin brother, and at one point they relate that Jesus kissed Mary Magdalene on the lips. The Gnostic gospels could also be considered an early-day document for women's equality. God, they considered, was neither male nor female and there was no earthly reason for the clergy to be run exclusively by men, who, they wrote, had no right to administer authority in the name of God.

This is not the rambling of heretics or the vicious propaganda of anti-Christians. It was the state of the religion as seen by an important founding sect. Many such writings and thoughts apparently abounded in the time of the early evolution of the religion, often by the bishops themselves, and they have continued to surface throughout every generation.

Now in the 1980s the challenge has been raised by eminent Catholic theologians in Belgium and Switzerland, whom the Vatican has gone to inordinate lengths to silence. The constant charge and challenge is that the virgin birth, the deification, the trinity and the resurrection were all man-made concepts, after the fact.

The course of early Christianity in hammering out a uniform code is best exemplified by a monumental theological conflict between Augustine, one of the foremost of all Christian thinkers, and a liberal rebel monk named Pelagius.

Both men had fled to North Africa in the wake of the barbarian invasion of Rome. As Bishop of Hippo, Augustine turned his home into a monastery in which he demanded celibacy, blind obedience and poverty of his monks. His regimented monastic style made a great impact on the course of the Church. His writings made more of an impact. Augustine argued for the doctrine of divine grace. He wrote that man's innate desires had to be suppressed, for he felt that man was incapable of making choices in life and was without the will power to redeem himself.

On the other hand, Pelagius felt that man controlled his own destiny and was responsible for his own failings. Such human impulses as sex were entirely normal. He further felt that man, with his basic goodness and basic ability to make decisions, had the option to choose Christianity for spiritual advancement or to seek other avenues. In any event such a decision should not be made out of fear or imposed upon him.

Pelagius and Augustine were soon locked in spiritual combat. The Augustinian grip on the human mind was supported by the Church. Pelagius was condemned and excommunicated and his arguments silenced. Pelagius had to be run out, for to have considered his ideas would have been tantamount to the Church voluntarily relinquishing its monopoly to judge human morality. Moreover the Church was not ready to admit there were avenues of salvation other than Christianity.

Christianity has grown to be the most popular of religious philosophies. Certainly the Church's self-proclaimed power to be able to deliver heaven constitutes the centerpiece of its power. Man will never be able to either prove or disprove the existence of heaven, for the dead have never told us whether heaven holds divine truth or is merely another human concept. It is obvious that the idea of the reward of heaven, born out of the fear of death, is implanted in the mind of almost everyone.

There are other insatiable magnets of Christianity, particularly among the downtrodden and suffering masses who have no control over their own destinies. They view their own agony on earth as an extension of the agony of Jesus. The poor, the weak, the hungry, the socially and politically abused are symbolically nailed to the cross every day of their lives. In Jesus they have the ultimate soul mate, a representative of the Almighty who has shared their agony and who now awaits them in a heaven which is characterized as a never-never land. Christianity emerged out of apocalyptic belief that life on earth is a torment, that earth is a doomed place and that the life experience is really a preparation for the kingdom of heaven, which one can attain provided one accepts the authority of the Church. Such a belief, in my view, devalues the human experience here on earth and dilutes man's greatest power, his power to make decisions.

The very symbol of Christianity, the cross, denotes human suffering. It tends, does it not, to throw a sense of joylessness over the religion; indeed the joylessness of life? The bones and bits of flesh and relics of saints which are kept sacred in every Catholic cathedral are constant reminders that martyrdom is truly the most glorious aspect of life. The cruelty of life, which must end on a cross, martyrdom, the identification of man's suffering with the suffering of Jesus, tragically appeals to people who are without the will or the power, by choice or circumstance, to direct the course of their own lives and must depend on such a discipline to get them through their terrible mortal experience.

Thus implanted, the dogmas and canons were thoroughly engraved, the opposition suppressed, and early Christian thought was forcibly unified; the Christian route to God and heaven was established.

There were to be no serious military threats to the Syria-Palestina region except for a brief Samaritan uprising during the reign of Justinian in A.D. 527.

In the year 614 a revitalized Persian nation, which had sparred with Rome off and on for centuries, invaded Syria-Palestina and conquered Jerusalem after a short three-week siege. As Persia broke into the holy city, all the love and devotion the Christians had poured into it went up in flames. Thousands of Christians were put to death and more thousands exiled with their Patriarch, Zacharias. The most beloved and sacred relic of Christianity, known as the "true cross," went into captivity with them.

As often was the case in Jewish history, the Jews sided with an invading army to lift their own oppression. This time the small Jewish community, mostly in the Galilee, allied with the Persians in the hope that Jerusalem would revert to them again. This ill-fated alliance was to cost the Jews dearly, for the Persian occupation lasted only fourteen years. During their occupation the Persians permitted the Christians to administer the city and many of their ruined shrines were rebuilt, most notably a smaller version of the Holy Sepulchre.

In A.D. 629 the Byzantines regained Jerusalem, returning the "true cross," and the Jews, remembered for their collaboration with the Persians, were massacred and the few surviving expelled.

A new force was rising out of the Arabian Peninsula. Islam had come into being under the authorship of Mohammed and this was to change the face of the holy city, the holy land, the region and the world, forever.

Islam

B eyond the grasp of the early empire builders, the Arabian Peninsula remained remote, inaccessible and unconquered. Life and culture in this punishingly cruel desert developed according to the harsh dictates of nature. It remained in a primitive state without a developing technology. Mere survival took eminent priority over education, medicine, agricultural technique or urban grandeur. In the northern segment of the desert nomadic bands evolved a culture grounded in the blood oath of the clan, which engaged in continuous tribal warfare. They raided the weak and plundered the caravans. Along the Red Sea in the west and on the Persian Gulf in the east, more agricultural settlement took place and there were overseas trading ports with enough craftsmanship and rare products to sustain them. Binding this vast, semi-charted, blisteringly arid land, was a crisscross bloodline of caravan routes, their goods riding on the humps of camels domesticated two thousand years before the advent of Jesus.

The life style of the peninsula was and remains alien to that of the balance of the world. The fight for existence was reflected in a brutal society. Strong men and strong clans emerged while the weak went under, with little pity shed on them. The peninsula consisted of dozens of tribal units that were never unified in a national sense but constantly shifted alliances. A system of absolute social order developed so that each man had a specific place within the tribe. The only way one could rise within the system was to destroy the man above and dominate the men beneath. Their ethics and sense of justice, totally foreign to Western concepts, called for cruel and final decision. The demands of survival left no room for convocations of scholars to equivocate in forums or parliaments to argue on democratic principles. The law of the desert was absolute.

Dozens of religious cults of various tribes were pagan and primitive. Their beliefs were dictated by the forces of nature. Colonies of Jews which had settled the more mercantile areas since the time of Solomon had lent many Judaic beliefs to the cults. Early Christianity, which was strong on the coast of North Africa, also filtered down to mingle with the Arab religious beliefs.

While the Byzantine Empire and Persia hammered away at each other and were bleeding each other into exhaustion, a power vacuum developed in the seventh century which was destined to be filled by a future Arab nation out of this peninsula.

Life was dull, dirty, repetitious and structured, with little room for humor and less for cultural and technical expansion. The daily search for sufficient food and water still left far too much time for one to find the shadow of a shade tree and daydream. Mirages of the mind abounded. Fantasy blotted out the cruelty of life, made great sheiks out of shepherds, made water where there was no oasis, made warriors out of cowards. Truth and fiction intermingled within the Arab mind so that, to the Arab, fantasy and reality were often one and the same. Fantasy was perpetuated with a language known for its overkill of exaggeration and verbal flights of imagination. The Arab describing the most simple scene can twist it into wild complexity. The act of an easy barter or purchase can become a play of monumental proportions.

The only way people could keep going day after day was to adopt a passive acceptance of their lot. The moment was ripe for a religion based on fatalism. There were actually two vacuums to be filled. One, the political/military vacuum with the decline of the reigning powers, and the second, a religious vacuum through creation of a faith to conform with their fatalism. Add to this the acceptance of fantasy as fact and the time was at hand for a dynamic personality to capture the Arab mind and unify it for the first time.

The word "Islam" literally means "the submission to God's will." It is not a partial or qualified submission, but an absolute submission, without question, discussion or protest. It is a total surrender of man to a deity and it is the ultimate form of fatalism. Islam is more than a religion, it is a complete way of life that governs every aspect of daily existence. No corner of life is too small to escape its rules, no relationship too remote to be exempt from its edicts. Islam teaches its followers not to think for themselves but to live by the decisions of others. When we examine exactly what the submission to God's will means in this context, we see that it is a form of mental sterilization, for it tells man not to aspire or hope but to accept. It is a tranquilizer, a defense for a lot of hot, hopeless, unhappy, struggling people, and it thrives where human helplessness is paramount and progress is stagnant.

There is no papacy or structure of authority, no ordained priesthood. A loose collection of holy men assumed dictatorial powers in interpreting the sole authority, the Prophet Mohammed.

In actuality, the term "God's will" means "the word of Mohammed," the "Messenger of Allah," whose writings are considered divine and above question. It is the most authoritarian of all the major religious philosophies, strangely suited to people who are at the mercy of cruel natural forces.

Mohammed was born in Mecca around A.D. 570. Little is known of his childhood except that he was orphaned at an early age. Like David before him, it is generally believed he was a shepherd and, like David, he formulated thoughts of the Almighty as he tended his flocks. The ideal of desert meditation reoccurred as it had in both Judaism and Christianity. Mohammed's youthful existence was one of extreme poverty as a caravan driver. During this period, one can assume, he traveled far and came into contact with Judaism and Christianity, which were at the roots of his own religious concepts.

He was able to escape the cycle of destitution through marriage to a wealthy widow, which freed him to spend his time in contemplation. Mohammed realized the unlimited political power the Arabs could attain should they unify. He also realized that such a unification could only come through adoption of a universal religion imposed through military conquest.

Continuing the parallels to Judaism, Mohammed went up to Mount Hira near Mecca at the age of forty to gain his commission from Allah. The Angel Gabriel told him that he was indeed the "Messenger of God." What he came down from Hira with were tenets that were extremely Judaic in nature. The centerpiece was monotheism, belief in one God with liberal use of the Jewish prophets and revelation. He adopted and simplified Judaic rituals and moral thought with prayers facing Jerusalem, establishment of a Sabbath, periods of fasting, charity, giving oneself to God. From Christianity, Mohammed lifted concepts of heaven, hell and the judgment day. Abraham, Moses and Jesus were among his prophets, Mohammed considering himself to be the ultimate and final prophet.

What evolved on Mount Hira was liberal usage of Judaism and some Christianity simplified so that the simplest and most illiterate Arab peasant could understand it. Preaching as the "prophet of the poor," he gained a flock of followers around Mecca, mainly among the slaves and farmers.

While his following grew he was held in contempt by most affluent Meccans and, had it not been for the influence of his wife and family, he surely would have failed. In A.D. 622 Mohammed learned of a plot to assassinate him and fled to Medina a few hundred miles to the north.

It is entirely possible that Medina was originally settled by Jews. When Mohammed arrived they were a minority but among the wealthy and influential. Here he turned his efforts to converting the Jewish community in the belief the Jews would flock to him. As was the case with Christianity, many early Moslem converts were Jews. Also as with Christianity, the main body of Jews rejected Mohammed's pretensions. Thus in denying a status of deity to both Jesus and Mohammed, the failure of the Jews to convert ultimately turned rampages of vengeance and hatred against them.

THE MIDDLE EAST

Mohammed was stunned at the rebuff. He changed much of the Islamic ritual to divorce it from its Jewish origins just as early Christianity had de-Judaized Jesus. Part of the process was to claim that the Jews had lied about Abraham and had falsified his words. One of the chief characteristics of the emerging religion was that it made no accommodation for the beliefs of others, so that anyone who was not a Moslem was looked down upon as an inferior or infidel.

Most of Mohammed's followers were ragtag, which gave him self-justification to lead a band of brigands who scourged the caravans and established the principle of conversion by sword and fire. Future wars of conversion became jihads or "holy wars," blending the morals of the desert into the religion and rejecting the notion that murder was the principal sin of man. In the ensuing years the Jews of the Arabian Peninsula were decimated.

In A.D. 622 Mohammed's chief lieutenant, Abu Bakr, joined him in building the first mosque in Medina, where the Prophet preached his messages from Allah, which were to become the Koran, the holy book of Islam. In the beginning nothing was written down. Mohammed's sermons and recitations were memorized and passed along orally and became the unifying code of the Arabs.

At the same time Mohammed's military power grew and he cast his eye to Mecca and the Kaaba, an ancient pagan shrine. According to legend, Abraham, who is also the Arab patriarch, traveled to Mecca and had erected the shrine to his son Ishmael, the Father of the Arab people. In A.D. 628 Mohammed's army fought the Meccans to a standoff but won the right of pilgrimage to the Kaaba by his followers.

Mohammed was a cunning operator, the complete leader. To enhance his political strength he appointed himself chief magistrate of Medina so that his religious and political powers stemmed from the same source. These powers were enforced by his military power. He had established himself successfully as the sole, supreme and final authority so that subsequent inheritors of Islam had to reiterate rather than interpret. In finalizing the religion he left little room for expansion, for the divine canon of Islam is that every utterance of Mohammed must be accepted as above question.

Mohammed died in Mecca on pilgrimage in A.D. 632, only ten years after he had fled to Medina, having forged an Arab nation. Within five years of his death Arab forces had conquered the Syrian province and in the year 638 Jerusalem was under siege by their armies.

THE JERUSALEM CONNECTION

With the death of Mohammed rule passed to his right-hand man, Abu Bakr, the first of the caliphs, who completed the conquest of the Arabian Peninsula and began the chore of compiling Mohammed's message in the Koran.

It had long been the dream of Mohammed to convert the Syrian province, a job which fell to the second Caliph, Omar. Omar's inspired forces stormed out of the desert and overmatched the threads of a wearying Byzantine army in a key battle along the Yarmuk River.

With aim being taken on Jerusalem, Bishop Sophronius, the Eastern Orthodox Patriarch, with a silken tongue sued for a peace that would spare the city. The takeover was conditioned on Omar's personally coming to Jerusalem. Few conquerors had passed up the temptation to plunder Jerusalem but Omar venerated it as an integral part of the new Islamic religion. The story of how Jerusalem came to be designated as an Islamic holy site demonstrates how far the Arab mind is capable of soaring from reality.

When Mohammed had been rebuffed by the Jews of Medina, one of the changes he ordered in the ritual was to cease facing Jerusalem during prayer, instead turning to Mecca and the shrine of the Kaaba. Yet, despite Mohammed's downgrading of Jerusalem and the Jews, he and succeeding generations of Moslems kept a reluctant sort of love-hate respect for Judaism as the old and parent religion. Since Jesus, Adam, Moses and Noah were locked

in as Moslem prophets and Abraham was claimed as the
Arab patriarch and Judaism and Christianity were used in
the creation of Islam, it was natural, almost mandatory, to
establish a foothold in Jerusalem. Both the Jews and
Christians had unalterable foundations in the holy city.
The problem with Islam was that it had neither history
nor experience in Jerusalem and therefore some connection had to be invented.

What was conjured up was a mythical visit by Mohammed
to Jerusalem in order to establish Moslem claims in the
city. The account of the prophet's visit goes something
like this:

Mohammed was awakened by the Angel Gabriel in
Mecca and advised that he was to take a night journey to
paradise. In preparation for the trip, Gabriel slit Mohammed's body open, removed and washed his heart and
when it was returned to him it was filled with faith and
wisdom. Sewn up and ready to travel, Mohammed mounted a magic mare named el-Buraq. This incredible beast
had a woman's face, a mule's body and a peacock's tail
and could travel as far as the eye could see in a single
stride.

Accompanied by Gabriel, who winged it, Mohammed
took no time at all to reach "the fartherest place." "The
fartherest place" is an obscure phrase in the Koran with
no further amplification. Moslem holy men have interpreted
"the fartherest place" to mean Jerusalem, although Jerusalem
is never mentioned by name. Non-Moslem scholars say
that the message could or could not have meant Jerusalem
and, in any event, Mohammed never took the trip or saw
Jerusalem in his lifetime.

Mohammed arrived, tethered his horse at the Wailing
Wall, then went up to the Temple Mount. Here he
discovered the Rock of Abraham's sacrifice, which had
also been the altar in the Temple's Holiest of Holies.
Mohammed then leapt from the Rock onto a ladder of
light which led to paradise. The Rock started after
Mohammed but Gabriel ordered it to remain and it obeyed.

Once again on his mount, Mohammed rode through
the "seven heavens." At one point he led the patriarchs,
the Old Testament prophets and the angels in prayer.
Moses was described as a ruddy-faced man and Jesus as
of medium height and freckled. Abraham, it appears, was

the mirror image of Mohammed. After gaining all the wisdom of Solomon, Mohammed was given the rare privilege of a private audience during which he saw God or Allah, unmasked. Allah wanted his subjects to pray to him thirty-five times a day but Mohammed talked him into a more practical five-a-day ritual. He then returned to Mecca the same night.

There is nothing wrong with this lovely fable, had it been accepted as such. However, in the complex, perplexing and fanciful Arab mind, this story has been taken as absolute gospel. A few chagrined Moslems may admit that it was really a vision or a dream but the overwhelming mass of practicing Moslems and their priests take the fundamentalist view that this is a literal account.

And thus Jerusalem was tied into the Islamic religion.

The conquest of the Caliph Omar began centuries of Moslem occupation. He did not go up to Jerusalem as a military victor but went alone on a camel. His first acts were to insure the sanctity of the Christian holy sites. When shown the Holy Sepulchre, Omar declined to go inside but prayed outside and today the site of his prayer is marked by a mosque.

One account has it that immediately after his arrival Omar asked to be taken to the Temple Mount. The Patriarch Sophronius hemmed and hawed, for the Christians had long used it as a garbage dump. When Omar reached it and found how it had been desecrated he forced Sophronius to crawl through the refuse on his hands and knees as atonement.

Omar erected a simple wooden mosque on the Mount to denote "the fartherest place" of Mohammed's journey. The original mosque, temporary in construction, was eventually replaced by the grand Al Aksa Mosque, which stands on the southern fringe of the Temple Mount plaza. The words "Al Aksa" are Arabic for "the fartherest place." Omar had nothing to do with the building of the dome over the Rock which has been misnamed the Mosque of Omar.

The Caliph Omar's rule was considered wise and moderate, with the Arabs retaining the established civil governmental structure headquartered in Caesarea. It should be noted that Jerusalem was not then and never has been the capital of any Arab nation. Over the objection of Sophronius, Omar permitted the Jews to return to Jerusalem.

THE UMAYYADS, THE ROCK
AND THE FARTHEREST PLACE

The Caliph Omar was assassinated as was his successor. Ali, the fourth successor of Mohammed, found himself plunged into a civil war with the emerging power of the Syrian Arabs. Ali was forced to abdicate the caliphate to Omar's former military commander and was also assassinated.

The center of Arab power now shifted from the Arabian Peninsula to Damascus as the Umayyad clan established a dynasty that was to last for ninety years through fourteen caliphs. The first of these caliphs had himself installed in Jerusalem, which was immediately upgraded because of its proximity to Damascus.

The Umayyads were to put an indelible stamp on their empire, changing the vernacular from Greek to Arabic, which was the language of the Koran, minting Arabic coins and erecting great and exquisite mosques. The Umayyad life style was one of grandeur and the joy of the flesh, which was echoed in magnificent desert palaces filled with fabled gardens, exotic birds, poets, dancing ladies and mosaic and fountained harems. The Umayyads were even better known for their military exploits. One Umayyad general landed by sea on the Iberian Peninsula and ordered the boats burned as he exhorted his troops, "The sea is behind you, the enemy before you, there is no escape save valor!" And valor they had.

By A.D. 711 Arab armies ranged from Spain to India. In less than a century after the death of the Prophet their empire was the largest in history. Making no pretense of gentle persuasion, the national conversions of Persia, Egypt, North Africa and Central Asia took place.

Early in the Umayyad dynasty the Caliph Abd El Malik and his son, the Caliph Waleed, began and completed the two structures that were to cement the Moslem connection to Jerusalem. The Dome of the Rock, the oldest existing Islamic shrine, and the Al Aksa Mosque were constructed for many considerations, not the least of which were political.

Even if Mohammed had never visited Jerusalem and even if Islam had no history in the city, the Moslems had an undeniable spiritual claim as the third party in this religious triumvirate. Arabs were indigenous to the region and formed the majority population most of the time.

The construction of appropriate shrines to consecrate the Moslem presence also contained heavy political and commercial overtones. When the capital of the Arab empire moved to Damascus a rival caliphate emerged in Mecca. To counter this and assure Umayyad prestige and authority, Jerusalem was upgraded dramatically as a Moslem holy place. Every devout Moslem was supposed to make a *haj* or pilgrimage to Mecca once in his lifetime. Now Jerusalem with its great twin shrines was offered by the Umayyads as an alternate site.

Jerusalem was also the best place for Islam to demonstrate its superiority over the other religions. Since the day it was completed, the Dome of the Rock has been the centerpiece of Jerusalem. It is about the same size as the dome of the Holy Sepulchre but from its perch on the Temple Mount the mosque is almighty in its reign over everything else. As for the Jews, their lone shrine was a part of the wall of Herod's Temple which groveled beneath the great Moslem edifice.

The final consideration was commercial. Pilgrimages were the original package tours. Jews came at Passover and Succoth in masses. Christian pilgrimages at Easter and Christmas jammed the city. Moslem pilgrimages either rivaled Mecca or were tied into the haj to the Arabian Peninsula. These floods of visitors required services and produced enormous revenue. Moreover, everyone who traveled up to Jerusalem was made aware of the "supremacy" of Islam.

THE FAR REACHES OF ISLAM

By the mid-700s the Islamic empire was ponderous in size, ranging from the gates of France to China. Shortly after the first flushes of glory when the Arabs had galloped out of the desert the empire became wracked with constant rebellions and political instability. Assassinations and intertribal, intercult, interclan warfare never ceased. Slave rebellions and surges of regional nationalism added fuel to the fires.

The Umayyads in Damascus had sown the seeds of their own destruction from the beginning and eventually a coalition of three major elements brought the Arab dynasty down.

Converts to Islam who were not of Arab lineage were downgraded, shorn of normal rights and blatantly discriminated against. They were the foot soldiers while the Arab elitists were the cavalry, both on the battlefield and on the social scale. Damascus remained indifferent and insensitive to the vast collection of nationalities who began to form up in opposition.

The second element of discontent was the Shiite sect, which emerged on the Arabian Peninsula and plunged it into civil war against the Umayyads. It was the Shiite contention that the caliphate and leadership of the Moslem world belonged to the direct descendants of Mohammed. Ali, the fourth caliph, had been their inspirational leader and had been assassinated by the Umayyads after they took power. In answer to one Shiite protest the Umayyads handed them the severed head of Mohammed's grandson.

The third and perhaps the most important element in the anti-Umayyad coalition were the Persians. With Persia's conversion to Islam, the Arabs had conquered a great ancient power with a long-standing civilization and a military and imperial tradition. The Persian hierarchy, although now Moslem, still considered themselves of a higher order than the johnny-come-lately Arabs.

Other unhappy groups were prone to join the anti-Umayyad party. The Abbasid war party, named for its leader Abbas, took to the field garbed in black and raised

THE ISLAMIC EMPIRE

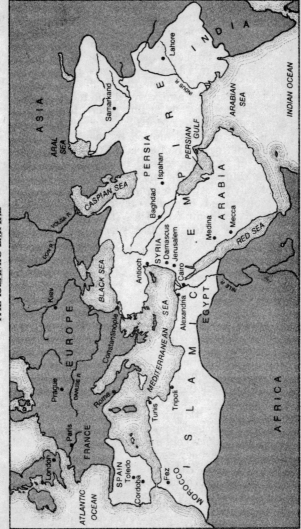

the black banner of rebellion. The house of Umayyad, bloated with patronage, corruption and excesses, was finally defeated at the battle of the Great Zab, a tributary of the Tigris River in northern Iraq. The revolution had comvulsed, then reshaped the Moslem world.

The coup was applied when an Abbasid general invited the remaining eighty Umayyad princes to a peace conference and had them all murdered at an opening-night banquet. Their bodies were covered and the feast continued. A lone escapee fled to Spain, where he established a separate caliphate in Cordoba.

Abbas then declared himself the new Caliph of Islam. The Shiite allies who had expected the caliphate to go to the heirs of Mohammed had been thoroughly betrayed and their course of vengeance was set.

Eventually the Abbasid dynasty would brazenly circumvent Mohammed himself. Previous caliphs served as "deputy to Mohammed." The Abbasids declared themselves "deputy to God" or the "shadow of God on earth," thus bypassing the Prophet.

Abbas, the first non-Arab Caliph, was succeeded by his brother Mansur, who continued the de-Arabization of the religion by moving the center of Islam farther east into Mesopotamia. In a lush valley along the Tigris he ordered a new capital to be built, envisioning it as the center of the earth. A hundred thousand workmen from all over the empire took four years to construct a circular city two miles in diameter. Within the walled citadel were housed magnificent palaces of government and the aristocracy. Beyond the citadel a center of commerce grew, the likes of which had never been seen.

In the year A.D. 762 Baghdad became the new crown jewel of Islam. International in character, it stood as a hub with spokes of the empire leading into it from all over the world. Here the mercantile arts reached an unprecedented high. The routes ranged from Ceylon and the East Indies to deep into the Volga and as far north as Sweden. An endless list of rare, plain and exotic goods poured into Baghdad from the pearl-diving grounds of Asia to the furs of the Russian steppes. The Chinese papermakers, taken prisoner in A.D. 750 by Islamic armies, established that art in Iraq a year later. Canals, dams and waterworks enhanced a blossoming countryside. Favorable terms for tradesmen and craftsmen lured them to the cornucopia of riches.

Others reached Baghdad as well: philosophers, historians, mathematicians, poets, musicians, physicians, astronomical scientists all opened the gates of Islam's golden period. Away from the rigid confines of Arab orthodoxy, Islamic scholars reached out to incorporate many of the Greek and Western philosophies into their own. A more liberal division of lands along with sophisticated structures of government and law followed, and great institutions of learning arose.

The Abbasid rule was more secular than religious, but it was entirely autocratic. A single man, the Abbasid Caliph, personally owned both the church and the state. One approached the Caliph's throne groveling and kissing the ground beneath him. For the first time in history a set of monarchs kept an executioner always at hand. If the Caliph was displeased it was his prerogative to behead the offender on the spot. A leather carpet was rolled up near the throne for such routine decapitations.

Although the Abbasids ruled for centuries, the Islamic world was awash with movements from such divergent societies as the Berbers of North Africa, to the Khorasanians among whom the Moslems came into direct contact with Buddhist ideas, to those in the heartland of Mecca. Rebellion was always in the wind.

The empire was so huge, so diverse, that it became unmanageable. The throne became dependent on mercenaries out of Central Asia but no empire can be held together with hired guns. A central national force was required but the Arabs had been downgraded and replaced. Fragmented, the Abbasid power declined and their boundaries began to shrink. Many Persian provinces simply took self-rule for themselves. Elsewhere independent caliphates emerged, first in Spain, then in Morocco and Tunisia.

The Shiite Moslems formed a sect called the Fatamids, named after Fatima, the daughter of Mohammed. By A.D. 969 they had come out of the Arabian Peninsula, conquered Egypt, founded the city of Cairo and a rival dynasty to the Abbasids. By the ninth and tenth centuries the political unity of Islam had been shattered, the Abbasid caliphate retrenched a little more than the immediate territory around Baghdad.

Islam had been in continual battle with the Byzantine Empire and at one juncture reached the gates of Constantinople before being repulsed. In western Europe a confederation of noblemen, known as the Carolingians, also became rivals of the Byzantines.

Harun al-Rashid, the fifth Abbasid Caliph, enlisted the Carolingians as allies against the Byzantines. The carrot was Jerusalem, an opportunity to allow the Carolingians, who were Roman Catholics, to break the Eastern Orthodox hold on the city. The caliph sent Charlemagne, leader of the Carolingians, a number of sacred Christian relics as gifts and granted him rights of protection over their holy places. Although Charlemagne upgraded the deteriorated conditions and improved facilities for pilgrims the move embittered the Eastern Orthodox Patriarch. By the end of the ninth century the Abbasid/Carolingian alliance faded, leaving the Christians of Jerusalem in conflict with one another, and both Latins and Orthodox became isolated from their administrative centers in Rome and Constantinople.

Living under Islam was iffy at best for the non-Moslem. At one point fighting around Mecca had interrupted Moslem pilgrimages and they poured into Jerusalem as an alternative and went so far as to build a mosque on the grounds of the Holy Sepulchre. The one attempt of the Byzantines to recapture the city was aborted within sight of its walls after the death of the Byzantine emperor.

Conditions for the Jews went from fair to middling, depending on which part of the empire their communities were in. The variances in discrimination ranged on a scale of one to ten but they were universally regarded as second-class people and lived under special laws. Their history as travelers, traders and skilled professionals caused every caliph to have his house Jews. The Moslem code disdained usury, the business of moneylending, so this loathsome profession was given to the Jews. In the heydey of Baghdad trade deals became too sophisticated to be handled by gold. Banking was invented, with letters of credit and checks that could be honored everywhere. Because of their background in moneylending, the Jews became involved in banks and banking but, all told, they skated on thin and tentative ice.

In A.D. 976 the Fatimid dynasty of Egypt swept into Palestine and captured Jerusalem. Under the Caliph al-Aziz the lot of Jews and Christians was enhanced but with his death came a tragic and rapid decline of events.

Al-Hakim, known as the mad Caliph, succeeded to the Fatimid throne and unleashed a binge of terror and bigotry. He ordered destruction of all non-Moslem sites in the holy land and halted all non-Moslem pilgrimages. The Church of the Holy Sepulchre was demolished and a series of outrages perpetrated on the Christian priesthood. Western Europe became aroused, the doors of suspicion burst open and bitter relations ensued. Things cooled down somewhat with the death of Al-Hakim, when an accord was reached that allowed a rebuilding of the church. Even so the Moslem and Christian worlds were heading for an inevitable clash.

The explosion came in a half century with the ascent of a new power in the Islamic world. Seljuk Turks, a nomadic tribe of Central Asia, had served as mercenaries throughout Islam's far reaches. They were violently orthodox in their beliefs and completely intolerant of others. Wherever the Seljuks touched down, non-Moslems were made to suffer grievously. The Seljuks gained control of Persia and in A.D. 1071 launched the conquest of Syria and Palestine. By 1077 Jerusalem had fallen to them and the aftermath was familiarly horrendous. The Christian community was pillaged, raped and their sites destroyed. To western Europe, this was the final straw.

The Fatimids were able to wrest control of Jerusalem from Seljuk hands but there was no turning back an aroused Christian Europe. In June of 1099 Fatimid guards looked down from the walls of Jerusalem to see the army of the First Crusade advancing on the holy city.

THE OLIVE PICKER AND
THE CITY GIRL

A mask of tragedy is universally worn by Moslem women. They have been reduced to the lowest form of human life on the planet. The bedouin woman was undoubtedly sold by her parents to a prospective husband for a number of goats when she was a teen-ager. In the first three years of marriage she bore three daughters, an insult to her husband's masculinity. During a windfall her husband took a second wife. She lay in their tent, divided from her husband and his new bride by a curtain of cloth. For two months she listened to their love-making, a process of total dehumanization. After fourteen children (her husband gave her a few years off as a gesture of good will) she spends a good part of her days sitting in a squalid alley in the Old City selling a few scraps of crop. Otherwise, she labors from sunup to sunset, scarcely able to give even primitive care to her enormous family. She has never laughed since childhood. Her only recreation is telling riddles with other women at a wedding or a funeral. After her day of laboring in an olive grove, her husband rides home on the donkey after spending his time sitting in the shade. She walks behind him.

The city woman was saved from the ultimate Islamic debasement by not having to wear a veil over her face. Even so, her eyes would mirror the agony of Arab womanhood. She cannot eat in a restaurant, see a motion picture in a theatre, dance, sing, or even travel to the next city unless accompanied by a male relative. She cooks and serves all the meals to her husband and his male relations and friends but is not allowed to sit at the table with them. If she is even suspected of having an affair, she will be murdered by her family in order for them to salvage their honor. The only figment of equality she has is to get out in the streets and riot and chant nationalistic slogans. Her marriage will soon be loveless and after a dozen children she will be drained of vitality into a listless exhaustion and undesirable for the most primal sexual function of her husband; a function which she is not permitted to enjoy by tradition. She is and will remain a birth-to-death prisoner of the home, a slave to her husband, chattel of her family, her husband's family and a society from which no one can escape to find human dignity and happiness.

The Crusades

In A.D. 755 Abd Ar Rahman, sole survivor of the massacre of the Umayyad princes, fled to Spain and in Cordoba established what was to be a seven-century Moslem presence in that country. Moslem Spain was the light of what was otherwise a dismal European continent wallowing through the muck of an age of abominable ignorance, lingering barbarism, rampaging disease, poverty, bigotry and bloodthirsty power fights, often between church and state.

Spain flourished in magnificent cities, bountiful fields and, mainly, a glorious era of human achievement. It was a time of poets and learned men during which the Jews played a vital role as the bridge between the Arab and Christian communities. Jewish translations of Greek philosophy as well as the Arabic works in mathematics and astronomy did much to penetrate the black curtain over Europe.

Among the Jewish immortals was the poet Solomon ibn Gabirol, who is mentioned in the same breath as Dante and Milton. Ibn Gabirol was once described by Heine as "a nightingale singing in the darkness of the Gothic medieval night."

Moses Maimonides, the physician-philosopher, also emerged from this vintage time and place. He is considered as perhaps the greatest Jew between the fall of the Second Temple and the emergence of the modern state of Israel, a span of some nineteen centuries. The most important of his works, *The Guide for the Perplexed*, completed in 1190, goes to the roots of a thinking man's desire to practice his religion as it establishes a rational basis for reconciling revelation with scientific truths.

But Arab Spain and its celestial capital of Cordoba stood virtually alone in a sea of contaminated minds and contaminated nations.

The heartland of Christian Europe was along the Rhine Valley, with the Franks on the west bank and the Teutonic Germans on the east. Until the Crusades, the Jews had been shut out of the mainstream of a feudal society, but existed reasonably well through their special skills, professions and particularly their knowledge of commerce. In many places there was a gaping hole between the masses of poor and the nobility and the Jews were invited to settle here and there to establish a middle class of artisans and merchants. In accordance with ancient tradition, Talmudic schools perpetuated the religion. Although ostracized from normal life, the Jews found solace among themselves.

As the Christians spread their teachings among simple, often tragically ignorant peasants overlorded by a sanctimonius, feudal and barbaric nobility, so did the scourge of anti-Semitism rise. Local indignities were commonplace, so that the Jew became a ready-made scapegoat for the disastrous failures of the society. Pope Gregory VII placed an official stamp on Jew baiting in 1078, enacting into law a number of disgusting anti-Jewish practices.

War fever to regain the holy places in Jerusalem gained momentum along the Rhineland. At first it appealed to people whose intention it was to loot the fabled Orient of its riches. These ranks were further swelled by the dregs and scum of this cesspool of a continent. The glory of Jesus was overpowered by a crude mob, hungry with greed and crazed for blood. Up and down the Rhine Valley religious zealots whipped up hatred of the Moslems, and this hatred was soon distorted into hatred of the Jews.

One libel after another was heaped upon the Jews in a carnival atmosphere akin to madness. The Jews had been blamed for the universal poverty, for the terrible epidemics, for famine, for the most ancient libel of the death of Jesus. New acid dripped from the perverted mouths of the

CRUSADER JERUSALEM

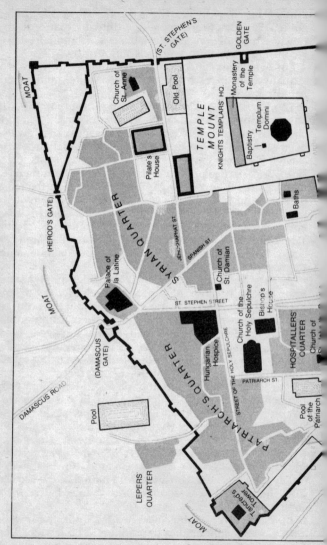

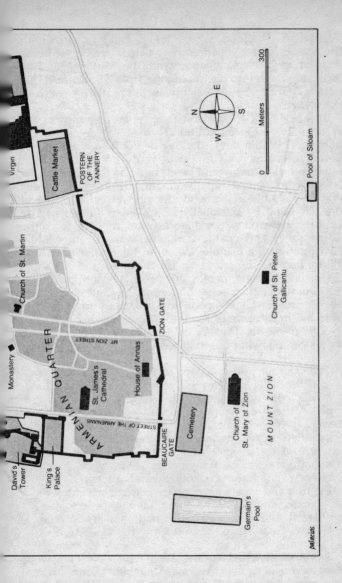

evangelists. The Jews, who, after all, had no quarrel with the Moslems over Christian holy places, were now being accused of a black alliance with the Moslems and of "coercing them into destroying the Holy Sepulchre." This haranguing of fanatics was openly supported by much of the Church.

In A.D. 1095 Pope Urban II convened a council in the French city of Clermont and called for the rescue of the holy sites. Within days, Godfrey de Bouillon, the Duke of Lorraine, commenced the great venture by vowing that the blood of Christ would be avenged by the blood of the Jews. Word spread rapidly among the growing hordes that they should first sanctify themselves before going to the holy land by personally killing a Jew for Jesus. The Crusade gathered size and momentum, moving down the Rhine Valley and on the traditional route to the Middle East through the Danube Valley. In town after town Jew killing became the warm-up for the holy land. In some cases, bishops and nobles attempted to stop the blood orgy but with little success. Many well-meaning churchmen offered the Jews conversion to Christianity to save their lives but in most cases the Jews chose suicide.

Gibbon in his *Decline and Fall of the Roman Empire* made the following observations:

> The example and footsteps of Peter [a monk known as Peter the Hermit] were closely pursued by another fanatic, the monk Godescai, whose sermons swept away fifteen or twenty thousand peasants from the villages of Germany.... The rear was again pressed by a herd of two hundred thousand, the most stupid refuse of the people, who mingled with their devotion a brutal license of rapine, prostitution and drunkenness... of these and other bands of enthusiasts, the first and most easy warfare was against the Jews ... many thousands of the unhappy people were pillaged and massacred, nor had they felt a more bloody stroke since the persecution of Hadrian.

As they marched to the First Crusade, Jews were slaughtered at Speyer, Worms, Cologne, Mainz, Treves, Lorraine, Neuss, Ratisbon, Metz, Prague, Wevelinghofen, Eller, Xanten, Mehr, Kerpen and Geldern.

In preparation for the Second Crusade, Jews were butchered in Speyer, Worms, Treves, Wurzburg, Aschaffenburg, Magdeburg, Carinthia, Halle, Ham, Carentan and Blois, where the entire community was burned at the stake.

Jewish massacres before the Third Crusade included Bray, Neuss, Vienna, Worms, Boppard, Speyer, Erfurt, Baden, Fulda, Frankfurt, Kitzingen, Ortenburg, Belitsa, Meiningen, Pforzheim, Arnstadt, Coblenz, Sinzig, Weissenburg and in Franconia and throughout Bavaria. Jew-killing fever spread to England, with massacres in Lynn, Norwich, Stamford, Bury St. Edmunds and a most horrible one in York. In France Jews were murdered in Troyes and Toulouse and in Austria and Germany there were further mass murders in Wurzburg, Nuremberg and Franconia where one hundred forty-six communities were annihilated. Spain joined the savagery in the early fourteenth century, beginning with a massacre in Navarre.

When the black plague rampaged through Europe in the fourteenth century it is estimated that upwards of twenty-five million persons perished, almost destroying the European civilization. This plague was blamed on the Jews for "poisoning Christian wells."

The killing of Jews continued in Swabia, Prague, Seville, Toledo, Valencia, Barcelona, Franconia, Breslau, Lisbon and ironically in Cordoba, where they had contributed so brilliantly to Spain's great era. When the Jews fled en masse into Poland and Russia they found no respite from the holy murders.

Jews were expelled from England, France, Austria, Bavaria, Portugal, Lithuania, the Papal States and dozens of major cities.

After all this the ghettos were instituted. Somehow the Jews managed to survive this four-century nightmare in crimson just in time to face the Spanish Inquisition.

Obviously the Jewish attitude toward Christians had been altered forever. It was rather difficult, was it not, to reconcile what happened with the teachings of Jesus?

THE CRUSADER KINGDOMS

When Pope Urban II called for the crusade at the Council of Clermont in A.D. 1095, the Byzantine Empire in the East was reeling under a series of defeats by the Seljuk Turks. The Byzantine Emperor, Alexius, called to the West for help and although the Latin-Orthodox church rift had continued there had been a period of stability. Anti-Moslem feelings in Western Europe overwhelmed other considerations and encouraged the gathering elements of the Crusade to assemble in Constantinople, come to the aid of the Byzantines and launch their operations in the holy land from there.

The first element to arrive in Constantinople was under the leadership of a fanatic monk, Peter the Hermit, and his associate, Walter the Penniless. This so-called "People's Crusade" had not only turned on the Jews in their march east but had raised considerable havoc in Hungary and Bulgaria. Arriving in 1096, they launched an ill-advised foray toward Jerusalem instead of waiting for the rest of the Crusade to join them. Their ranks were decimated by the Turks, although Peter the Hermit escaped.

Another force under command of the brother of King Philip of France was shipwrecked crossing the Adriatic with great losses and the other units, traveling by land and sea, had a hellish journey. During mid-1097 and late 1098 they gathered near Constantinople. The largest army was under Raymond of St. Gilles, the Count of Toulouse, who at the age of fifty-five was considered the leading light. The other major leaders of the continuing story were Godfrey de Bouillon, Duke of Lorraine, and his brother Baldwin. All told, some four thousand mounted knights and twenty-five to thirty thousand infantry had assembled and were under the command of an array of nobility that caused the crusade to be named "The Crusade of the Barons." Rome's emissaries in the form of a bishop, priests and monks assured the Latin interests.

The Byzantine Emperor Alexius, in exchange for support, provisions and passage, compelled the Crusade leaders to take an oath to restore all conquered territory and annex all new territory to the Byzantine Empire. The Crusaders agreed only with considerable reluctance and launched operations across Turkey into the domain of the Seljuk Turks. In 1098 Godfrey de Bouillon's brother Baldwin became involved in a region of Armenia called the County of Edessa and split off from the main force.

More important was the siege of Antioch, a major city on the northern tip of the Syrian coast. Antioch's Moslems held out despite naval reinforcements by the Genoese and English. Wary of a Turkish counterattack, the Crusaders appealed to the Emperor Alexius to send in extra troops. When Alexius declined, the enraged Crusader leaders felt they had been betrayed and were no longer under obligation to uphold their oath to him. On June 3, 1098, the Crusaders broke into Antioch, massacred the Moslem population, threw out the Eastern Orthodox Patriarch, installed a Latin Patriarch and eventually established a Latin Kingdom of Antioch.

The Crusader army had been decimated by epidemic and loss of key leaders but the rank and file were restless. After leaving a garrison force at Antioch the main force continued down the Syrian coast where they were joined by other elements, including Tancred, a Norman nobleman, and Robert of Normandy, who was a brother of the English king.

In the meanwhile the Shiite Fatimids of Egypt had thrown the Seljuk Turks out of Jerusalem and therefore became the prime enemy of the Crusaders. The city was strongly garrisoned, well provisioned, and any attack on it could quickly bring a relief force out of Egypt.

In the late spring of A.D. 1099 the army of the first Crusade assembled on the Palestinian coast. Their numbers were down to some fifteen thousand but they had been hardened by their epic journey and some grueling warfare. The port of Jaffa had been abandoned to them and provisions arrived on Genoese ships, enabling them to proceed toward Jerusalem. They did so, however, without adequate food, water and preparation.

The population of Jerusalem consisted of twenty thousand Moslems and a handful of Jews. In light of the advancing Crusader army, the Christians had been expelled from the city, an act that could be deemed merciful, a mercy not reciprocated by the Crusaders later.

The Moslems, commonly referred to as Saracens, had a well-trained army of Egyptian Fatimids. In advance of the enemy, the Saracens stripped the fields, poisoned the wells and destroyed the timber in a large area of the Judean hills to deny the Crusaders provisions, water and siege materials. The villagers of the countryside poured into Jerusalem's walls for protection, swelling the population to forty thousand.

On June 7 the Crusaders arrived and encamped and a war council was called to determine the deployment of forces. The steep Hinnom and Kidron valleys on the southern and eastern sides of the city were ruled out. Godfrey de Bouillon took the far eastern position on the northern wall opposite today's Herod's Gate. Counterclockwise and next in line opposite today's Damascus Gate were Flemish forces under the command of Robert of Flanders. The Norman nobleman Tancred massed on the northwest corner of the wall opposite a battlement called Goliath's Tower. The most difficult position fell to the Provençal unit under command of Raymond of St. Gilles, who held the western side opposite David's Tower (the former Herod's Palace) at today's Jaffa Gate. Historically this last position had always held some sort of fortress or garrison. The Provençals realized the strength of the defenses opposite them and shifted slightly to the south opposite Mount Zion.

Once in place, the Crusaders were anxious to do battle. However, they were woefully unprepared for siege. Their water supply came from a single clean spring which was totally inadequate for the number of troops. By June the hills had grown arid with hot winds coming up from the desert and they were faced with a sudden and immediate crisis of thirst.

There was no timber about to build siege towers and no

carpenters in the ranks to build them. A final sense of urgency swept the ranks when the news reached them that a relief army had left Egypt and was moving up the coast toward the Fatimid garrison at Ashkelon.

An ill-advised frontal assault was launched with crudely slapped-together scaling ladders which the Saracens easily beat off with hot oil, stones, arrows and an ugly weapon called Greek fire by which flames were shot through an early-day mortar tube.

After an agonizing reappraisal the Crusaders settled in. An adequate water supply system was installed from distant sources near the coast. When a small fleet of Genoan ships were blockaded by the Egyptians in Jaffa, Godfrey de Bouillon convinced them to break up the boats for their timber and used the ship's carpenters to erect siege towers.

Moving now with zealous speed, they finished three huge towers complete with drawbridges in short order. Their front sides were plated with armor and coated with materials to prevent them from being burned down by the Greek fire.

After a three-day fast, the priests led a procession around the walls, carrying banners of the saints, shouting up to the defenders, singing hymns and praying. They were looking for a repeat of the miracle of Jericho but the walls did not come tumbling down. In fact, the defenders derided them jeeringly from the walls. On the Mount of Olives, Peter the Hermit delivered a final tirade of a sermon.

On July 10 the three siege towers were positioned on Mount Zion, opposite Goliath's Tower in Tancred's sector and in Godfrey de Bouillon's position near Herod's Gate. On July 14, under cover of a rain of arrows and fireballs, the towers were rolled forward against the wall.

A day of furious combat found the Mount Zion tower collapsed and the other two seriously damaged. During the night the Saracens threw everything they had at the two remaining towers, but they held. The following morning a breach was made by Godfrey de Bouillon and this was soon followed by a breach by Tancred. With the Crusaders swarming on the walls, the Saracen defenses suddenly collapsed and they fell back onto the Temple

Mount in that sector. On the opposite side of the city
Raymond of St. Gilles broke through the western side late
in the evening. The defenders in that area dropped back
into the Citadel, sued for peace and were able to bribe
their way to freedom. They were to be the only survivors
save a few hundred prisoners, for what followed was the
worst religious massacre in human annals.

The Jews, whose quarters were near Godfrey de Bouillon's
breach, gathered inside their main synagogue, where the
Crusaders locked them in and burned them all to death.

T he rest of the forty thousand defenders and civilians
were butchered despite Tancred's guarantee of amnesty,
which was disobeyed. Men, women and children were
dragged from their homes, cornered in alleyways and on
rooftops, found praying in mosques and hacked to death
as they cried for mercy. When the defenses collapsed
many people swallowed their gold and jewels, hoping to
have them for another day. In their maniacal lust for
treasure, the Crusaders followed decapitation and dismemberment by slitting open the corpses with daggers to
retrieve the gold. The Crusaders' fury continued until
every street and alley ran red; in some places the blood
flowed so high, it washed over the ankles of the executioners. When all had been murdered except a few hundred prisoners, the Crusaders claimed houses, confiscat-
ing them by placing their shields on the doors.

Wrote one of the Crusaders, William of Tyre:

> It was impossible to look upon the vast numbers of
> slain without horror; everywhere lay fragments of
> human bodies and the very ground was covered with
> the blood of the slain. It was not alone the spectacle
> of the headless bodies and mutilated limbs strewn in
> all directions that roused horror in all who looked
> upon them. Still more dreadful it was to gaze upon
> the victors themselves, dripping with blood from
> head to foot.

Prisoners were made to clean up the streets, remove the remains beyond the city walls and burn them. With their handiwork done, the Crusaders dressed in fresh uniforms and walked barefooted, in a show of reverence, to the Holy Sepulchre, prostrated themselves and thanked God for their victory.

The Knights set aside their swords and shields to deal with the business of politics. Raymond of St. Gilles remained faithful to his oath to the Byzantine Emperor, Alexius, and advocated that the new territories conquered be added to that empire. He argued that Jerusalem had been isolated for centuries and even with its liberation it remained in a precarious position in the middle of two warring Moslem caliphates and a hostile world of Islam. The Byzantines were in a far better position to defend Jerusalem because of Constantinople's proximity.

However, Raymond of St. Gilles was overwhelmed by Latin interests who contended the city had been won by a Frankish army under Catholic banners and was no longer under obligation to Alexius. The Pope's representatives were absolutely determined to end Eastern Orthodox domination of the holy places. It was reported that Raymond of St. Gilles was offered the crown of Jerusalem but refused it under the condition of Latin rule. Rivalry was so intense among the commanding knights that no king was declared. Instead Godfrey de Bouillon was named "Defender of the Holy Sepulchre."

Raymond of St. Gilles left Jerusalem and set out on other adventures, attacking territory along the coast north of Beirut. Eventually his relatives carved out a Latin Kingdom of Tripoli (not to be confused with Tripoli in North Africa) after his death.

Godfrey de Bouillon died a year after his arrival in Palestine, a death that brought his brother Baldwin down from the County of Edessa; he successfully thwarted the brewing conspiracies over succession. On Christmas Day of the year A.D. 1100, Baldwin was crowned King of Jerusalem by the new Latin Patriarch in the Church of the Nativity in Bethlehem. Although the Orthodox were permitted to remain, there would be no mistaking the Catholic character of the new state. The Latin Patriarch, as emissary of the Pope, became an equal power within the state. The Orthodox monopoly of guardianship of the holy sites was broken, while Latin holdings increased vastly from scores of new churches, monasteries and convents to landed estates in the countryside.

Baldwin's first chore was to make the kingdom defensible. The task was simplified by taking advantage of the ongoing rivalry between the Fatimids in Egypt and the Turks who had taken over Baghdad. With the aid of Italian maritime power, and an assist by the Norwegians, Baldwin secured the coast by annexing Caesarea, Acre, Beirut and Sidon and by alliances with the Latin Kingdoms of Tripoli, Antioch and the County of Edessa in the north. He occupied the Transjordan region and extended to the Red Sea, effectively driving a wedge that split the Islamic world in half.

With the Crusade done, the majority returned to Europe, leaving but three hundred knights and a few thousand soldiers. They were relatively safe so long as they stayed buttoned up behind walled cities but the roads and the nights belonged to roving bands of Saracen brigands. A string of Crusader fortresses, garrison cities and castles were interlinked in the Galilee and Lebanon to assure safety of the roads and quick Crusader reaction to trouble.

The defense of the kingdom was based around two orders of knights. The Templars, a group of Frankish nobles, took their name from the Temple Mount, which they had confiscated as their headquarters. The Dome of the Rock and the Al Aksa Mosque were converted into churches, a monastery and housing for the order. They stabled their horses in a hall beneath Al Aksa in the mistaken belief that it had been the stables of Solomon.

The less aristocratic order of St. John, composed of monk-knights, had an area near the Holy Sepulchre. They were fiercely dedicated as defenders of the Holy Sepulchre and stood out because of the red cross on their white uniforms. Known as the Hospitalers, it was their duty to care for pilgrims and run the medical establishment. A third knightly group, the Teutonic Order of St. Mary, also ran an establishment in the holy city.

The Christian population of Palestine had never been dominant and immigrants were needed. Baldwin encouraged all Christians, Orthodox as well as Latin, to settle the holy land, and free land and homes were offered. The Jews were evicted from their quarter, which was taken over by Syrian Christians, Jacobites, and Egyptian and Ethiopian Copts. An Armenian Quarter was established on Mount Zion where they built the Cathedral of St. James. A small Spanish colony existed near the Damascus Gate and the Provençals held the opposite end of the city near Zion Gate. Hungarians had an enclave near New Gate, adjoining the main Christian quarter, and Georgians from the Caucasus settled outside the walls several miles removed, near the ancient Monastery of the Cross. Most mosques were made into churches to accommodate the variety of languages. The principal defenses of the city were in the Citadel, or David's Tower, which became the king's residence, and in Goliath's Tower, which had been renamed Tancred's Tower.

A few hundred Jews were tolerated in a small area near the Jaffa Gate where they ran the business of dyeing cloth and other materials. On occasion a few outstanding Jews, such as the Rabbi Benjamin of Tudela and Moses Maimonides, were permitted to visit the city.

As further inducement to settlement, taxes were cut and trade went unrestricted to caravans and maritime cities. These efforts, defensive and commercial, were pursued with Frankish stubbornness until the fragile hold on the country became secure.

At any given time one could find twenty-five or thirty Christian nationalities intermingling, from Norwegian to Indian. When restrictions on the Jews and Moslems were relaxed the city took on the look of a perennial oriental bazaar. Baldwin wore the silken robes of an Islamic prince, sat cross-legged on carpets and pillows at his banquets and was referred to as the "Frankish Sultan."

A new building boom blended the heavy Gothic of the Crusaders with the more delicate arches and domes of the East, and somehow they all mixed together well. Fifty years went into remodeling the Holy Sepulchre, with its four separate sanctuaries put beneath a single roof.

Crusaders built streets of covered, vaulted arches which carried such exotic names as The Street of Bad Cooking, The Street of Herbs, The Street of Barbers where pilgrims went to clean up after their journey and before visiting the holy places, and The Covered Street, housing the main bazaar, a function it still carries on.

The most famous surviving Crusader church, St. Anne's in the Syrian Quarter, is associated with a lovely tale of Baldwin's chicanery. In order to shed his wife so he could marry into the fabled wealth of Adelaide of Sicily, he had her placed in St. Anne's as a nun. So that the nuns would keep her locked away and quiet, Baldwin used Adelaide's dowry to grant large subsidies to the church. When Adelaide's money began to run out, Baldwin renounced her just in time to escape excommunication on a bigamy rap.

SALADIN

Saladin was an Armenian Kurd, a Moslem who was raised in Damascus, where his father was governor. At the time Damascus was a great center of Islamic learning and it was here he became obsessed with the mission of a jihad or holy war to the Crusades, for the massacre of 1099 had never been forgotten. Saladin was one of history's true giants, magnificently geniused in the governing arts, and he rose quickly, succeeding an uncle as vizier of Egypt. This position, as right-hand man of an often secluded caliph, was one of almost unlimited power. By the age of thirty-one he was in complete control as the Sultan over both Egypt and Syria. He was the greatest benefactor of the Sunni Moslems, who constitute the great majority and are nowhere as rigid and fanatic as the volatile, martyr-seeking Shiite sect. The Jerusalem Christians were able to retain their precarious foothold; however, the situation was touchy and required only the proper incident to hurl the armies of Christ and Mohammed against one another. In 1186 the Latin Prince of Antioch broke the truce by engaging in attacks on caravans of Moslems making the pilgrimage to Mecca.

Saladin declared a holy war and moved out of Egypt with an army of eighteen thousand under his personal command. Crossing the Jordan, he took up position south of the Sea of Galilee.

The Crusader King of Jerusalem, Guy de Lusignan, called on his allies, Raymond of Tripoli and the Prince of Antioch, then emptied his own garrisons and moved to intercept Saladin. The Crusader army was about the same size as the Saracen force but it constituted the entire might of the Franks.

The Sea of Galilee is a lake that stands below sea level, turning the area into a tropical furnace during the summer months. Considering the weight of Crusader armor, the heat would have a seriously debilitating effect on both men and horses. By contrast, Saladin's cavalry rode light and was far better equipped to contend with the devastating heat.

Saladin made a maneuver of blocking the road to Tiberias and sending in a small force to capture the city in hopes of luring the Crusader army out into the open. Against the better judgment of some of the knights, Guy de Lusignan moved from his encampment near the road from Nazareth in a fierce forced march. Night found them half crazed with thirst and maneuvered onto the arid Plain of Arbel at the village of Hattin. The Crusaders had their backs to sheer hills topped by the rocky "Horns of Hattin." With Saracen-made grass fires blowing in their faces, thirst maddening them and Saladin's cavalry breaking their co-ordination, the Crusaders became trapped and confused. The infantry fled to the lake for water and when Saladin's final charge came the knights were either killed or were taken prisoner. It became a rout in which the Crusader force was utterly decimated.

By demolishing the foolhardy Frankish army, Saladin had crushed the Crusader power in Palestine in a single stroke. Both the offending Prince of Antioch and Guy de Lusignan were taken prisoner but Saladin was a most

civilized man and later gave both their freedom. The third
Crusader leader, Raymond of Tripoli, was able to break
out and escape back to his kingdom.

Saladin followed up quickly, seizing coastal ports to
prevent Crusader reinforcements. Only Tyre far to the
north and Tripoli, farther north, remained in Crusader
hands. By mid-September Saladin was moving on Jerusalem.
In advance of the Saracen army a familiar scene was
replayed with the population of the Frankish settlements
in the Judean hills fleeing into Jerusalem and swelling the
city to sixty thousand souls.

Within the city the situation was maniacal. During the
long period of peace the Franks had neglected to maintain
the walls and many parts were in disrepair. There were
but a handful of knights and a tiny garrison force. The
situation seemed so desperate, a delegation of citizens
arranged a truce and went to Saladin's encampment.
Always looking for avenues of settlement and compromise,
Saladin made them the magnanimous offer of allowing
the Franks to retain the city for some eight months. If, by
that time, Frankish armies arrived, Jerusalem could remain theirs. If, on the other hand, no rescue force was
coming, the Christians would give up Jerusalem quietly
and leave. Although facing certain defeat, the delegation
refused the offer, perhaps hoping a miracle would save
them.

This was followed by another bit of weird diplomacy.
Balian, the Crusader Lord of Nablus, a Palestinian barony,
had been among the knights to escape the slaughter at
Hattin and had fled to Tyre. He personally went to Saladin
and petitioned for permission to enter Jerusalem to fetch
his wife and children. Saladin granted this on the condition Balian swear an oath not to take up arms.

Once inside Jerusalem, Balian was pounced upon by
the Latin Patriarch Heraclius, who beseeched the knight
to lead the defense of the city. In face of Balian's vow to
Saladin, the Patriarch offered instant absolution and warned
him that failing to defend the holy city was a far greater
sin than lying to a heathen. Balian wrote to Saladin asking
to be relieved of the oath and in a bit of uncommon
chivalry Saladin granted the request. Moreover, the Moslem
leader arranged safe passage to Tyre for Balian's family.

The first act of the new commander was to knight the sons of all noblemen over the age of sixteen. Next, he stripped the gold and silver from the Holy Sepulchre, melted it down and purchased soldiers from among the throngs within the walls.

Saladin came in from the west on September 20 and deployed his army from Tancred's Tower on a line down to the Citadel. After a few skirmishes he found the defenses too strong and shifted his forces eastward from the Damascus Gate to the Valley of Kidron, and set up his siege machines backed by a cover of infantry and his magnificent cavalry of ten thousand horsemen.

Within the city there were scenes of complete madness. Mothers cut off the hair of their daughters in hopes of preventing their rape. Monks and nuns in hysterical prayer paraded around with the Syrian "true cross" which they had kept after losing the Latin "true cross"; purveyors of poison sold out, treasures were stuffed into cistern bottoms, prices for food became ludicrous and riots and general mayhem added to the bedlam. The Crusader massacre of 1099 weighed heavily on their minds.

Saladin made his breach in the same spot that Godfrey de Bouillon had made his eighty-eight years earlier. With Saracens swarming on the walls, Balian was miraculously able to arrange another truce to play his final card. Facing Saladin once more, Balian again made vows. This time he vowed that if he did not get an honorable surrender he would first slaughter the five thousand Moslems being held on the Temple Mount, after which he would destroy Al Aksa and the Dome of the Rock. Finally Balian vowed his men would kill every woman and child in the city, put it to flames and then come out and fight to the last man.

Saladin was obviously impressed with Balian's sincerity. The terms were that the Franks and other Latins would be granted forty days to liquidate their affairs and leave the city. Although they could take their fortunes with them, each man, woman and child who left Jerusalem would have to pay a ransom. The Jaffa Gate alone would be left open for this purpose. Moslems would be allowed into the city immediately to buy Catholic houses so the ransoms could be paid. Any unransomed Catholic would be sold into slavery after the forty-day period. Armenians, Syrians and other Eastern Orthodox Christians would remain unharmed, as Saladin said he had no quarrel with them.

This arrangement was to have the effect of compelling wealthy Catholics to buy the freedom of their poorer brethren. What ensued was a disgrace. The Latin Patriarch Heraclius left Jerusalem with his entire treasury, not ransoming a single soul other than his immediate entourage. This act so outraged Saladin's emirs that they demanded the Patriarch's enormous wealth be confiscated but Saladin remained true to his word. Likewise, the less than noble Knights Templars paid ransom for a mere seven thousand people, all connected with them somehow, and took the vast bulk of their own fortunes with them.

The ransomed left in three groups led by the Templars, the Hospitalers and Balian. The Saracens escorted them north to Christian territory where Saladin forced Genoan and other ships to carry them off. A large band of refugees lit out for the Christian enclave at Tripoli where they hoped to resettle but Raymond, the ruling noble, who had fled the field at Hattin, closed the borders and refused to let them enter.

As a result some fifteen thousand unransomed Franks and other Catholics remained in Jerusalem. Saladin freed the paupers and other unfortunates. His brother is said to have purchased freedom for a thousand more: the balance went to the slave markets of Damascus.

The Eastern Orthodox Church was left alone, its followers unharmed. Later, at the request of the Byzantine Emperor, guardianship of the Holy Sepulchre returned to Orthodox control.

Saladin also rescinded the ban on the Jews and they returned, first from around the Galilee, and later from all over Western Europe, with the major group of rabbis coming to settle from England and France.

When he made his entrance into Jerusalem, Saladin had the cross removed from the top of the Dome of the Rock, purified the twin shrines and rededicated them to Islam.

All that remained of the Frankish incursion was the port of Tyre. Survival of this single Christian toehold was made possible by Western rule of the sea, as Saladin simply did not have the ships to stop reinforcements. Control of Tyre permitted the Third Crusade under Richard the Lionhearted of England and Philip II of France to take place in A.D. 1191, some fifty years after a Second Crusade had collapsed.

Richard was everyman's Crusader, honorable and ruthless, chivalrous and bloody, all at the same time. The French arrived first and laid siege to Acre, which was defended by Saladin's nephew. After a rough crossing, during which he conquered Cyprus from the Byzantines, Richard joined the French and they combined to take Acre. Squabbles between the two kings finally compelled Philip to depart for France, leaving Richard in charge of the Crusade. After a breakdown in negotiations with Saladin, Richard ran up a string of coastal victories which included the capture of Jaffa.

Once inland, the luck of the Third Crusade ran out. Richard was stopped in September of 1192 on a high hill named after the prophet Samuel within sight of Jerusalem's walls. With the main objective of his crusade now unreachable, Richard refused to look toward the city. Saladin, decent as always, made a status quo truce which would allow for the continuation of Christian pilgrimages, which, incidentally, he never stopped even during the fighting. He permitted the knights of Richard's army to come to Jerusalem to pray at the Holy Sepulchre provided they entered the city unarmed. Saladin also received the Bishop of Salisbury, who traveled with the crusade, and permitted two Latin monks to return to the Holy Sepulchre as partial guardians. After fifteen months in the holy land, Richard departed for England.

Saladin returned to his beloved Damascus. This loftiest of Islam's princes died a year later, penniless, for he had given his vast personal fortune to the advancement of the Sunni Moslem culture. Saladin must occupy an extraordinary niche in history. In a number of ways he showed many of the same qualities as David. He was totally devoted to his religion in a constructive way. He always sought alternatives of diplomacy and compromise to avoid bloodshed. His word was to be totally trusted. He was forgiving of his enemies. He was tolerant of religions other than his own.

All his adult life he had been gearing for the holy war to liberate Jerusalem and avenge the Crusader massacre of 1099. He had been considered a heathen by his enemies. Yet, when he had them quarried, his overpowering sense of humanity won out and he spared them. He was the true giant of Islam after the Prophet.

As we have seen so often in the past, the death of a great leader invariably led to the split of the empire he had created. And so it was with Saladin. The empire was divided among his sons, who immediately reinstituted the struggle between Cairo and Damascus, with both sides using particularly vicious armies of Turkish mercenaries.

The Franks retained their shrunken coastal kingdom but were able to hold a sort of balance of power by siding with either Egypt or Syria, whichever was to their immediate advantage.

A Fourth Crusade, to be directed against Egypt, the leading Moslem power at the time, was called by Pope Innocent III in 1198. Although the maritime power of Venice was heavily involved in trade with the Egyptians, it allied itself with the Crusade and agreed to provide ships. From then on, this Crusade went amuck, never reaching Moslem nations or the holy land, but instead taking over the Byzantine Empire.

In 1203 the Fourth Crusade invaded Constantinople, sacked it brutally and created an unholy Venetian/Crusader kingdom out of the Byzantine provinces. When the Byzantines recaptured it decades later with the help of the rival Genoan maritime kingdom, the city had lost its ability and principal function as the front line against the Turks and other invading Asians. The sacking of Constantinople also was the cause of the final and permanent split between the Roman Catholic and Eastern Orthodox churches.

The emotional, often fanatical pull of the crusading ideal again swept Europe and in A.D. 1212 resulted in an enormous tragedy. A "Children's Crusade" made up of thousands of youngsters set out from the Continent to be lost at sea or sold into slavery.

A Fifth Crusade, the final one directly run by the papacy, launched an invasion of Egypt in 1217. It went into battle without the promised support of Frederick II of Germany, Holy Roman Emperor who pleaded vital internal business and was released from his vow. This loss, along with military interference by an attending cardinal, ruined any chance of its success. The commanders awaited Frederick II to no avail and launched an ill-fated attack on Cairo. What distinguished this particular Crusade was the presence of Francis of Assisi, founder of the Franciscans, who was allowed to enter Jerusalem by grace of the Moslem Sultan. He established the Franciscan Order as the future guardians of the Holy Sepulchre.

A decade later the Crusaders were to regain control of Jerusalem by one of the more bizarre episodes in the city's history. The finger had long been pointed at Germany's Frederick II for his failure to attend the Fifth Crusade. He had been maneuvered by Pope Gregory IX into marriage to Isabelle, daughter of Jean de Brienne, who had been pretender to the throne of the defunct Kingdom of Jerusalem. This marriage gave Frederick II somewhat of a claim on the title, which would also leave him free to annex Cyprus. It was enough for the Pope to try to lock him into launching a Sixth Crusade.

Among Frederick II's lesser titles was that of King of Sicily, where he lived much of the year and where he had many close Moslem friends. Frederick II was an extremely advanced man with cultured tastes, among which was an appreciation of Islam and a high regard for the Moslem achievements in the sciences. One gets the feeling he wasn't particularly stirred to make a Crusade; he loathed Pope Gregory IX, and he had reasonable doubts about the validity of his rights over Moslem rights to Jerusalem.

He turned back, claiming personal illness, after only a partial launching of the Crusade in the summer of 1227. This act so enraged the Pope, he excommunicated Frederick II.

At the moment Jerusalem was under the rule of the Sultan al-Kamil of Egypt, another of Saladin's nephews. Al-Kamil had his hands full with the Syrians, who had unleashed gangs of Turkish mercenaries on Palestine. By going into an alliance with Al-Kamil, Frederick II was able to gain by treaty the return of Jerusalem. The Treaty of Jaffa also returned to Latin rule the cities of Nazareth and Bethlehem as well as a corridor to the sea. It was an absolute model of religious toleration, with the Moslems retaining sovereignty over the Haram esh Sharif.

The Pope, desirous of ejecting the Moslems altogether, denounced the treaty. Nonetheless Frederick II traveled to the holy land without papal blessing. He went up to Jerusalem and in the absence of any Latin clergy placed the crown of the kingdom on his own head in the Holy Sepulchre. After ordering necessary repairs around the city, he left his representatives and departed.

The Frankish knights soon gained control over Frederick II's people and likewise renounced the Treaty of Jaffa on the argument that it was invalid because of Frederick II's excommunication. The knights threw out the Emperor's representatives, went into a counteralliance with Damascus and joined the Syrians and their Turkish mercenaries in an attack on Egypt.

The Egyptians replied with their own savage army of Khwarizmian Turkish mercenaries, who ravaged both Palestine and Syria. In 1244, the Khwarizmians captured Jerusalem, slaughtered the cream of the Frankish and Latin communities, including the leaders of the Templars and Hospitalers. The women were taken off for mass rape and the city and the holy sites again plundered.

A few years later the Egyptians dismissed their Khwarizmian mercenaries and took direct control of the city. What Jerusalem had been reduced to once more was a miserable, broken, desolate outpost. For all intents the Christian Era was done and no Christian nation would rule here again for the next seven centuries.

THE ETHIOPIANS

Earliest presence of another nation in Jerusalem was that of the Ethiopians; it stems from the visit of the black Queen of Sheba to Solomon about 1000 B.C. Their offspring is said to have founded the Ethiopian dynasty and introduced Judaism into that land. Ethiopian emperors referred to themselves, among other titles, as the "Lion of Judah." During an ancient Passover pilgrimage the Ethiopians were converted to Christianity by the Apostle Philip. Allied with the Egyptian Copts, their religion remains outside the influence of the Orthodox and Latins. They have been present in Jerusalem since A.D. 386 on land they claim was given to them by Solomon. This site, near Calvary, was sanctified by Helena. The Ethiopian monastery of Deir es-Sultan consists of a chapel and a collection of mud huts atop the hill of the Holy Sepulchre. Within the great church they have another chapel where the Roman soldiers cast lots for the garment of Jesus. However, direct access from their monastery into the Holy Sepulchre has been denied by their brother Egyptian Copts, who own the keys to the passageway. The Ethiopians live in terrible poverty and keep abnormally long daily hours of prayer, using their tall crossed crooks to keep them from toppling over. Two hundred and eighty days of each year require some sort of fasting. Yet, in their privation, they seem closer to the life of Jesus than many other sects.

The Long Decline

To the Moslem, proof of his religion's superiority had been manifested by the magnitude of the Islamic empire. The Moslem, in his own eyes, had elevated himself above the infidel, disdained the infidel's culture and religion and believed himself to be a higher order of man. The effect of the Crusades was to devastate these notions.

The Moslem saw an "inferior" civilization force its way onto his private turf, defeat him militarily, establish a presence in his midst and defecate on his religion. This new reality destroyed any chance of evolving a peaceful co-existence. The West was now his everlasting enemy and the Moslem personality took on a characteristic of intense xenophobia.

Eventually the Christians were ejected, for the Moslems believed that in good time Allah's will was bound to come through on their behalf. But they had peaked, and aside from the Ottomans toppling an already crumbling Byzantine Empire, Islam would grow little further in universal greatness. The Moslems would replace the infidels as the backward peoples of the world.

A second shock, invasions by the Mongols, furthered Moslem retrenchment. The Moslems settled into what they were, a regional religion through which nature's unkindness and man's cruelty could be embalmed by fundamentalism into acceptances that made life bearable.

In the mid-1200s, just as the Crusader epoch was winding down, Genghis Khan had united the Tartar tribes of Mongolia and swept into Persia, reaching as far as Egypt. By A.D. 1258 Baghdad had fallen and the Abbasid Caliph-

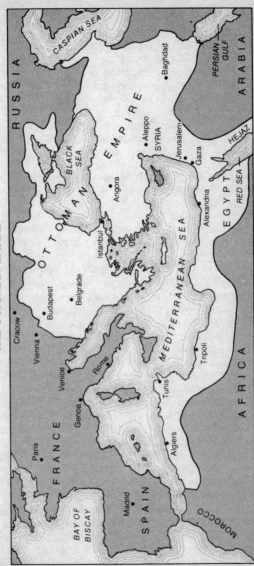

THE OTTOMAN EMPIRE

ate was terminated. The bestiality of the Mongols can best be depicted by their standard procedure of making pyramids of the skulls of the conquered.

Some historians argue about the effects of the Mongol invasion upon Islam. It certainly did them no good. In Iraq the magnificent irrigation works and canals in the Tigris Valley were destroyed and such destruction, where water maintained life in a delicate balance, had a permanent impact. Damascus fell to the Mongols and was plundered. Other Moslems were squeezed into a no man's land on the Byzantine borders. The spirit of learning and nationalism declined. Once powerful caliphates broke up into smaller sultanates.

The Mongols ultimately were ejected, as the Crusaders had been, but Islam's moment of international magnificence was done.

THE MAMELUKES

The various Islamic caliphates had come to depend heavily upon mercenaries to sustain them in power. The prime breeding grounds for these fighting men were mainly in the Central Asian Turkish-speaking provinces.

One such group of this breed were the Mamelukes, named for an Arabic word which literally means "the owned." These were slaves, a mixed bag of Turks, some Mongols, Kurds and Circassians. Their servitude was in the form of soldiering. Like other mercenaries before them, the Mamelukes often overcame their masters and seized power. They were to rule Egypt for two hundred and fifty years. When the Mongols crossed into Palestine in A.D. 1260, it was the Mamelukes who turned them back and then annexed Jerusalem into their empire.

For Jerusalem it heralded a skid in the city's fortunes that kept on a downhill course until modern times. Except for some improvements in the Islamic establishment, Mameluke rule could best be characterized as one of benign neglect. The city they inherited was desolate, its population down to a mere two thousand. Although the Mamelukes did not engage in any notable massacres of non-Moslems, there were always varying degrees of persecution, directed mainly against the Christians, who no longer had ambitions to regain the holy land.

Mameluke administrators were an absolutely deplorable lot, with taxations of the type that made permits for churches, synagogues and personal home building an impossibility. In the small Christian and Jewish Quarters, buildings went to seed because of the weather, a series of terrible earthquakes, and because repairs were not permitted.

The Church of St. Anne was confiscated and turned into a mosque and the Hospitalers' headquarters were converted into a Moslem hospital. Mameluke monopolies squelched rival commerce and drove prices sky high. Christian pilgrimages all but dried up.

The few hundred Jews clung to their foothold, where an ironic tradition began. Jews who wished to be buried as close as possible to the Temple Mount began the cemetery on the Mount of Olives and over the centuries it was to become the most sacred burial site of the Jewish people.

The major contribution of the Mamelukes was directed to the Moslem establishment. A number of beautifications were made on the Haram esh Sharif and some needed repairs to the Dome of the Rock and Al Aksa. A number of Moslem theological schools were established with adjoining mosques in what was a rather feeble attempt to make Jerusalem appear to be a major center of Islamic study.

In truth, Jerusalem had been demoted to the status of a backwater town administered by a low-ranking Mameluke deputy from the controlling province of Damascus. The Moslem theological establishment did nothing to assert that Jerusalem was one of the great cities of Islam. The original intent of the Umayyad dynasty to make the city a rival to Mecca and Medina was no longer valid.

It was a city becoming cobwebbed, collapsing through a lack of care, poor in economy, misruled, overtaxed and with discrimination against its minorities. Add the natural disasters of plague, earthquake and famine. At no time in the two-and-a-half-century Mameluke rule did Jerusalem contain over ten thousand people. If indeed the city had once been part of Islam's grand plan, that had long been forgotten.

THE OTTOMANS

By the middle of the fifteenth century yet another group of warrior Turks were on the rise. The house of Osman, commonly known as the Ottomans, had spilled out of their Central Asian lairs and moved westward. As mercenaries, the Ottomans proved too tough and independent to be controlled for long. They overtook their masters and built a power base by chipping away at the borders of the Byzantine Empire. The Ottoman thrust was spearheaded by Europe's first standing army, composed of Christian youths drafted during the Balkan conquests and converted to Islam and of former prisoners of war. This corps, called the Janissaries, was under direct command of the Sultan, and celibacy as well as other strict regulations were imposed on them. The Janissaries were privileged, loyal to the central authority and vital to Ottoman success.

In 1453 Constantinople fell to the Ottomans, denoting the official end of the Roman Empire. Constantinople's name was changed to Istanbul and the Sublime Porte, as the sultans' court at Topkopi Palace came to be known, dominated the Moslem world for the next four and a half centuries. At its zenith the empire included all of North Africa, the entire Fertile Crescent, southern Russia, the Balkans, Greece and Turkey.

In the year 1516 under Sultan Selim, the Ottomans defeated the Mamelukes, annexed Egypt, Syria and Palestine and entered Jerusalem without resistance. Palestine was relegated to a district of the Syrian Province and Jerusalem was often administered from Gaza. The city did not rise in political importance or Moslem religious status for the succeeding four hundred and fifty years.

The most significant of the sultans came early in the dynasty when Suleiman, son of Selim, assumed the throne in 1520 and reigned until 1566. In Jerusalem, Suleiman the Magnificent, as he came to be called, did what any Moslem potentate should. On the Haram esh Sharif the exterior walls of the Dome of the Rock were covered with a facade of marble and mosaic tiles and the windows in the drum of the dome were set in gilded glass. A few charitable institutions were established, mainly by Suleiman's wife, for the benefit of Moslem students. Suleiman's enhancement of the Moslem presence was minimal, particularly considering that the Ottoman creed called for the protection, preservation and expansion of Islam.

Concerning repairs of a non-Moslem nature, Suleiman was aware of the city's importance to the infidels and wanted to encourage those revenue-generating pilgrimages. The walls were in a sorry state, leaving the city open to bedouin raiders. Suleiman's major work was to have the walls rebuilt. This roughly followed the line of the Roman wall of Aelia Capitolina and excluded Mount Zion once again. The work took some three years and remains today around the Old City.

THE GATES

From the time of David onward, the gates of Jerusalem have been added, subtracted and moved, depending on the defensive theories of each new ruler. The gates installed by Suleiman remain to this day.

Pride of the reconstruction was the Damascus Gate, given that name because it faces Damascus. The most lavish of the gates, it was the greeting place for visiting dignitaries and remains the central artery in and out of the Old City.

Moving clockwise about four hundred yards to the east from Damascus is Herod's Gate or the Flower Gate. This location has been the general point of attack against the city and was the area of the breaches of the First Crusade and of Saladin.

Two gates remain on the eastern side of the Old City facing the Valley of Kidron, Gethsemane and the Mount of Olives. One originally named St. Stephen's Gate after Christendom's first martyr is better known as the Lion's Gate from its decorations. The Lion's Gate stands just a few feet north of the Temple Mount and an equal distance from the First Station of the Cross.

A few hundred yards down from the Lion's Gate, a

double gate known as the Golden Gate once afforded
direct access to the Temple Mount. Set a few yards below
the plaza, the twin openings were called the Door of
Mercy and the Door of Repentance. It was bricked up by
the Turks, largely because of Moslem superstitions that a
Jewish messiah would enter through it. Jesus is believed
to have come through the Golden Gate on that fatal day.

On the southeastern corner of the wall, where the
present excavations of the City of David are going on,
single, double and triple gates with access to the Al Aksa
Mosque were also bricked up. In the area of the Western
Wall there are all sorts of archaeological diggings, which
have unearthed arches over covered streets, bridges, broad
steps and other accesses to the Temple Mount.

The first open southern gate, the Dung Gate, was so
named as the former passage to the city dump. This also
borders the original City of David and is today's main
entrance to the Western Wall.

Farther southwest the ground rises sharply to Mount
Zion and the Zion Gate, a bullet-riddled monument of the
recent wars. On Mount Zion, outside the wall, are the
traditional sites of the Last Supper, Mary's place of death
(not her tomb, which is in the Kidron Valley adjoining
Gethsemane) and King David's Tomb.

Along the western side of the Old City, the Jaffa Gate is
equal in importance to the Damascus Gate in commerce,
locale and, more so, historically. Immediately inside the
Jaffa Gate one finds the site of Herod's Palace, which was
also the Citadel and later held the residence of the Crusader
kings. This has traditionally been the strong point of the
defenses. David's Tower hovers above it. This is actually a
minaret constructed on the remains of one of the Herodian
towers and is completely misnamed. Inside the Jaffa Gate
one finds the Anglican Hospice, with the Maronite convent and monastery close by, and the site of "Hezekiah's
Pool" just over the street.

The seventh and final gate, the New Gate on the
northwest corner, is the area where Tancred the Crusader
attacked and is the most inconspicuous of the entrances.
It serves the Christian Quarter with St. Saviour's Franciscan
Church, the Christian Brothers College and the Latin
Patriarch's residence just inside.

The Ottomans were not known as great builders or

architects. Their work on Jerusalem was mainly restoration. The walls, fortifications and water works were installed by Suleiman to assure Jerusalem's defensibility.

Very little else can be said of a complimentary nature of the Ottoman years. Their rule was corrupt, cruel and cunning and they reduced the holy land and the holy city to dust and ashes. The pasha of the Syrian Province had two basic duties insofar as Istanbul was concerned. His job was to keep his territory secure and to collect his quota of taxes for the sultan. Whatever could be stolen, skimmed, extorted, bribed, taxed or otherwise milked out of his province over and above the sultan's cut was welcomed by Istanbul. The Turks were the champion pluckers of all time, keeping the non-Moslem communities anemic and allowing them outside transfusions only to be able to suck their blood again. Corporal punishment was constant and known for its perverted brutality. A favorite Turkish discipline was the whipping rod, applied to the soles of bare feet and often leaving the victim crippled for life.

Overtaxation of villages and leaving them undefended led to an ultimate destruction of the farmlands. When an exorbitant levy was not met, an entire village was often tumbled and the land fell to swamp and erosion. Bedouin goats, a menace since the time of Abraham, ravaged the delicate balance as they dug the earth with pointed hoofs and tore up any and all existing vegetation. Outside the cities the highways were nests of bandits who preyed on the weak and undefended. Villages and fields were constantly raided by bedouin looters.

THE OTTOMANS AND THE JEWS

During the fifteenth and sixteenth centuries the battering of the Jews on the European continent continued without respite. Pope after Pope, with few exceptions, continued to fuel the sport of Jew baiting with forced conversions to Christianity, the institution of the ghetto, special Jewish clothing, taxations, barring Jews from owning land and practicing professions and trades.

Martin Luther, who published his 95 Theses at the same time the Ottomans conquered Palestine, kept the fires of hatred against the Jews glowing brightly.

Expulsions all over the Continent and a particularly traumatic expulsion from Spain sent this desperate people scurrying for new places to survive. France shut her borders and, after settlement in Italy, papal harassment brought on further persecutions and an ultimate expulsion from there. In the beginning the Ottomans needed Jewish expertise and they fared reasonably well in havens in North Africa and along the Levantine coast.

Jews began to arrive in Palestine in large numbers but the acquisition of land and permits for new buildings as well as the repair of old ones were subject to astronomical payoffs and little could be done to raise the Jews above the destitution level. In Jerusalem they settled in a quarter adjoining Mount Zion in the southern part of the city close to the Western Wall. No Jew under Ottoman rule was permitted to go to the Haram esh Sharif, the Jewish Temple Mount. The Jerusalem colony was Sephardic, Jews of Spanish or oriental descent, and they carried on as struggling craftsmen or impoverished peddlers.

In a slow season the tax collectors generated revenues by snatching a leader or important rabbi and holding him for communal ransom. At other times synagogues were boarded up until a communal "debt" was extorted. On other occasions synagogues were burned to set in motion the cycle of demanding blood money for new building permits.

Despite this Jews arrived in thousands as the persecutions continued in Europe. After living for centuries in an atmosphere of death and dismemberment, various mystical messianic cults swept through the Jewish ghettos and they eventually turned toward Jerusalem for their salvation. Ultra-Orthodox Hasidics arrived to await the messiah and they were to become particular targets of Ottoman barbarism. Bearded, earlocked, dressed in the ghetto costume of the Russian Pale, these Ashkenasi or European Jews came under the full weight of bigotry, scorn and derision and were finally expelled from Jerusalem.

They settled in the Galilee in the holy cities of Tiberias and Safed and in Hebron. Their main source of income was through a tradition which was called the *hallukah*.

Almost every Jewish home in the world kept a *pushka*, or collection can, to raise money to sustain their brethren in Palestine.

The Jews had neither abandoned nor given up claim to the holy land. When history permitted them to return to Jerusalem they responded, and in numbers. Now they persisted. The Ashkenasim were allowed to return to the city and after years of typical Turkish gouging they built Jewry's most magnificent shrine, the Hurva Synagogue, in 1743. They came in such numbers that the Jewish Quarter was jammed with synagogues and by 1850 they were quickly becoming the majority population.

THE OTTOMANS AND THE CHRISTIANS

The Latin Church had seized the lion's share of the holy places during the Crusades. With the departure of the knights, Catholic fortunes took a turn for the worse.

The schism, hostility and continuous bickering between the major Christian denominations were delicious morsels for such dishonest brokers as the Turks, who were soon running a shell game between Latin and Orthodox Christians. The administrative capital of the Eastern Church was in Istanbul and they pressed their claim with the sultans for a greater share of the Jerusalem pie. In 1551 the Turks expelled the Franciscans from their headquarters on Mount Zion, a monastery called the Coenaculum, the traditional site of the Last Supper. Forced to move into the Christian Quarter, the Franciscans established St. Saviour's Monastery, which has remained their headquarters ever since.

Within a few years the French kings opened their purses and persuaded the Sublime Porte to reverse its position by granting France permission to rebuild the principal chapel in the Holy Sepulchre and giving the title to the Latins.

By the time the first Protestant pilgrims arrived in the middle of the sixteenth century the Turks were thoroughly enjoying their operation of the holy-land hustle. The Latin

Church had come on hard times. The Hundred Years' War, the Black Death and finally the schism precipitated by Martin Luther had left the monastic orders in a sorry state. It was during this period that Ignatius Loyola, a former Spanish officer turned monk, founded the Jesuits. He came to Jerusalem with six of his disciples, vowing, among other things, to convert the heathens of Islam to the true Church. However, the Franciscans would allow no one to cut into their territory and had the Jesuits expelled.

Begun by Suleiman the Magnificent, a vicious poll tax was levied on all non-Moslems, which forced the Christian establishment to struggle to remain. At one point or another the Holy Sepulchre had monks and chapels of the Latins, the Orthodox, Syrians, Armenians, Maronites of Antioch, Nestorians from Mesopotamia, Egyptian Copts, Ethiopians, Georgians, Melchites of the Byzantine Church and Jacobites. The jockeying for position and control within the Holy Sepulchre became very un-Christianlike business and Turkish avarice was so great that all but four of these sects were forced to close shop.

Christian pilgrims arriving at the port of Jaffa were at the tender mercy of Turkish customs officials. The quickest way to gather the necessary documents, stamps, seals and signatures was through the bribe, also an effective way to recover lost luggage. The road to Jerusalem was perilous and required paid escorts and tolls with a little something thrown in for the police.

Jerusalem of the fifteenth and sixteenth centuries held less than two thousand Christians, mostly monks and clergy, with a few Christian women dressed as Moslems, covering their faces and rarely appearing in public. Boozing and prostitution were very much part of the scene. Seeking admission to the Holy Sepulchre set off another round of Turkish fleecing. The Turks loathed the infidels and considered the Holy Sepulchre an abomination in comparison to the Dome of the Rock. All told, it was a rotten place to live and a worse place to visit.

Christian rivalry flared into bloodshed more than once. Pilgrims were often shocked to witness Franciscan friars and Greek monks flailing away at one another, biting, kicking and bashing each other over the head with their crosses within sight of Calvary and the Tomb of Jesus. The hostility broke into a fierce riot during the Easter services of 1757, forcing the Sultan to issue a decree which greatly reduced the Latin possession. This set off a howl in Turkey by ambassadors of the Western nations.

The Sultan's document, a masterpiece of confusion, sliced up the Holy Sepulchre and the Church of the Nativity like a mosaic. Decades-long arguments ensued over who had the right to wash what steps, who owned the keys to what corridor, whose candles and incense holders hung in which order, who could hold mass where and when, who could cross what courtyard at what times. Carpets were cut at odd angles so if one stepped off an odd-shaped rug he was instantly transported from Rome to Istanbul.

During this period the tradition of praying at the Stations of the Cross was established. There are different beliefs as to which route Jesus took to his death. Various events described in the Scriptures were arbitrarily set in the Antonia fortress, along the Via Dolorosa and within Calvary. These were marked but the number of stations varied from time to time and it was not until quite recently that the fourteen stations were standardized and agreed upon.

By the end of the eighteenth century Britain had become the world's greatest colonial power. Rule of the seas to protect her shipping lanes was paramount to that power. The Levant and Egypt became key geographic points in the imperial game. In an effort to be able to interdict British naval forces, Napoleon invaded the region. First he took Malta, which was defended by the Knights of St. John, the former Hospitalers of Jerusalem. After Malta's fall on June 10, 1798, the French invaded Egypt and within a few weeks the entire Nile Valley was in their hands.

In order to block a Turkish relief force, Napoleon moved north into Palestine in February of 1799. The British allied with Turkey and Napoleon's advance was halted at Acre, forcing the French to return to Egypt.

Although Napoleon's advance into the Middle East had been thwarted, the skill and invincibility of his army in Egypt sent Europe into an anti-French alliance which included the Austrian Hapsburg Empire, Russia, the Ottomans and Britain. Against this array Napoleon was forced to retire from the region.

Napolean made a devastating impact on the Moslem world. The French were the first land army of the West to intrude on Moslem territory since the Crusades. Their obvious military, administrative and technical skills shocked the slumbering Islamic world, which had continued to fantasize about its superiority.

The Moslem mind has largely remained puzzled by the complexities and skills of the Western world, which created the Industrial Revolution. The rigid Moslem environment gave little room for a man to expand his mind. Islam told him everything: when to pray, when to sleep, eat, have intercourse, dispense justice, how to govern, how to behave in every aspect of business life, of social life, in fact, it held tight rein over every facet and value of life. Minds under such restrictions simply could not cope with Western organization. The European continent was democratizing, with emphasis placed on man's individual freedom and his individual right to action. This was totally opposite from the Moslem experience. Unable to absorb the benefits of the West into their own culture, the Moslems became frustrated and their xenophobia heightened.

In 1831 Turkey was weakened by a crisis in Serbia as well as by the Greek War of Independence. Mohammed Ali, the Pasha of Egypt, seized the moment to rebel against the Sultan, liberated Egypt and conquered the Syrian Province. For a decade there was a breath of fresh air in Jerusalem.

With the French moving in on North Africa, the British coveting Egypt and both of them after Palestine, the Ottomans spiraled toward inevitable decline. They were propped up by "here today and gone tomorrow" alliances as they benefited Western ambitions.

The British were the first to make an official appearance in Jerusalem, establishing a consulate in 1838. This was soon followed by French, Prussian, Sardinian, United States, Russian, Austrian and Spanish consulates.

The second British consul, James Finn, who served between 1845 and 1862, had been tremendously moved by the plight of the Jews in Europe. He is credited with helping the Jewish community in Jerusalem as Britain became a sort of unofficial protector. With Finn's devotion, the Jews were able to break down much of the Ottoman game and continue the community's progress. Jews were now earning high positions and new freedoms in Europe and they lent additional support to strengthening the Jewish position in Palestine.

With the Ottomans under the influence of the Western powers, the fortunes of the Eastern Orthodox Church in Jerusalem declined. In 1852 the Sultan issued a decree finalizing the division of the holy places stone by stone. Far from resolving the issue, it set off a fury. Russia, the defender of the Eastern Church, demanded that the Sultan allow all members of the Orthodox Church in the entire Ottoman Empire to come under protection of the Czar. England and France rushed to the side of the Ottomans against growing Russian ambitions and in protection of the Latin establishment. The result was the Crimean War. The massive land war was fought largely on the Crimean Peninsula of southern Russia. A half million men died, disease being the major killer.

With all the blood spilled over Jerusalem, it is mandatory to look at the condition these Turks left the holy city and the holy land in.

Wrote Chateaubriand in 1806:

The houses of Jerusalem . . . resemble prisons or sepulchres. On seeing these stone houses set in a stone landscape, one might wonder whether they are not the distorted monuments of a cemetery in the midst of a desert! Go into the city, nothing will console you for the bleakness outside. You lose your way in little unpaved streets which rise and fall over uneven ground, and walk along in clouds of dust, or over loose pebbles . . . vaulted bazaars succeed in taking away the last light from the desolate city. A few wretched shops display only poverty to one's gaze, and frequently these shops are closed for fear a cadi (a Moslem holy man who acts as a judge) will pass by. There is no one in the streets, no one at the gates of the city, except that from time to time a peasant glides along in the shadows, hiding beneath his clothes the fruits of his toil in fear of being robbed by the soldiery...the only sound heard in the city is the occasional galloping of a desert mare; it is a Janissary bringing back the head of a bedouin or going to plunder a fellah (peasant)....

Or consider the observations of Mark Twain in *Innocents Abroad*, which was written in 1869 after his trip to the holy land.

Of all the lands there are for dismal scenery, I think Palestine must be the prince. The hills are barren, they are dull of color, they are unpicturesque in shape. The valleys are unsightly deserts fringed with a feeble vegetation that has an expression about it of being sorrowful and despondent. The Dead Sea and the Sea of Galilee sleep in the midst of a vast stretch of hill and plain wherein the eye rests upon no pleasant tint, no striking object, no soft picture dreaming in a purple haze or mottled with the shadows of the clouds. Every outline is harsh, every feature is distinct, there is no perspective—distance works no enchantment here. It is a hopeless, dreary, heartbroken land....

...Palestine sits in sackcloth and ashes. Over it broods the spell of a curse that has withered its fields and fettered its energies...Nazareth is forlorn... Jericho the accursed lies in moldering ruin...Bethlehem and Bethany, in their poverty and humiliation... renowned Jerusalem itself, the stateliest name in history, has lost its ancient grandeur and is become a pauper village....

There was never a permanent Turkish settlement in Palestine or Jerusalem. Under the Ottoman pashas an Arab aristocracy emerged and played the Ottoman game. These Arab families inherited much of the land and the true power and continued the Ottoman legacy of corruption and larceny. The land was tilled by feudalism. Reigning Arab families milked their control over the religious institutions and the bedouins finished off what was not already wrecked. No, the Turks did not settle Palestine. Their surrogate Arabs did nothing but further the abuse and rape of the country. In seven and a half centuries of consecutive Moslem rule, Jerusalem was never elevated as one of their proclaimed holy places. It was drained of life and vitality. If indeed the Moslems bleat for Jerusalem their abysmal record forfeits those claims. Claims made, incidentally, only after the Jews had restored the city to greatness.

The Return to Zion

By the early 1800s the population within the walled city became a crush, particularly in the Jewish Quarter. The Jewish community was rag poor, lived in abysmal squalor without medical facilities or proper sanitation and with rationed water. Their poverty increased during the Crimean War of 1854–56, when the Russian Czar ordered a halt to all charitable donations from Russian Jews to Palestine. Each night the Turks closed the Old City gates and, inside, a dusk-to-dawn curfew was in effect.

The first man to really alleviate this condition was a British Jewish stockbroker, Sir Moses Montefiore, whose entire life was spent in the service of his people. He made seven pilgrimages to the holy land, no simple journey in those days, the last being at the age of ninety-one.

Montefiore also made innumerable visits to the world courts in the cause of simple justice for the Jews. During the middle of the Crimean War, with Britain an ally of the Turks, Sir Moses traveled to Istanbul for an audience with the Sultan and petitioned him to be able to purchase land outside the walled city. The Sultan was persuaded and issued a decree of permission. After scrutinizing possible sites and much oriental haggling, some land was bought on the western side of the city across the Hinnom Valley opposite Mount Zion. Montefiore's efforts were strongly supported by the philanthropy of two American Jews from New Orleans: Gershom Kursheedt, a publisher, and Judah Touro, a businessman.

234

Two years after the land purchase a windmill was constructed on the site. The entire adventure was filled with risk. There was the wrath of avaricious landlords of the Old City. They didn't want people moving out and the accompanying loss of rents. Moslem fanatics were also determined to keep the Jews locked in their quarter. The greatest danger was the omnipresence of bedouin thieves and marauders. By 1860 a long rectangular building capable of housing some fifteen to twenty families had been erected. It was called Mishkenot Sha'Ananim, meaning "Houses of Tranquillity," a hopeful misnomer. Shortly thereafter a quarters called after Yemin Moshe (the right hand of Sir Moses Montefiore) was built on neighboring land. This Montefiore Quarters, as it came to be known, went through several changes of function. At first it was considered too dangerous to live outside the walls and each night the Jews returned to the protection of the city.

Sir Moses Montefiore lived to be a centenarian and never stopped his benevolent works for his fellow Jews. After a devastating plague in 1864 he made the contribution that brought in a decent waterworks to the Jewish Quarter. Medical care had been in the hands of Christian missionaries. Sir Moses hired the first Jewish doctor, a chap named Frankel, and established a small hospital in the Old City.

The daring of one Jew, Joseph Rivlin, finally broke the barriers that had prevented settlement outside the walls. Some buildings, used during daylight hours, had been constructed about a half mile from the New Gate along the Jaffa Road and Rivlin dared to live in one of them. Each morning when the city gates were opened, Rivlin's relatives rushed out to see if he was still alive. He weathered the storm and more houses were added to a quarters which came to be known as Nachlat Shiva. Fifty families joined the venture and by 1869 had succeeded in establishing the first permanent habitat outside the Old City.

About the same time as Nachlat Shiva took root, a group of oriental Jews established successful quarters opposite the Citadel and Jaffa Gate called Mahane Yisrael. The big project that really changed the face of Jerusalem happened in 1874 with the starting of the Mea Shearim, a housing project of ultra-Orthodox Hasidics. The project was subsidized by benefactors from Hungary, Poland and

Russia with individual donors buying small apartments and granting use of them to families in Jerusalem to "hold" for the owners until they could come to Jerusalem to die.

After Mea Shearim there followed an outburst of small stockadelike neighborhoods, mainly in the vicinity of the Jaffa Road. Joseph Navon, ancestor of the Israeli President and a very important Jewish leader of the time, established the Mahane Yehuda Quarters in 1887 with the help of a Christian banker. Most of these quarters were fortresslike, with the houses connected so the outer walls formed a protective shield. Entrances were through gates which were locked by night. These were largely self-contained communal units made up of families of the same nationalities or religious sects. An inside courtyard generally held a community center, a synagogue, a school and some sort of minor medical facility.

There were colorful quarters of Yemenites and Persians and Kurds wearing their native costumes. A lovely and more open neighborhood was established by the Bukharans, who were more affluent, as they had left part of their families in the old country to keep businesses going and income coming. Six of these neighborhoods contain the name of the beloved Sir Moses Montefiore, whose foundation supplied much of the funds.

In concert with the housing developments came the first hospital, a Rothschild donation, and a Hebrew press which printed not only religious texts and books but four news publications. A school of higher learning for boys was followed by the opening of the Bezalel Art Academy.

By the end of the century thirty-five thousand Jews formed the majority population of the city, living in sixty separate quarters plus the Old City. Thirty-eight distinctive nationalities of Jews could be counted, each with their separate cultural backgrounds and unique synagogues.

THE MEA SHEARIM

Nowhere is Jerusalem's diversity of cultures more evident than in the Mea Shearim, another of its cities within a city. The Hasidics (meaning "the pious") came into being in Eastern Europe as a result of Christian excesses during medieval times. Driven to fanaticism, the Hasidics have maintained an uncompromising set of values and dogma ever since. The centerpiece of their existence is to pray, study and wait for the messiah. They are a poor lot, mostly shopkeepers, dependent on charitable contributions from Orthodox Jewry to sustain them. The name Mea Shearim, meaning "a hundred gates," is taken from a passage in Genesis. Founded in 1874, its charter noted that the quarter was being built for Hasidics, the successors of the biblical Pharisees. First constructions were protective row houses with interior courtyards. The entire quarter is crammed, without modern facilities, and poverty stricken; its few thousand inhabitants making it an anachronism resembling a Polish ghetto of several centuries ago. On entering the quarter women are admonished to dress modestly. Their own women paddle about in drab, sacklike dresses seemingly from the same three bolts of cloth. Shorn heads of married women are covered with kerchiefs. The men move in quick fidgety motions, as though weaving and bobbing in prayer. They are all dressed in black, long kaftans, beaver hats or fur headdress, their knickers usually tucked into high socks. They are bearded, black for the young and white for the old. They wear earlocks in memory of King David, who is said to have worn them. It is a total religious settlement with its own tiny, dimly lit synagogues, unpainted in living memory. There are ritual baths and, in the markets, omnipresent signs that all vendors and merchants are bound to pay a tithe, or one tenth of their earnings, as was paid to the Temple in biblical days. Voices of young boys reciting in unison from the Talmud-Torah schools are heard at the turn of most corners. Yeshivas of higher learning also flourish. The various sects are built around outstanding rabbis whose influence is near sacrosanct. The word "God" is too sacred to speak and is never heard or seen written on the graffiti-filled walls. Life is geared to the Sabbath and the holidays with an explosion of energy. The Thursday shopping is followed by women bringing their unbaked loaves to the communal bakery while the men purify themselves at the ritual bath, then proceed to the Western Wall, after which the night is spent in Talmudic discussion in their small dismal synagogues. On the Sabbath the inhabitants are forbidden to work, ride in a car, speak on a phone, write or cook. Cars from the outside are apt to be greeted with blockades and stones. Yiddish, a bastardized German and the language of the Eastern European ghettos, is the spoken tongue. Hebrew is saved for prayer. The separation of the sexes is paramount and women don't amount to much except as servants of the men. There is no nonsense, little laughter, little room for young people to grow inside the bounds of the stifling restrictions and crowded living space. Yet there is virtually no crime. A great percentage of the young flee the ghetto but enough remain to continue the traditions. One sect, the Naturei Karta, refuses to recognize the State of Israel because it wasn't established by the messiah. Blind to other beliefs and out of step with modern society, they have retrenched defensively because of the hostility toward them. Many of the Hasidics are true Zionists. The Mea Shearim stood on the front line during the War of Independence and they fought with great valor, holding their quarters against Arab attacks.

ARAB SETTLEMENT BEYOND THE WALLS

Shortly after the Jews began moving out of the walled city, the Arabs also built a number of neighborhoods, mainly in a northeastern direction around the Nablus Road. On the south side of the city Abu Tor, on the road to Bethlehem, was established in the late 1870s. The Arabs, who were not under the same security threat as the Jews, ventured to farther corners such as the Katamon, an isolated settlement several miles southwest of the city. Arab buildings were more conventional, with individual houses and long main streets, in contrast to the garrisonlike Jewish structures.

CHRISTIAN GROWTH

The streets of the Old City were finally paved in 1865 by gangs of chained prisoners and roads were built to connect the new suburbs. Carriage highways were constructed to connect Nablus, Jericho and Bethlehem, and a badly needed road was constructed to the port of Jaffa. This latter road was done in preparation for a pilgrimage by the Emperor Franz Joseph who was en route to the grand opening of the Suez Canal. Before the Jaffa Road was built, the trip to and from the coast had taken two days along a torturous winding course through the Judean hills. The carriage highway cut the journey down to seventeen hours.

Throughout the ages Christians and Moslems had shown a distinct lack of respect for each other's holy places. Until 1860 St. Anne's Cathedral had been used as a stable by the Turkish military. Shortly after 1860 it was cleaned up and returned to God's work when the Sisters of Zion, an order of Catholic nuns, established a convent and restored many of the sites attributed to Jesus that surrounded the Antonia fortress and the First Station of the Cross.

In 1870 the Palestinean Exploration Society came into being and produced the first photographs as well as the first field maps of the country. Today, an original black and white print of the period brings up to several thousand dollars.

The new art of archaeology saw the American Edward Robinson make a dig following the line of the third wall of Agrippa and Charles Warren explored the foundations of the Temple Mount. Englishman Charles Wilson made the most exciting find, an archway that was a continuation of the Western Wall into a covered street. It is believed that the arch supported a bridge to and from the Temple Mount to the Upper City.

The French developed a number of churches and schools, their major work being the Notre Dame de France Hospice, just outside the wall in the area of Tancred's Corner. A French Jewish convert founded the Convent of Notre Dame of Zion for the purpose of converting other Jews, but with little success.

Leading directly out of the Damascus Gate was a string of hospitals built by the Germans, Italians, English and Rothschilds. The British Order of St. John's established an Eye Hospital on the Hebron Road. There were numerous orphanages, a highly regarded Dominican Bible School, hospices, the prestigious Schmidt's College for girls and a scattering of new churches in the vicinity of the walled city, not the least of which was a unique octagonal Ethiopian church near Mea Shearim. The Queen of England and the King of Prussia joined to erect a mission on the Nablus Road which eventually became the Anglican Cathedral of St. George.

During these years the Russians and Germans, whose motives had heavy political overtones, made the greatest impact on the Christian development of the city.

THE AMERICAN COLONY

Horatio and Anna Spafford were Chicagoans whose charitable works began with the rehabilitation of the city after the great fire of 1871. Two years later Anna Spafford was in a shipwreck in which four of her daughters drowned. In 1878 they lost a son to scarlet fever. The Spaffords were thrown out of the Presbyterian Church for rejecting the doctrine that their suffering was in retribution for their sins. In 1881 they headed to Jerusalem with a small group of friends to live and work as close to Jesus as they could and founded a colony inside the Old City in a house near the Damascus Gate. The "House on the Gate" was soon a salvation center for destitute Arabs living in unfathomable squalor. Other Christian missionaries loathed the Americans because they made no attempt to convert their Moslem wards. After the death of Horatio from malaria, the group struggled and came under tremendous pressure to abandon the city. The colony was saved near the turn of the century when they were joined by a group of Swedish families. Together, they purchased a former Turkish pasha's palace beyond the walls. The colony flourished for a time as a total communal unit. Disdaining outside labor or salaries for themselves, they planted their own fields, including cotton, made their own cloth, had their own carpenters, shoemakers, blacksmiths, dressmakers, and ran their own livestock. It was a lively place with an art and literary club, a choir and even a brass band. They were among the first to go in for photography. Early Zionist leaders studied the colony as a prototype for the kibbutz and incorporated many ideas into the new movement. During the First World War the Turks left the city destitute and the American colony saved thousands of lives through their soup kitchen. After the war the colony began to unravel, its members drifting off. Eventually it was turned into a hotel but remained in the Spafford family. It was Bertha Spafford Vester, a surviving daughter, who continued the colony's charitable works and became a minor legend. At the House on the Gate, Bertha established a handicraft school for Arab girls. By learning a trade so they could earn money, they were able to avoid being sold into marriage at the age of twelve or thirteen. A clinic tackled the ponderous health problems of the Moslems. Nutritional and stomach ailments lead a list which includes sanitation-oriented diseases and respiratory ailments due to the lack of heating. Typhoid and hepatitis are particularly severe. Burns are always a problem because so many children play in unattended kitchens. Education is now a major part of the clinic's program because until recently Moslem mothers did not make the connection between cleanliness and health and many sick children were left in the corner to die. Until 1948 the Spafford House was the only health-care center for the Arabs in the Old City and surrounding countryside. Today its expanded program is run by Oral Roberts University with a full staff of doctors and treats some 14,000 Arabs a year.

THE RUSSIANS

The czars had long considered Russia the protector of the Eastern Orthodox religion. Russia had fought the Crimean War partly on the issue of holy sites in Jerusalem. Russia had and still harbors dreams of breaking into the warm waters of the Mediterranean. Even after the Crimean fiasco, the Russians pressed their presence in Jerusalem. In 1870 they purchased a large plot of land several hundred yards beyond New Gate, a former Turkish parade grounds, and established a major church with facilities for the thousands of Russian pilgrims who came each year. One unkept secret has it that a number of the "priests" are actually KGB agents.

On the Mount of Olives the Russians built the exquisite multi-onion-domed Church of Mary Magdalene just above the traditional site of Gethsemane. On the crest of the Mount of Olives stands the Russian Convent and Church of the Ascension. The tower is one of the distinguishing landmarks of the city and can be seen from great distances.

An eight-ton bell, cast in Russia, was dragged from Jaffa to Jerusalem by the hands of pilgrims, a task of the dimension of slaves moving great stones in building the Pyramids. Progress was a few miles a day, requiring a lot of hymn singing and prayer. The Russian pilgrims were the most colorful, devout and ecstatic, their voices blending in a continuous singing of canonicals and sacred music. If one is fortunate enough at prayer time to slip into the Church of the Ascension or the Russian convent in Ein Kerem, the suburb where John the Baptist was born, the singing of the nuns is an experience not apt to be forgotten.

After the Russian Revolution, their pilgrimages dried up under Communism. Today, a strict head count is kept by the Kremlin of the remaining White Russian nuns, with replacements hard to come by. The Red Russian nuns at Ein Kerem can be replaced only when a nun dies. Her body is shipped back to Russia for proper identification, after which a replacement is sent; so this contingent remains constant.

THE GERMANS

There has been a German presence in Jerusalem since the Teutonic Order of Knights established themselves during the Crusades. The Germans came back very strongly in the latter part of the nineteenth century when the country drifted toward its World War I alliance with the Turks.

The new German presence began in the 1860s with the construction of a large orphanage beyond the walls to house Syrian orphans, and this was followed by a hospital for lepers and a school for Arab girls.

In 1873 the German Templars founded the German Colony in the southwest between the Montefiore windmill and the Greek Colony. It was the most beautiful residential district of its time, with tree-shaded streets, lovely individual homes and a strangely European and comfortable look. This neighborhood was to absorb a large number of engineers and military people sent from Germany to help get the Turks organized on modern lines.

Where the Mount of Olives joins Mount Scopus the Germans built another towered edifice, the Augusta Victoria Hospital complex. Aside from its commissioned duty as a medical center, it had a key position on a ridge that gave it military importance. The complex was commandeered from time to time, for instance as regional headquarters for the Turko-German forces during the First World War.

Inside the Old City the German Lutheran Church of the Redeemer was built as close as they could acquire land to the Holy Sepulchre. The site is a hillock called Mount Muristan, its tower affording a unique view of the interior of the walled city.

The German presence was magnified by a visit from Kaiser Wilhelm II at the turn of the century. The Emperor did not arrive by donkey as did Jesus or aboard a mule like the modest Caliph Omar, but riding a white horse in the midst of bombastic pageantry. An old legend had it that the city would be conquered by a king on a white stallion who would enter one of the city's gates. In order to pacify the fears of some of the more superstitious, the Kaiser did not enter through a gate but a special breach was made in the wall for him to go through.

On Mount Zion Wilhelm dedicated a piece of ground purchased by the German Catholic Society for the Holy Land which was the traditional site of the death of Mary. Later, a major structure, the Benedictine Abbey of Mary's Dormition, was built on the spot.

An important side show of the Kaiser's visit was his meeting with Theodor Herzl, the founder of Zionism, who sought recognition for a Jewish homeland in Palestine. Although Palestine was an Ottoman province, the Zionists sought to enlist the support of every government it could. Wilhelm was non-committal toward the delegation but the mere fact he conferred with them at length was heartening for the new movement.

By the beginning of the new century, with the impetus of Zionism, the Jewish population in Jerusalem had grown to forty-five thousand. There were fifteen thousand Christians at the time and ten thousand Moslems. The Jewish city began to take on standard urban functions—with newspapers, banks, theaters, shops, old-age homes, hotels, museums, restaurants and the like. Joseph Navon promoted a railroad line which the French built and in a sense this marked the beginning of the end of Jerusalem's eternal isolation.

ZIONISM

The so-called phenomenon of Zionism was no phenomenon but an inevitable happening. Until the American Revolution no Jew anywhere had enjoyed the privileges of equal citizenship since the fall of the Second Temple nineteen centuries earlier.

In Western Europe Jewish conditions had improved manyfold. Some Jews became internationally prominent, wealthy, powerful and respected. A flood of doctors, lawyers, politicians, scientists, writers, musicians, businessmen and thinkers all enhanced the human race by Jewish contributions hundreds of percentiles greater than

their meager numbers. Even in this enlightened atmosphere the odors of anti-Semitism lingered on. The new
discriminations were milder in form, yet the discomfort of
the Jew in his native or adopted land never fully disappeared. Even in subdued forms, vicious outbreaks of
anti-Semitism were always simmering and periodically
boiled over.

In Russia and Poland, with a population of several
million Jews, there was a continuation of the viler and
bloodier forms of persecution.

It is reasonable to say Jews lived tentatively almost
everywhere. Nowhere else in history had a people lost
their nation and been subjected to so many attempts to
eliminate them, and managed to survive. Thus the Jew
never gave up spiritual claim to Palestine and Jerusalem
any more than the Moslem could ever give up spiritual
claim to Mecca. When there was no Jewish settlement in
Palestine it was only because it was not permitted. When
it was permitted, no matter how severe the conditions,
the Jews always returned.

Zionism had an official starting date in 1897 but for
centuries the need and hope for a return existed in every
new generation. Hereto the Jews who went back to Palestine
were mainly religious. They were devoted to prayer, study
and awaiting the messiah, hardly a breed to build a new
nation. Yet, without the persistence of the ultra-religious
Jews and their devotion to Jerusalem, the link might well
have been broken.

By the mid-1800s pre-Zionistic movements were being
intellectualized all over Europe and America. In Russia
and Poland physical movement was taking shape. In 1860
the French Baron Edmond de Rothschild, one of the
greatest of all Jewish benefactors, established a foundation
which permitted Jews to go out onto the land in Palestine.
Huge acreages which had fallen into disuse because of
Arab neglect were available.

In the ten years that Mohammed Ali's forces occupied
Palestine the pasha levied severe taxation and instituted
conscription to draft Palestinian Arabs into his army. The
result was a mass Arab exodus. Entire villages fled to the
Transjordan region, leaving many more tracts of land
available.

As Rothschild's foundation began seeking land, Arab

land sharks and feudalistic absentee owners were only too happy to dump land on the Jews at outrageous prices; land which they believed would never be productive again. Rothschild established several complete farming villages, provided the implements, homes, synagogues, hospitals, stock and seed. He sent agricultural experts from his estates to provide the Jews with farming expertise, as most of them didn't know one end of a cow from the other. Despite their isolation and the perils of the Palestinian countryside, the villages took root and became reasonably successful. But there was something lacking: a Jewish tradition of peasantry. While Rothschild's experts and trial and error were creating a minor success, it all added up to transplanting a European system into Palestine. The Jews became small-acreage farmers, using Arab stoop labor. This was fine for a few villages here and there but it certainly was not the way to redeem a derelict agricultural establishment. What was needed was an entirely new concept of dealing with the land. Jews were going to have to do it through their own toil. The idea of communal farming and living and self-sacrifice began to surface.

Movement to Palestine and its redemption was speeded after the assassination of Czar Alexander II in 1881. The libel was spread that the murder had been the work of the Jews. The first anti-Jewish pogrom began in a town in the Ukraine in the spring of 1881 and within days it had erupted to three dozen cities in the area. By the end of the year the entire Pale (areas where Jews were permitted to live) in Russia and Poland was in a frenzy of Jew killing.

The progrom is a particularly ugly affair. The Eastern Orthodox Church was especially venomous toward the Jews and perpetuated the libels that flared into these massacres. The pogrom was often led by drunken, thick-witted Cossack horsemen who tore through a Jewish village or section of town and flattened and burned everything in sight. Shops were smashed and looted, synagogues gutted and sacred books and Torahs desecrated, pathetic little plots of land were stomped under, cottages tumbled, beatings, beard pullings, humiliations and indiscriminate murders wreaked devastation on man, beast and property. Between 1881 and 1914 over two and a half million Jews fled Russia. By 1882 twenty thousand destitute Jews had arrived in Palestine. Most of them went up to Jerusalem.

The man of Zion was Theodor Herzl, a Hungarian-born Jew who was a journalist in Vienna. He was what was considered an assimilated Jew, one who completely conformed to the European life style and was respected and comfortable in his environs. He had a change of mind as the pogroms spilled over into his own Vienna with a horrible outburst of Jew baiting.

By 1896 Herzl had assumed a leadership role in European Jewry and penned and published *Der Judenstaat* declaring to all of mankind the urgent need for the establishment of a Jewish state and the rebirth of Jewish nationalism. In the same year Herzl traveled to Constantinople to try to persuade the Sultan to relinquish Palestine to the Jews. The Sultan did not succumb to the monetary temptation but many restrictions on Jewish immigration were relaxed and additional conditions were granted to enable settlement of evacuated lands. A year later the movement became official with a charter congress in Basel, Switzerland. It is well to quote the founding principles of Zionism because of the future distortions of Arab propaganda.

The promotion, on suitable industrial lines, of the colonization of Palestine by Jewish agricultural and industrial workers.

The organization and binding together of the whole of Jewry by means of appropriate institutions, local and international, in accordance with the laws of each country.

The strengthening and fostering of Jewish national sentiment and consciousness.

Preparatory steps toward obtaining government consent, where necessary, to attain the aims of Zionism.

Extreme care was made to emphasize that only legally available land would be purchased. All public, Ottoman and international law would be scrupulously adhered to and the consent of all involved nations would be secured.

The return to Zion was an absolute historic necessity. No one can argue the case for forcing Jews to remain in Russia, Poland, the Arab countries and those other places where they had undergone century after century of abuse. Zionism is one of the most beautiful philosophies ever conceived, a movement in which all brothers serve and give to save brothers in peril.

The deliberate distortion of the truth about Zionism was patterned on Hitler's "Big Lie" technique: the repetition of a libel until people begin to think of it as the truth. If one were to believe Arab propaganda, the Jews seized Arab lands and were advance agents of Western imperialism. These lands, in fact, had been abandoned, raped and feudalized by the Arabs.

A second wave of pogroms swept over Russia between 1903 and 1906, with particular gore in the Ukraine, Bessarabia and Byelorussia. By the beginning of World War I fifty thousand more Jews had landed in Palestine.

In this group came the young idealists flushed with the calling to redeem this desolate country with Jewish labor, Jewish self-help and Jewish defense. They went out to the festering malarial swamps, to the unyielding rock and desert, to denuded earth, and they brought it back to life. A gleam of white towns dotted the landscape, an energy of building was heard. Most of these pioneers lived their lives with little in the way of material reward, but in commitment to sacrifice. This also was the beauty of Zionism.

They were the ones who, as in the time of Moses, had been the sons of the slaves of the Russian Pale, who reinstated Hebrew as a national language, who founded Tel Aviv from a sand dune, who plowed with one hand on the gun and one on the plowshare, who rode the night to cut down bedouin thieves, who faced the Turkish monsters.

By the onset of World War I there were a lot of trees growing in Palestine where they had not grown for hundreds of years. Jerusalem blossomed and progressed. Although it was obviously perilous for the Jews to stand against the Turks during the war, they did so, by coming to the support of the Allies en masse.

ARAB NATIONALISM

At the beginning of the twentieth century the two major crocodiles cruising the Mediterranean were Britain and France. The French had chomped off Tunisia and Algeria from the Ottoman holdings while His Majesty's Government occupied Egypt and controlled the Suez Canal. Czarist Russia still had visions of warm-water ports and Italy yapped on the fringes, waiting for a bone to be tossed her way. These four lovelies constituted the heart of the Allied powers.

Although seriously weakened, the Ottomans still held vast Arab areas, including most of the Arabian Peninsula, Palestine, Syria and Iraq. Their major strategic position was the Sinai Peninsula on the opposite bank of the Suez Canal which constituted a nightmare to the British and their shipping lanes.

Germany upped the threat to the canal as she moved toward a permanent alliance with the Turks as part of her own ambitious imperial Eastern movement. One could imagine the growing British discomfort as the Germans were getting to within breathing distance of the canal.

While the Allies plotted to devour the Arab world, a new element of Arab nationalism entered the picture. Arab feeling toward the Turks was generally one of bitterness and hatred, and clandestine movements were afoot to shake the Ottoman yoke.

The key personality among the Arab dissidents was the Sharif Husain, leader of the Hashemite family of Arabia, who claimed direct descent from the Prophet Mohammed. The Hashemites were accorded the traditional role of "Keeper of the Holy Places of Mecca," a position and title more honorary and ceremonial than actual.

In order to better observe the Sharif of Mecca, Husain was elevated by the Sultan to Emir of Mecca with some official status as "Protector of the Holy City." In reality it was a figurehead post under a Turkish governor.

Husain failed to take the bait and continued to pursue his immediate objective, which was to win local autonomy. His area was known as the Hejaz and included Mecca and Medina as well as a thousand miles of Red Sea coastline directly opposite the British in Egypt. The Red Sea was linked to the canal and constituted the single most important trade route in the world.

At the outbreak of World War I the Turkish Sultan put on his Islamic hat and called for all Arabs to join in a holy war against the infidels, a call that was scarcely heeded. Husain thought himself in the perfect strategic political position to play the Turks against the British. He sidestepped the Sultan's call to arms, claiming that with the British Navy in control of the Red Sea the Hejaz was simply too vulnerable to a takeover. The British had already instituted a grain blockade against the Hejaz in a not too subtle effort to coerce the Arabs into joining them.

Husain sent his second son, Abdullah, to Egypt to play a little political poker with Lord Kitchener, the British agent and consul general, and ask for arms and aid to be able to rebel against the Turks.

However Husain's third son, Faisal, was suspicious of the British and went to Istanbul to see if he could talk the Sultan into granting the Hejaz autonomy. When this was rather stupidly refused, Faisal immediately became involved with the Arab dissident movements.

In July of 1915 Husain initiated a correspondence with the British high commissioner in Egypt, Sir Henry McMahon. Husain felt he was in a position to raise his ante from mere local autonomy of the Hejaz and to take his chances with the British was the best route. He offered Arab support to the Allies in the form of a rebellion in exchange for an independent Arab nation at the end of the war. Husain wasn't bashful. He demanded a gigantic area, an Arab nation that would extend from southern Turkey to the Indian Ocean north and south and from the Persian border to the Mediterranean east to west. Husain had in mind being king of this vast region.

The British side of this correspondence turned out to be one of the seamiest, most underhanded, monumental diplomatic double-crosses in history. McMahon's replies became masterpieces of double-talk. What Husain and the

Arab nationalists were left with was a lot of heartfelt understandings, loopholes and evasions. The Arabs were deliberately led to believe that Palestine would fall into this Arab nation. However, what they didn't know was that the entire body of McMahon letters were a sham, not legally binding and exercises in trickery. All Husain really had going for him was a vague gentleman's agreement and history proved he was not exactly dealing with honorable souls.

If Husain was in the dark about the British double-dealing with the Zionists, the Zionists were also in the dark about British dealings with the Arabs. Both Husain and the Zionists were in the dark about the triple-dealings of the British with their French allies, who had gone into an ultra-secret agreement for the British and French to carve up the region between themselves. What the French did not know was that their good friends the British also intended to give them the shaft by acing them out of Palestine.

THE SYKES-PICOT SELLOUT

The Allies had to settle a number of conflicting claims. On March 9, 1916, a secret treaty, the Sykes-Picot, named after its chief negotiators, was signed by France and Britain and approved by the Russian and Italian allies. The treaty blatantly ignored Jewish aspirations for a Palestinian homeland as it blatantly ignored Arab aspirations for an independent Arab nation. An Arab state would indeed be created but the power of the state would be divided between France and Britain.

France would control the Arab state from Aleppo to Damascus and the Mosul Province inland. Britain dealt itself in to influence the area from the Red Sea to Iraq, an area that included the Negev Desert of southern Palestine and the cities of Haifa and Acre.

The word "infamous" is almost always used to describe this bit of surgery. Unfortunately for the perpetrators, a revolution broke out in Russia and she abandoned the war. The Bolsheviks broke into the Winter Palace in Petrograd (Leningrad) and a copy of the treaty was discovered and published.

Despite the obvious sellout, Husain was in too deep to back out and on June 5, 1916, his troops took Mecca from the Turks but failed in their attempt on Medina. Although he modestly declared himself "King of the Arabs" his erstwhile Allied partner only recognized him as "King of the Hejaz."

THE BALFOUR DECLARATION

The brilliant Russian-born scientist, Chaim Weizmann, had taken the mantle of leadership of the Zionists after the death of its founder Theodor Herzl. From an impoverished family of fifteen children in the Russian Pale, he had emigrated to England and risen to become one of the world's foremost organic chemists as well as one of the great political leaders in modern Jewish history. It was said of Weizmann that he could argue a leopard out of its spots.

Weizmann's chore during the First World War was to win legal world recognition for a Jewish homeland. There was general sympathy for the Jews in England, and they had conducted long dialogues with the Zionists. At one juncture Uganda was offered for Jewish settlement and at another point the Sinai Peninsula was mentioned. Although the Jews had heated debates over any and all offers, nothing but Palestine, their ancient homeland, was ever truly considered. As Weizmann said, "I read the Bible from one end to the other and never saw the name of Uganda mentioned once."

Lloyd George, the British Prime Minister, and Lord Balfour, the Foreign Secretary, both envisioned the establishment of a strong Jewish presence in Palestine as a way to atone for the horrors committed against this race. Zionism also fitted neatly into Britain's secret plans to take over Palestine after the war. A British-ruled, Zionist-oriented Palestine offered them the most reliable ally they could find. The Zionists were actively recruited as present and future allies.

On the other side, Germany and the Turkish Sultan were not averse to a strong Jewish presence in the Middle East. With both sides courting them, the Zionists had some leverage to play with.

Chaim Weizmann had an ace up his sleeve. In 1916 he invented a process in the production of munitions which was years ahead of anything known and this was needed by the British war effort.

In 1917 the British War Cabinet authorized the Declaration by Lord Balfour favoring the establishment of a Jewish homeland in Palestine and presented it to the British Lord Rothschild. The Balfour Declaration was later approved by the Allies at a conference at San Remo and incorporated into the Mandate of Palestine later conferred upon Britain by the League of Nations.

The Jewish Palestinian role in the war was nominal. Several battalions of volunteers wore British uniforms, including a Private David Ben Gurion. One unit, the Jewish Mule Corps, took part in the Allied debacle at Gallipoli when they tried unsuccessfully to force the Strait of the Dardanelles.

In Palestine, the Jews and Arabs both suffered grievously at the hands of the Turks. The Jews got it for their overt sympathy for the Allies. Food was withheld in many localities as a punitive measure. In Jerusalem, some twenty thousand persons died of famine and disease.

The Arab revolt was to become one of the most overglamorized events in the war, made so by the postwar writings of a wildly romantic British officer, T. E. Lawrence. The Arab forces were mostly involved in guerrilla actions and did some measurable damage in the Transjordan, particularly in slicing up vital rail lines. Faisal, the son of Husain, led his Arab troops into Damascus, a high-profile symbolic event, for the city was deeply embedded in Arab history and sentimentality. He proclaimed himself King of Syria, a title which included Palestine by ancient historic precedent.

In 1915 a huge British force jumped off from Egypt for the invasion of Palestine but was halted along a Turkish line that ran from Gaza to Beersheba. It would be November

1917 before the British, now under the command of General
Allenby, won Gaza in a third battle. Lloyd George was as
good as his word that he would present the British people
with the Christmas present of Jerusalem. Met at the
Citadel by the various leaders of the religious communities,
Allenby humbly made his entrance on foot. For the imme-
diate future, Jerusalem and Palestine would come under
British rule.

THE AFTERMATH

The political fallout at the end of the war left both the
Arabs and the Jews far short of their goals. As both sides
tried to cash in the IOUs from the Allies, they were to
discover the British and French too enmeshed in secret
deals and personal greed to honor their promises.

At the end of the war Faisal seemed to hold an advanta-
geous position. He was King of Syria and his father,
Husain, King of the Hejaz. Faisal, enthroned in Damascus,
was respected among the Arabs as a descendant of the
Prophet. He appeared to be an outstanding leader. He
met with Chaim Weizmann and saw no conflict with a
large Jewish settlement in Palestine which, Faisal believed,
was part of his kingdom. He reckoned the Jews had
greatly benefited the region and would continue to be a
progressive element so long as they were good subjects
under Arab rule. Rude awakenings were not long in
coming.

The Allied postwar maneuverings need not be covered
here conference by conference, but the net result spelled
disaster for the Arabs. Syria had declared her independence under Faisal in 1920, with an area which included
Lebanon and Palestine. Iraq also proclaimed independence on the grounds that it had contributed to the Arab
revolt.

The British didn't like these declarations of independence very much and the French liked them less. The
French snatched Syria, gave Faisal the boot, and the
British took over Iraq. In the squabble of the two allies
over Palestine, Britain eased the French out and took

absolute control through having it declared a mandated territory.

Next to get it were the Zionists through an outrageous act of British perfidy. From Roman times Palestine had been part of the Syrian Province and administered from Damascus. The British changed all that by thwarting French attempts to continue this ancient system. Also since earliest biblical settlement, Palestine had always included the lands on both sides of the Jordan River. The British were to change this too.

They decided it would be in their interest to create a new nation out of part of the Mandate to serve as a British base. Thus the emirate of Transjordan was invented out of Palestinian land on the east bank of the river. It was a piece of territory occupied sparsely mostly by bedouins.

However, the east bank of the Jordan was also ripe for settlement by the Jews on the grounds that it was part of the Mandate, which had been internationally sanctioned and which was committed to the Balfour Declaration. The British, arbitrarily and without the consent of the world community to modify the Mandate, said in effect, "The Balfour Declaration ends at the Jordan River."

On the surface the British presented the emirate of Transjordan as another piece of tokenism to the Arabs but the disguise was thin, their intentions obvious and their violation of the Mandate blatant. The British reached once more down to the Hejaz and plucked up Abdullah, the second son of Husain, and plopped him in Amman with the title of Emir of Transjordan. Thus the Hashemite emirate of Transjordan came into existence, ripped out of the Palestine Mandate. It was not a piddling piece of territory but represented seventy-seven per cent of the land mass of the Mandate, ruled by a puppet under British direction. Arab propaganda carried with it a standard bromide that the Jews are strangers to the region. If anyone was a stranger in Palestine and Iraq, it was their transplanted Hashemite puppets, put there to do the bidding of the British and, when the British whistled, Faisal and Abdullah danced.

Faisal and Abdullah were both to meet the standard ending for Arab monarchs: they were assassinated. Their father, Husain, whose trust of the British started the entire cycle of sellouts, ended up losing the Hejaz to his archrivals the Saudis, whose conquest of Mecca gave them the entire peninsula. Husain died in exile. T. E. Lawrence and the other British officers connected with the Arab revolt never lived down their country's shame.

The thrust of Arab nationalism was largely due to the ambitions of a single family. Before they were all reduced to puppets, their intention was merely to exchange one autocratic monarchy for another. There never has been a successful Arab government based on democratic principles.

On the other hand Zionism was and remains democracy in its purest form, the only one ever introduced successfully into that part of the world.

Seventy-seven per cent of the Palestine Mandate was removed from the map by political surgery in the establishment of a phony kingdom rigged up to serve British imperial interests. Only seventeen per cent of the original Mandate eventually went into the creation of the state of Israel. Until 1920 the Jordanians were not a people. After 1920 they were an invention. Jordan and its population are just as much part of Palestine as Israel is and no amount of Arab revisionism can change that fact.

The British Mandate

⚜

THE SEVENTEENTH RESURRECTION

In 1918 Chaim Weizmann laid the cornerstone for a future university on Mount Scopus. This institution would teach its courses in the Hebrew language, a tongue which had been used only for prayer for centuries. Although the institute would not open for several years, the cornerstone symbolized the coming Jewish nation and the rebirth of its ancient language. The precedent for the revitalization and modernization of a dead language was unique. The laying of the cornerstone also signaled the seventeenth rebirth of the city of Jerusalem.

Although Jerusalem had not been physically damaged during the war, those years had taken a severe toll, amounting to the loss of a third of the population. The Old City was an archaic slum, without proper sanitation, electricity or running water. Roads, civil services, schools and medical facilities were threadbare from the putridity of four centuries of Turkish misrule.

The British initially represented a corruption-free breath of fresh air as they assumed the Mandate from their first headquarters at the Victoria Augusta complex. Sir Ronald Storrs, the first governor of Jerusalem, decreed that all new building had to be faced with Jerusalem stone to give the city a look of eternal continuity. Nothing much more of a positive nature can be said of Storrs.

In 1925 the Hebrew University was dedicated, followed by the founding of the Jewish National Library and the beginning of the Hadassah Medical Center, one of the fine institutions of healing in the world.

With Ottoman corruption becoming a memory, the way was open for new highways and an upgraded waterworks and public facilities like bus lines. Public health and education were dramatically upgraded for the Arabs. The Jews ran these facilities for their own.

In 1924 one of Jerusalem's most beautiful churches was dedicated. The All Nations, alongside the Garden of Gethsemane, covering the Rock of the Agony, is striking with its alabaster stained glass windows. A few years later the Scottish presence came with the Presbyterian Church of St. Andrew. In 1929 an addition of major importance was made to the city by a Rockefeller donation. The Palestine Archeological Museum, later known as the Rockefeller Museum, was founded across the road from Herod's Gate and is important for its continued archaeological work. A raft of new digs continued to unearth the past. Bethel and Ai were identified and the Valley of Kidron was preserved. The most prominent of the archaeologists, E. L. Sukenik, was later to be involved with one of the great finds of all times, the Dead Sea Scrolls.

St. Peter in Galicantu was built in 1931 and two years later the landmark YMCA was designed by the architect who had done the Empire State Building, giving Jerusalem its first swimming pool. Jerusalem's first international class hotel, the King David, opened its doors. By the 1930s there were fifty-one thousand Jews in Jerusalem out of a population of ninety thousand and it sported a symphony orchestra and a national theater.

The end of the First World War brought an immediate influx of immigrants, some thirty-five thousand more Jews mainly from Russia and Poland. They entered the country in what is referred to as the Third Aliyah or the Third Rising. My father, whose name was then Wolf Yerushalmi, was an immigrant of the Third Aliyah from Russia. He was eventually driven out by recurrent malaria and other maladies. Our family name, before it was shortened to Uris, means Jerusalemite.

Land was unloaded on the Jews by absentee Arab owners who were mostly living it up in Beirut, Cairo and Paris. Unquestionably their greed displaced a number of

Arab peasants. Had the Arabs cared for their brethren in the same manner the Jews did, the story of Palestine might have taken a different turn.

The number of kibbutzim or communal farms increased rapidly and not only flourished agriculturally but introduced light industry. Many Jews, particularly from the family-oriented oriental communities, could not function in the total communal atmosphere of the kibbutz. Needing more individual freedom, such as a small plot of land and a private home where the family could live together, they formed the moshav movement. Between the two movements, tens of dozens of new settlements sprang up.

Despite the new look of the countryside and the new look of Jerusalem and the progress that was visibly seen in the birth and growth of Tel Aviv, there was serious trouble in the holy land. The British Mandate was a disaster from the first day and remained so for the entirety of its existence.

THE HILL OF EVIL COUNSEL AND THE TWICE-PROMISED LAND

When the British moved from the Augusta Victoria to a new Government House on the ridge of one of Jerusalem's southern hills, it was an unmistakable omen of things to come. The hill had been known since biblical days as the Hill of Evil Counsel.

Faisal had been evicted from Syria by the French and, with this, his ambition to be king over Palestine was finished. Still smarting from the Allied betrayals, the Arabs of Palestine were now to witness thousands of Jews pouring in from Europe. In 1921 they rioted in protest throughout the country, killing and injuring dozens of Jews. The sharpness of Arab anger caused the first of the British appeasements that set the tone of a Mandate in which they were damned if they did and damned if they didn't. There was no possibility that Britain could pretend to continue a role as the honest broker between two communities totally out of agreement with one another. Faisal, who had previously consented to a large Jewish population in what he believed was to be part of his kingdom, renounced this position after he was ousted.

Chief instigator of the 1921 riots was Haj Amin al-Husseini, of a prominent Jerusalem family. He stirred up the Arabs with the rankest sort of Moslem bigotry, then fled and was sentenced to fifteen years in prison in absentia. Sir Ronald Storrs was replaced by Sir Herbert Samuel, a British Jew, who was given the title of high commissioner. Samuel's Jewishness was more cosmetic than vital to Zionist interests.

The first of a series of British White Papers, from the pen of Winston Churchill in the Colonial Office, was published and it began the modifications of British commitment to the Balfour Declaration. Churchill's Catch-22 was to peg new Jewish immigration upon "economic absorption capacity," a nebulous and convenient ploy. It was not a real problem, as agricultural and industrial expansion under the Jews had brought enormous economic benefits to the Arabs as well.

The economic absorption gimmick was designed to give the British leverage over the Yishuv, as the Jewish community was called. It is a key point in the history of the times that, when the Jews brought prosperity to Palestine, tens of thousands of Arabs either returned or came to the country to reap the benefits. A large part of the Palestinian Arab population was no more indigenous to the country than the Jews who were immigrating at the time. Likewise Arab nationalism was a direct offshoot of Jewish nationalism. The Arabs had shown almost no inclination for self-rule until the Jews showed their own inclinations.

The first White Paper was followed by the recall from exile of Haj Amin al-Husseini and, lo and behold, Sir Herbert Samuel conferred on this vicious creature the exalted title of Grand Mufti of Jerusalem, making him overlord of the Moslem religious establishment and lining him up for leadership of the Arab community. In 1922, just a year after he had unleashed the riots, Husseini had not only beaten a fifteen-year jail sentence, he was president of the Supreme Muslim Council of Palestine.

Nor did Sir Herbert do anything but sit on his hands when the Colonial Office lopped off three quarters of the Mandate by creating the Emirate of Transjordan. Nor did the high commissioner, who piously attended synagogue each Sabbath eve, do anything about the continued ban on allowing the Jews to enter the Haram esh Sharif, the Jewish Temple Mount.

The Yishuv moved forward and developed a strong infrastructure of governmental and administrative capabilities that made Jerusalem a capital in everything but name. The Jewish Agency, an umbrella group of a wide range of self-help departments and activities authorized by the British became a government within a government. The World Zionists kept the hand and voice of international Jewry progressing in support of the Yishuv. A National Assembly governed those aspects over which the Jews had autonomy. The Histadrut, a powerful labor organization, ultimately became the largest builder and employer in the country as well as a union. A National Land Fund established by world Jewry continued its purchases and a vast understructure of charitable, medical, educational, religious, immigration, settlement, agricultural and industrial institutions operated independently of the British and actually made the Yishuv a quasi government.

After the 1921 riots the Yishuv realized they couldn't depend on British protection and quietly went about the business of forming a self-defense organization born of the tradition of the Jewish watchmen who had protected the earliest settlements. The Haganah formed units on every kibbutz, moshav and Jewish town and its members underwent extensive paramilitary training. Although the Haganah had a growing military capacity, it remained a model of restraint, engaging in necessary defense operations, and did not go into the business of vengeance seeking.

As the Jews organized the Arabs took the opposite tack. They not only rejected the plan for an Arab Agency but fought every idea that meant co-operation with the Yishuv. In so doing, Arab spite denied the Arab population the institutions designed to benefit them. Within the Supreme Muslim Council, Haj Amin al-Husseini and the other leading Arab families became bogged down in personal feuds and power plays. The result was that the Muslim Council had little effect on the well-being of the Arab population. Arab nationalism in Palestine was nothing more than a manifestation of personal ambition and a reaction to Zionism. The blood feuds and the vendettas, long the hallmark of Arab politics, continued as usual. Amost nothing of a progressive nature came from the Arab community, which was virtually devoid of self-help programs; their only goals were the assumption of autocratic power and their only base of unity an all-consuming hatred of Jews.

The relative peace of the 1920s, due in no small measure to the growing efficiency of the Haganah, was shattered by a new round of Arab riots in 1929. Haj Amin al-Husseini's continued appeal to the Palestinian Arabs was centered on Jew hating. Each year at Yom Kippur, the Jewish Day of Atonement, the holiday is ended by the blowing of the shofar, the ram's horn. This particular year, Husseini's henchmen, in consort with the Moslem clergy, spread the libel that the blowing of the shofar would be a signal for the Jews to come up from the Western Wall and take over the Moslem shrines on the Haram esh Sharif.

Vicious anti-Jewish riots ensued, mostly against defenseless Hasidics in the isolated cities of Hebron and Safed. In Hebron seventy Jews were slaughtered and this ancient community was driven out of the city.

After the 1929 riots, the British came up with another of their White Papers, this one authored by Lord Passfield, which placed further restrictions on Jewish settlement. The British by now had completely drifted away from their commitments of the Mandate and the Balfour Declaration. Chaim Weizmann was so enraged, he resigned from the Jewish Agency in protest.

Worsening trends mounted rapidly. With immigration under strict control, *aliyah beth*, or illegal immigration, came into being. The writing was on the wall for the Jews of Germany with the rise of Hitler and thousands slipped into Palestine by a number of ruses. Some came as tourists or crossed over the borders from Arab countries or with fake marriage certificates. The Haganah was soon heavily engaged in running this operation. The kibbutzim and moshavim were perfect hiding places for illegals, where they could be given new identities. By 1935 Chaim Weizmann had become distraught over the pending fate of European Jewry and returned to leadership of the World Zionist Organization.

As the Yishuv continued to upgrade the fighting capacity of the Haganah and the defense of the settlements, they remained restrained and were able to maintain contact with the British on some matters. Inevitable splinter groups broke off from the Haganah. Under the dynamic leadership of a Russian-born Jew, Zev Jabotinski, the Revisionists took the point among the Zionists in matters of activism and nationalism. Founder of the Jewish Legion in World War I, Jabotinski likewise was in on the founding of the Haganah. Finally Jabotinski broke away from the Haganah. The military arm of the Revisionists became the Irgun Zvi Leumi, better known as the Irgun. They were smaller in number and operated their units mainly in urban areas. As the British betrayal of the Mandate grew, the Irgun was the first to take the fight directly to them.

In 1936 the Arabs staged a full-scale revolt, beginning with a six-month general strike and clashes with the British. Palestine was interlaced with heavily fortified police stations called Taggart Forts, after their designer. In the revolt several Taggart Forts were overrun and the Arabs rampaged through their own population by intimidation and coercion. In his effort to terrorize the Arab community, the Mufti turned on rival families, and in 1938 six thousand Arabs were murdered by one another. They struck at the Jews wherever they could find easy pickings but gave the Haganah a wide berth.

The British invited the Haganah to join them in suppressing the revolt and by co-operating the Haganah was upgraded to a semi-legal status. A tremendously effective force called the Special Night Squads were trained by a zealous pro-Zionist British Officer, Orde Wingate, a sort of Jewish T. E. Lawrence. Wingate's people were formidable and commanded the fear and respect of the Arabs. They also were the first to take the offensive against the Arabs, a new dimension that made the Arabs think twice before hitting hitherto defenseless targets.

Sixteen thousand British combat troops and three years later, the Arab revolt had been put down. Haj Amin al-Husseini once again fled, this time toward Nazi Germany, where he ended up broadcasting for Hitler and recruiting Arabs into Axis units.

During the riots a British investigating team, the Peel Commission, concluded the Mandate was no longer operable and called for a partition of Palestine into Jewish and Arab entities and the internationalization of Jerusalem and Bethlehem. At first the Yishuv considered using the partition as a method to get Jews out of Europe legally without British interference but when it got down to specific boundaries the leadership concluded that what had been assigned to the Jews would not make a viable state.

Abdullah, the Emir of Transjordan, liked the partition plan, for he had in mind annexing the Arab portions into his kingdom. He was overruled by the Supreme Muslim Council, who wanted nothing less than a Palestine without Jews.

With the Second World War on the horizon, it was apparent that the British ability to govern was exhausted. Yet, on the eve of another war, the British believed it was still in their interest to pacify the Arabs. The Arabs responded with a spiritual alliance with Germans. Even with the Arabs spitting in British faces, another White Paper was penned by Sir John Woodhead which negated the right of the Yishuv to acquire further land in Palestine and called for a plan to phase out all Jewish immigration.

THE SECOND WORLD WAR
TO THE END OF THE MANDATE

"We shall fight the war as if there were no White Paper and fight the White Paper as if there were no war," said the Yishuv leader, David Ben Gurion, on the eve of the conflict. Within days 136,000 men, the entire Jewish population between the ages of eighteen and fifty, registered for national service.

Despite Jewish eagerness to fight Germany, the British were none too anxious to arm and train people who stood to be a potential enemy once the war was over. The British rounded up the cream of the young Jewish commanders, forty-three men who had fought in the

Wingate-trained Special Night Squads, and imprisoned them in the ancient Turkish jail in Acre. Those Jews who were accepted into the British Army were shuttled to units reserved for second-class colonials as trench diggers and menial laborers.

Nor were the British inclined to rescind or even suspend the White Paper out of fear of aggravating the Arabs. This policy led to the tragic sinkings and loss of hundreds of lives on two derelict and overloaded Jewish refugee boats.

The British policy of continued appeasement of the Arabs became unmistakably clear. The Yishuv went about the business of preparing for future eventualities. In 1941 the Haganah formed a small standing army of young people called the Palmach, its first commander being Yigal Allon. Their battalions trained in secret in the shelter of the kibbutz, in the Judean hills and on the desert.

A year later, in the Biltmore Hotel in New York, a convocation of world Jewish leaders took off the gloves by overruling their own plodding and passive leaders and stated Jewish aims for Palestine in clear terms. With the calamity befalling European Jewry and total British abandonment of the Balfour Declaration, world Jewry rallied behind the Biltmore Declaration, which defined the goal of Zionism as the creation of a Jewish state in Palestine.

By the middle of the war the Yishuv had made such obvious contributions to the Allied cause that the stiff necks of the British began to unbend. Co-operation between the British and the Haganah increased as preparations were made to form a resistance movement in the event Palestine fell to the Germans. Several dozen Jewish parachutists who had been born in various occupied European countries were dropped behind German lines to organize Jewish partisan units. Seven of them were killed, including the martyred Hannah Senesh.

Early in the war a thousand Palestinian Jews were taken prisoner in Greece in an ill-fated British expedition. My uncle, Aaron Yerushalmi, was among those captured and became known as the man who could not be kept behind bars, making several escapes and ending the war with Tito's partisans in Yugoslavia.

The Haganah gave a large assist to the British in the

invasion of Syria by the pro-German Vichy French. It was in this operation that the greatest of the Israeli warriors, Moshe Dayan, lost his eye, later donning his world-famous eye patch.

Churchill finally relented and allowed the Yishuv to form its own fighting unit with its own flag. All told, thirty thousand Palestinian Jews fought in the British Army, including four thousand women. They saw action on the Western Desert of North Africa, in Ethiopia and in the final battles in Italy in a front-line Palestinian Brigade.

Although the British controlled a number of Arab states, none of them made any meaningful military contribution to the Allies. Elsewhere the Arabs under French domination did nothing and there was great sympathy all around for the Germans. Although Egypt was a British base, it was also the heart of Arab nationalism and Arab officers, including Anwar Sadat, "distinguished" themselves by being sent to prison for pro-Nazi activities. At one juncture, when it appeared that Rommel's Desert Corps would conquer Egypt, Cairo was festooned with swastikas to greet the liberators.

With the war tilting toward an Allied victory, the Arabs began to put heavy pressure on the British on the Palestine issue and, despite Arab performance, or lack of it, during the war the British all but caved in to their demands. The Yishuv, which had acquitted itself so well, was to taste ashes.

More and more information began to filter out of Europe about the Nazi death camps. Instead of standing up on their haunches and screaming to the heavens for the Nazis to cease this most horrible of all human slaughters, America and England joined in a diplomatic conspiracy of silence. With the war entering its final phase, the British once more turned on the Haganah and the Yishuv.

By 1944 Menachem Begin, who had escaped the Holocaust, assumed leadership of the Irgun, defined Great Britain as the enemy and launched a battle against them within the Mandate. In October of the same year the British rounded up two hundred and fifty-one Irgun suspects and exiled them to Eritrea in Africa. The Lehi or Stern Gang, a volatile offshoot of the Irgun, assassinated

Lord Moyne, the British Minister of State for the Middle East. By the war's end the Irgun and Stern Gang were locked in combat with the British.

The Yishuv would see peace come as a double catastrophe. The Royal Navy was now given the unforgivable mission of preventing the survivors of Hitler from reaching Palestine. Clement Attlee had succeeded Churchill as Prime Minister and his Labor Party was committed to renew and redeem Britain's commitment to Zionism. However, Attlee had appointed a slovenly bully boy, Ernest Bevin, to the post of Foreign Minister. It was a disaster for the Yishuv, for Bevin was a rank Jew baiter.

On the Continent many members of Jewish units serving with the British in Italy quietly drifted into secret Haganah activities. A unit of the Haganah in charge of illegal immigration known as the Mossad moved its operators in. They searched for Jewish survivors, bought any sort of transport, often settling for unseaworthy vessels, and ran the British blockade with refugees. Dramatic and often bloody rammings and boardings by the British Marines and Navy ended with internment in a detention camp near the old Crusader fort of Athlit.

In Palestine the Haganah began operations similar to those of the Irgun and Stern by attacking and freeing the refugees held in Athlit and hiding them in the kibbutzim. They hit the railroads, sank patrol launches, attacked Taggart Forts, airfields, radar installation and coast guard stations. Let it be clearly defined that, in contrast to the war waged in recent years by the Palestinian Liberation Organization, the Jews concentrated on military targets against armed soldiers and did not parallel the cowardly PLO actions of massacring civilians, children in schoolrooms and infants in nurseries.

With the British building up their Palestine forces toward the high of a hundred thousand troops, Bevin repudiated his own party's pro-Zionist position and ordered operations against the Jews in an attempt to break their backs.

Alarmed at the deteriorating situation, President Truman urged formation of a joint Anglo-American Commission which recommended immediate admission of a hundred thousand Jews into Palestine. After first agreeing, the

British reneged. In response to this, the Haganah blew up every bridge in Palestine on a single night.

June 29, 1946, marked Black Saturday for the Yishuv when the entire executive of the Jewish Agency was arrested and massive searches were launched countrywide to find the Jewish arms caches. At the same time the order was issued that all future illegal immigration boats should be seized and taken to Cyprus where the refugees were interned in what was to become an enormous detention camp filled mostly with survivors of the Nazi extermination camps.

A month later the Irgun blew up the south wing of the King David Hotel, which housed some of the British command, and killed eighty British, Arabs and Jews. With an uncontrolled inferno close at hand, the Jewish Agency was reconstituted and it ordered a halt in military operations for breathing room to talk. Its own army, the Haganah, obeyed but the Irgun and Stern refused. Throughout 1947 the Irgun attacks continued, climaxing with an Irgun raid on the Acre prison in which they freed a great number of their comrades. The ugliness of the situation bottomed out when the British hanged seven Irgun men. Retaliation was immediate, with the hanging of two British soldiers and booby-trapping their bodies.

In May 1947 one of the most incredible diplomatic flipflops of the century occurred when the Soviet Union, a bedrock enemy of Zionism, strangely and unexpectedly came out in support of a Jewish state in Palestine.

A United Nations Special Commission on Palestine recommended the partition of Palestine into separate Jewish and Arab states and the internationalization of Jerusalem. In one of the most dramatic moments in Jewish history, the plan was adopted by the United Nations in November of 1947 and was immediately accepted by the Yishuv. Partition was unanimously rejected by the entire Arab world.

The British targeted the end of the Mandate and withdrawal of their forces for May 15, 1948. The Yishuv was now confronted with the danger of declaring their independence in the face of seven Arab armies who swore to annihilate them. Even as the sorry history of the Mandate was ending, the British engaged in outright perfidy against the Jews by doing everything in their power, in the time left, to see to it that the Arabs won the upcoming war.

With the adoption of the United Nations resolution in November 1947, the undeclared war for the land of Israel had already begun.

Siege

The year 1947 ended and the days until termination of the Mandate on May 15, 1948, ticked off precariously. No sooner had the United Nations voted for partition than individual countries threw up their hands and cried "Neutral!" It was painfully apparent no one would lift a finger to implement the decision. As 1947 ended, it seemed suicidal for the Yishuv to declare independence in May. Most nations concluded that the combined Arab strength was certain to crush the Yishuv. Perhaps, as the end was coming, they reckoned they could arrange some sort of humanitarian truce to salvage what was left of the Jewish population and thereby salvage their own consciences.

The Yishuv's arsenal was pathetic, a collection of mishmash weaponry, some of a vintage predating the turn of the century. Boer War rifles, homemade mortars and ammo, an air force consisting of a couple of planes of the Piper Club variety, no tanks, perhaps a dozen pieces of decent field artillery. The Jewish supply line was tortuous, with everything having to come over the Mediterannean, and they had neither merchant fleet to carry the stuff nor navy to protect it. Mossad agents bought up anything they could get their hands on in Europe and rushed it to Palestine in derelict ships and obsolete transport planes forced to land on hidden and treacherously inadequate airstrips.

In the Yishuv's favor, they had three battalions of tough young Palmach under the command of a great leader, Yigal Allon, and a well-organized citizen militia in the

Haganah. This force was supplemented by a few thousand Irgun and Stern who continued to operate independently in the cities. The Jews also had the hidden weapon of having no option. It was stand and fight or be driven into the sea.

The entire Arab world took the position that it would be better to let Palestine return to swamp and erosion for the next thousand years than to share an inch of it with the Jews. Their war drums banged out messages filled with typical exaggerations. Haj Amin al-Husseini returned from Germany to Lebanon to be in at the glorious kill. But even as the Arabs harangued with their bloodcurdling rhetoric, they had really whipped themselves up into a massive self-deception. They had long fantasized themselves as the heirs of the great Arab armies of the early days of Islam. After losing to every Western army for centuries, they at last had someone they could beat. The Jews, after all, were a lowly people completely lacking courage who whined in prayer houses and wept before an old wall. Moreover, the Jews would be outnumbered ten to one in manpower with an even wider Arab ratio in the number and quality of arms. The Arab armies were not modern but they had long-range artillery, fighter planes and bombers, tanks, heavy machine guns and an overwhelming logistical advantage in short, direct overland supply lines.

In reality the Arabs had not fielded a first-class army for centuries. Yet in Damascus, Baghdad, Cairo and Beirut they greased each other up and sold themselves on their invincibility. Tragically, they sold this attitude of arrogance and superiority to the Arabs of Palestine. The Palestininan Arabs were certain that if the Yishuv dared to declare its independence their annihilation would follow immediately. In many cases the Palestinians were urged by Arab leaders to clear out so that the destruction of the Jews could be accomplished with greater ease. This incessant bragging was so boisterous that it constituted the first step in the creation of the Palestinian refugee problem.

The only Arab ruler who seemed to be in touch with reality was Abdullah, the Emir of Transjordan, whose proximity and dealings with the Yishuv had given him a more respectful view of Jewish capabilities. Abdullah was not particularly anxious to get involved in the fighting,

preferring to work out an accommodation with the Jews,
give them their state and later annex the Arab portions of
Palestine into his own kingdom.

Abdullah was forced to go along with the other Arab
governments as a show of unity and he had already
received warning by the assassinations of moderate Arab
leaders who wanted to negotiate an agreement. Abdullah
owned the only truly fine Arab fighting units, his British-
commanded, -armed and -trained Arab Legion.

So anxious were the Arabs to get the rumble going,
they opened the conflict the instant the partition vote had
been completed. Before the formal war began, the Arab
League subsidized an army of irregulars of four thousand
men who were the first to cross the border into Palestine.
When the call went out to the Arab world for an army of
liberation, a number of adventurers, red hots, and nationalists swarmed on Damascus and mixed with the dregs of
the society and gangs of scum.

Their leader was Fawzi el-Kaukji, a Lebanese adventur-
er of the cutthroat variety, who had made an earlier name
as one of the chief instigators of the 1936–39 riots. Kaukji,
who had also spent the war in Nazi Germany, was enamored with all things German including their insane hatred
of Jews. Adorned with an Iron Cross he had won in the
Turkish Army, he was deluded to the point of envisioning
himself a Prussian field marshal.

Kaukji knew opportunity when he saw it and felt that
his irregulars could defeat the Jews before the regular
Arab armies entered the fight. Abdullah didn't much like
the idea of the irregulars but, with their support by the
Arab League, there wasn't a thing he could do to stop it.
In March 1948 the irregulars crossed into Palestine over
the Allenby Bridge right under the eyes and noses of the
British, who promptly looked the other way.

Kaukji's first target was Tirat Zvi, a kibbutz of religious
Jews isolated near the Jordan River who had but a hundred and fifty people of fighting capability. In picking a

soft touch, Kaukji reckoned he could create a panic among the Jews and then go on an uncontested rampage throughout the Galilee and grab all that lovely loot for himself.

Five hundred irregulars made an arrogant frontal assault in five waves. The Orthodox Jews of Tirat Zvi chopped them down. The Arabs lost communication and coordination, the rain poured down on them and, seeing their field of dead, they limped off in search of greener pastures.

The easiest touch they could now find was the Bab el Wad, a ravinelike stretch of road into Jerusalem. Here Kaukji's forces could take up high positions along the road and shoot down on Jewish traffic without being shot at. Yet his sobering defeat at Tirat Zvi had to be avenged and he needed an important victory to establish his credibility.

Kaukji's next target was the kibbutz Mishmar Haemek. Its fall would cut the road between Tel Aviv and Haifa. He beefed up his force with all the heavy pieces and armor he had and arrayed over a thousand troops for the assault.

The British intervened long enough to enter the kibbutz and advise them to evacuate. What was unknown was that two battalions of Haganah were training in the area and it was a rare instance that every man had a rifle. During the night the Haganah slipped into Mishmar Haemek and when the irregulars rushed at them they received a rude reception and were chased halfway back to the border. In his report Kaukji said he had been hit by dozens of tanks and heavy artillery in what was a childish attempt to cover the cowardice and ineptness of his soldiers.

The balance of the contribution of the Arab Army of Liberation was of the coffeehouse variety, taking potshots from a safe distance and returning to the backgammon game. What had been learned was that every kibbutz, moshav and town in Jewish Palestine was going to have to be taken by bloody conflict. Of the hundreds of Jewish settlements, less than a dozen fell during the entire war.

BAB EL WAD AND THE BURMA ROAD

The main Arab effort of the war concentrated on western or Jewish Jerusalem. The Plains of Sharon near the sea were thick with Jewish settlement from Tel Aviv to the Plain of Aijalon where Joshua had once made the sun stand still. From this point a road ascended up to Jerusalem, negotiating ten miles of twisting, steep, ravineline country called the Bab el Wad. From ancient times, as the Romans and others could testify, this gorgelike terrain had been a natural for ambushes. The hills looking down on the road were in Arab hands, led by Kaukji's irregulars before they went to their disastrous defeat at Mishmar Haemek. Not only did the Arabs command the Bab el Wad, they had strong positions which sealed off both ends of the road.

Near the entrance to the Bab el Wad stood the Trappist monastery of Latrun, famous for its products of the grape. Opposite the monastery on a rise of high and commanding ground was a Taggart Police Fort. During the first phase of the battle for the road, the fort remained in British hands.

At the other end of the Bab el Wad, eight miles up in the hills as it approached Jerusalem, was an Arab village at the base of a long steep height called the Kastel which had once held a crusader fort.

Within days of the United Nations partition vote, the battle for this key piece of road began. Initially the British went through the motions of keeping the Bab el Wad open, but Jewish transport was constantly being stopped by them and searched for smuggled weapons. It became incumbent for Jewish women to hide grenades, ammunition and small arms beneath their clothing where no decent Englishman would venture. When the British were not patrolling the Bab el Wad, which was just about all the time, the Arabs from nearby villages and Kaukji's irregulars lined the steep hills and made a turkey shoot out of Jewish traffic.

The Jews were compelled to plate their vehicles with makeshift armor and travel the Bab el Wad in convoys.

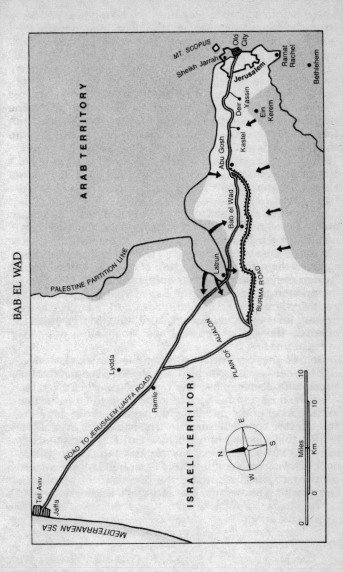

BAB EL WAD

These had to slug their way through, taking heavy losses. In a short time the Bab el Wad was littered with the wreckage of vehicles, some of which have been preserved and left along the roadside as monuments.

By blowing up sections of the Bab el Wad, the Arabs had effectively sealed the road and by spring of 1948 Jewish Jerusalem was cut off from the rest of the Yishuv. The British did nothing to prevent the Arabs from attacking the convoys and made no effort to reopen the road. In Jerusalem, the Arabs held the eastern half of the city so the Jews were totally isolated and under siege. By April 1, 1948, Ben Gurion was compelled to move the headquarters of the Jewish Agency to Tel Aviv but as he did so he issued a determined order to the Haganah to open the Bab el Wad.

Heretofore the Palmach had operated only in small units, usually no larger than a platoon. Operation Nachshon, named for the first man with Moses to leap into the Red Sea to test the waters, changed all that. Operation Nachshon signaled the first offensive action of the war, with Shimon Avidan commanding the Har El Brigade (God's Hills) with the mission to force open the Bab el Wad long enough to get three large convoys of supplies into the besieged city. In the first three weeks of April the Har El Brigade removed the Arabs who had held dominating positions over the road.

One of the key battles was for the Kastel. A unit of eighty men was assembled under the command of a young Jerusalemite in his early twenties named Uzi Narkiss.

Uzi Narkiss and his people made it up the long incline to the Kastel in the middle of the night without detection and effected complete surprise. The battle was over shortly after they opened fire, with the entire village stampeding to get out. The next day Narkiss turned the village over to a Haganah contingent of older militia, some ninety men from Jerusalem, under the command of Mordechai Gazit, who later became one of Israel's leading generals.

Word of the capture of the Kastel by the Jews flashed from Arab village to village and to Jerusalem with disbelief! The coffeehouses emptied and Arabs assembled with their weapons at the base of the hill, more of a mob than a disciplined unit. When enough of them had gathered, they charged up the hill, Teddy Roosevelt style, in a frontal attack only to be hurled back by Gazit's men. The Arabs, who can be excellent fighters from fixed defensive positions, showed a marked distaste for the co-ordination, skill and stamina required for a determined offensive effort. During a war, as they attacked kibbutz after kibbutz, this flaw took on a repetitious pattern. Without a determined leader to rally them, the Arabs became unable to sustain their drive and after a time simply drifted off the field of battle and back to their villages.

With the Kastel momentarily in Haganah hands, the Yishuv lost no time loading up relief supplies for Jerusalem as the Har El Brigade cleared the hills above the Bab el Wad. Warehouses on the docks and settlements were cleaned out of essentials in a frenzied around-the-clock operation. By April 30, three convoys had pushed their way to Jerusalem with 175, 250 and 294 trucks. The route, which was normally driven by car in a half hour, took each convoy between seven and ten hours. The final convoy lost three dozen vehicles but for the moment western Jerusalem was saved!

Titular commander of the Palestinian Arabs in the Jerusalem sector was Abdul Kadar Husseini, nephew of the Grand Mufti. He was a charismatic character and a quality leader, adored by the Arabs as a demigod. Abdul Kadar came under immediate pressure to retake the Kastel with the threat that the task would be given to his archrival, the brigand Kaukji, and his irregulars.

Abdul Kadar immediately assembled a force, deployed it intelligently and kept the Kastel's defenders pinned down under fire until Gazit's men were worn down and getting desperately low on ammunition.

Just about all the ammunition in the Yishuv had been expended when a leaky tramp steamer, the *Nora*, zigzagged through the British blockade with a cargo of arms and ammo. Uzi Narkiss and a dozen Palmachniks were able to get into the Kastel through Abdul Kadar's line with fifty thousand rounds of ammunition with no time to spare.

During a respite in the fighting, Narkiss and Gazit examined their perimeters, where a number of Arabs had fallen. It was then they discovered the body of Abdul Kadar. Narkiss quickly left the Kastel to get this information to headquarters.

When the news of Abdul Kadar's death reached the Arab side they were galvanized into action! Every Arab village from Hebron to Nablus rushed men to the Kastel by taxi, bus and truck. They poured up the slopes in a human sea, reminding one of the Russian steamroller waves of infantry.

Gazit ran from position to position, kicking his weary men awake, throwing boxes of ammunition to them, firing and shouting orders. The Jews could not shoot fast enough to stop the surge. As the Arabs swarmed into the Kastel, the Haganah was compelled to retire.

The emotion that had triggered this rampage continued to erupt in pure grief when the Arabs found the body of their beloved leader. Firing into the air, stamping their feet, weeping hysterically and shouting oaths to heaven, they carried the slain martyr down from the Kastel. In an oddity of oddities the Arabs left only forty men under the command of a schoolteacher to defend the position. They had come only for the purpose of recovering Abdul Kadar's body.

The Haganah returned in quick order, this time led by a young Palmach officer, David Elazar, known by everyone in the Yishuv as Daddo. Daddo was to become chief of staff of the Israeli Army later and, ultimately, the scapegoat for the disastrous opening days of the Yom Kippur War of 1973.

The funeral of Abdul Kadar, whose opened pine coffin was passed over the heads of tens of thousands of hysterical Arabs, was a masterpiece of Moslem grief and rage. As they swarmed through the Damascus Gate, they jammed every inch of the narrow ways in the Old City where he was accorded the ultimate honor by being buried on the Haram esh Sharif.

Fearing that the Arab Legion would cross the river and

attack West Jerusalem, the Har El Brigade was taken out of the Judean hills and shifted to Jerusalem. By the beginning of May, with but two weeks left to declare independence, the road was shut again and without the Har El available to clear the way a relief convoy was considered too risky.

On the night of May 5 three Palmach scouts set off on a wild odyssey, moving into the Judean wilds using shepherd's trails and old Roman roads in an attempt to find an alternate route to Jerusalem that would by-pass Latrun and the Bab el Wad. Because of their intimate knowledge of the hills and the history of the land they reached Jerusalem the next morning and flashed the word back to Tel Aviv. Ben Gurion immediately ordered a task force to work from both ends to build up the route so it would be wide enough for vehicles to negotiate.

The Latrun fort was now in the hands of the Arab Legion where they had a view of all activity toward Jerusalem so work had to be done by night. The building of the "Burma Road" was largely engineered by an American colonel, Mickey Marcus, who had come to Palestine as a volunteer charged with organizing the supply and transport sections of the Haganah. Marcus was tragically killed during the operation, mistakenly shot by one of his own sentries. It was brinksmanship all the way as the defile pushed through precipitous rock slides and sheer plunges, sometimes the width of a goat trail. Test runs over the route revealed the first jeeps through had to be winched up in numerous places. In other places, supplies had to be unloaded and carried on backs to traverse impassable sections.

The two ends of the task force linked up in a matter of three weeks and with some daredevil, steely-nerved driving the impassable and impossible became a fact. The back-door route into Jerusalem, built under the noses of the British and Arabs, was entirely in Jewish hands. Water pipes were laid alongside the Burma Road to replace the pipes blown up by the Arabs in their attempt to beat the Jews into submission through thirst. With the successful passing of the first convoys on the Burma Road, the battle of the road had been successfully won by the Yishuv.

THE AGONY OF WEST JERUSALEM

From the moment of the partition vote the life was being squeezed out of West Jerusalem, reflecting the situation of the entire Yishuv. The Jewish Agency had no funds to continue on or to buy arms with. In the dead of a bitter winter Golda Meir arrived in America with little more than an overnight bag. She aroused and rallied the American Jewish community and raised some fifty million dollars, vital to the Yishuv's survival.

The Arab world was chomping at the bit to get at the Jews. In advance of the regular armies, Abdul Kadar represented the ambitions of his uncle, the Grand Mufti, and Kaukji and the irregulars had crossed the borders.

Back-stabbing among Arab leaders followed historical lines. The Grand Mufti had overt ambitions to rule Palestine and didn't particularly like Kaukji's army of liberation to set up too much of a claim on "his" turf. On the other hand, the Arab League, which supported the irregulars, were not all that much in love with the Grand Mufti, feeling his Nazi activities would create world sympathy for the Jews.

Against both the Grand Mufti and Kaukji was Abdullah of Transjordan, who envisioned expanding his country by taking Palestine for himself.

Syria and Egypt were not without ambitions to snatch up pieces of Palestine, Syria wanting Haifa and Egypt the Negev and Gaza strip. When the various spheres of interest were sorted out it appeared that the Yishuv was being thrown to a pack of ravished jackals. Also following historical lines, the Arab leadership was not motivated to liberate Palestine for the Palestinian Arabs but were in it for personal ambition or national interest. Self-determination and legitimate rights for the Palestinian Arabs were phrases never heard or known in those days. The bright rally flag of the Arab world was simply the total destruction of the Jews.

When the last United Nations vote was cast in November 1947 Palestine erupted from one end to the other with tens of dozens of Arab attacks which killed hundreds of

Jews, mainly by ambush or where they could catch people unarmed or isolated. In the face of this, the Haganah remained cool and concentrated on building up their capabilities. The Irgun and Stern were under no such restraint and terror and counter-terror raged, particularly in Jerusalem.

Throughout December 1947 Arab atrocities went unchecked by the British, who gave them a free hand to snipe, ambush, indiscriminately bomb crowded theaters and markets and toss grenades. Water pipes into West Jerusalem were blown and the Bab el Wad was shut. The British, for the most part, threw up their hands and shrugged, claiming inability to cope with the situation despite their army of a hundred thousand men.

Meanwhile the British were quietly beefing up the arms of the Arab Legion, commanded by the Englishman Sir John Bagot Glubb, who was also known as Glubb Pasha. The British had promised to keep the Legion in Transjordan until their May withdrawal but their posture was so overtly pro-Arab, no one believed them any more.

In Jerusalem, in those areas where the Jewish and Arab sections met, the British set up mazes of barbed wire enclaves, appropriately named Bevingrad after the British Foreign Minister. The announced intention was to keep the two communities separated but it was a convenient ruse to strip and search Jews for weapons.

At the same time it was no trick for the Arabs to smuggle in arms from bordering countries. These were openly sold in the Old City. On their sacred Haram esh Sharif, pro-Abdullah forces built up an enormous cache in the underground passages of the Al-Aksa Mosque and in the Dome of the Rock itself. The Temple Mount became a military observation post as well as a sniper position against the Jewish Quarter. There were no British arms searches on the Haram.

With the barbed wire entanglements impeding passage into the Old City, the British were able to restrict movement into the Jewish Quarter. The one direct access, through the Zion Gate, was sealed up. It was obvious the British intended to pressure the Jewish Quarter and try to force the sixteen hundred Hasidics out and turn the Old City over to the Arabs.

Dov Joseph, a Canadian-born lawyer, was Jewish gover-

nor of Jerusalem and went about masterfully and tenaciously
mobilizing his people in preparation for siege and battle.
Water would be the most critical problem. Joseph ordered
a survey of all the cisterns in West Jerusalem. They were
all repaired, filled and treated with chemicals, then capped
with cement. It was determined that there was a reserve
of twenty-two million gallons, a paltry amount for a
hundred thousand people. With an excruciatingly sparse
ration it could last for some three months at the rate of ten
gallons a day per family. When the Arabs blew up the
water pipes into West Jerusalem and the British refused to
allow them to be repaired or guarded, the Jews were
forced onto their rationing program.

Each day water trucks opened a number of cisterns,
emptied them and distributed the liquid gold to the various neighborhoods. A prescribed ritual was followed. A
gallon or so was set aside for essential drinking and
cooking. The balance went through a series of declining
usages, so it could be used over and over for personal
washing and cleaning the most vital pots and pans, then
brushing teeth and perhaps some laundry. The final use
of the day was to give the toilet its single daily flushing.
There was no water for showers, gardening and lawns or
basic sanitation. Streets became thick with dust from the
desert and, as the Jews were dehydrated, the city took on
a look of browned-out bleakness.

There was no fuel for individual use. What there was
went to hospitals, military transport and places like bakeries.
Candles replaced electric lights. The Jerusalem housewife
had to do her cooking on a bonfire of wood scraps in her
yard or on her balcony. Wood was always a scarce item in
Judea, so people began to dismantle their homes, furniture,
railings, window sashes or anything made of wood.

The only greens were dandelions as the ration fell to the
near starvation level of six hundred calories a day.

A small makeshift airstrip of single-engine size was later
set down in the Valley of the Cross so baby formula,
drugs, some ammunition and the leaders of the Yishuv
could be carried in.

The arms situation was equally grave. The Jews had a
total of five hundred rifles, twenty-eight light machine
guns and a few mortars, some of the homemade variety.
The mortars were constantly shifted from front to front to

give the illusion that the Jewish arsenal was larger than it was.

The immediate Haganah problem was to straighten out a defense line and keep communications open to the various isolated neighborhoods and enclaves. Haganah attempts to capture the heights of Nebi Samuel and the Augusta Victoria both failed. Eventually the Arabs were ejected from the Katamon district and the Jews were able to hold onto Mount Scopus but they were isolated. The Hebrew University, National Library and Hadassah Hospital were shut down as Scopus could be reached only through Arab Jerusalem. The Jews settled for a "demilitarized" status in order to save the buildings which were manned by a tiny garrison force. Government House on the Hill of Evil Counsel, which had headquartered the Mandated government, was also demilitarized and eventually turned over to the United Nations truce-keeping operation.

In February and March of 1948 the British in collaboration with an Arab terrorist, Fawzi el-Kutub, who had been trained as an SS commando by the Nazis, unloaded three devastating bomb blasts in West Jerusalem. The Palestine Post was the first to go, followed by a bombing of the main Jewish business district around Ben Yehuda Street. Finally, the Jewish Agency was blown up.

A bit south of Jerusalem on the Bethlehem Road, a lone Jewish kibbutz, Ramat Rachel, near the Tomb of Rachel, clung to a hair-thin line to connect it to the city. The kibbutz had the unenviable task of having to stop Arab troop movement from the south.

THE DEIR YASIN AND HADASSAH MASSACRES

The escalating savagery climaxed with a pair of massacres, one Jewish and one Arab, that epitomized the tragedy consuming Palestine.

The Arab village of Deir Yasin on the approaches to West Jerusalem had long been suspect as a launching point for attacks against Jewish traffic. Inside Jerusalem the Haganah commander was faced with the fact that the Irgun and Stern Gang continued to operate independently. When the Haganah and its elite force, the Palmach, won their victory at the Kastel, the Irgun and Stern felt they also had to win an important victory of their own in order to maintain equity.

On the night of April 8, 1948, the Irgun and Stern jointly attacked Deir Yasin in the middle of the night with over a hundred troops. They were unable to effect a surprise and a vicious house-to-house battle ensued. Although the Irgun had experience in attacking British police forts, this kind of fighting was not their forte. They were more of an urban guerrilla force while the Stern Gang's specialty was assassination.

As the fighting got hot, captured houses were blown up. This caused growing panic among the Arabs, who had women and children tangled up with their fighters. With fire pouring in every direction, the Irgun's discipline apparently collapsed in confusion and then in frenzy. Fleeing Arabs were shot down in what turned into an uncontrolled orgy of shooting. When it was done, two hundred and fifty men, women and children had been killed.

Deir Yasin immediately became the battle cry for vengeance in the entire Arab world. The stories that emanated from the survivors of the massacre reported Jewish atrocities of a kind never heard of before.

The Jewish leadership of Palestine immediately denounced the massacre. The Irgun and Stern argued just as vehemently that they were only responding to armed resistance. What really happened at Deir Yasin in the smoke, screaming, confusion and breakdown of discipline will never really be known. The result was a black mark on the Jewish people that they would have a lot of trouble living down.

Without intending to defend the indefensible, this kind of behavior is not consistent with the Jewish character or Jewish history. The PLO, by contrast, uses the murder of children and non-combatants as a matter of policy. By any accounting, Deir Yasin was a unique, isolated occurrence never sanctioned by the authorities. For decades the history of Palestine has been filled with Arab massacres and if one were to write a book called the Massacres of Palestine, the Jews would be guilty of a single page in a large volume.

The aftermath of Deir Yasin was an Arab magnification of the event beyond all truth. Eyewitness stories grew ridiculously fanciful and the Arabs went on to expand the event, trying to make the world believe that the Arab population fled Palestine exclusively as an aftermath of Deir Yasin. No doubt the massacre had a shocking effect. However, none of the hundreds of Arab atrocities against the Jews forced the Jews to flee Palestine.

The true cause behind the Arab flight was that their belief in their own infallibility had been deflated. In the throes of a mob scene on the streets, in the hallucinations of their wild rhetoric, they had elevated themselves to supermen in their own eyes. They had always disdained Jewish fighting ability and for centuries had easy pickings in kicking the Jews around. It was not Deir Yasin but the sobering reality of their own weakness that brought on the refugee problem. The bursting of the bubble came with defeat after defeat, the near comic Kaukji and his irregulars, the failure of Abdul Kadar to capture the Etzion Bloc, four religious settlements south of Jerusalem, and his loss of the Kastel, the gutty determination of the convoys and the failure to blow the Jews out of Jerusalem.

The Arabs came to understand they were in a serious war which they had started by their refusal to go to the conference table. They had been so positive of their ability to destroy the Jews that when they learned it wasn't going to happen they panicked and fled. Moreover, they were encouraged to leave Palestine by Arab governments who wanted smooth sailing when they came in to destroy the Jews.

Deir Yasin was a sick happening but, make no mistake, the Arabs were already abandoning villages and towns and cities by the dozens. They fled Haifa, they fled Jaffa, they fled Tiberias, they fled Acre and over a hundred villages with scarcely a shot being fired at them. The bully's bluff had been called and the bully suddenly came face to face with his own ineptness.

Nothing could more clearly illustrate who caused the Arabs to flee than the situation in Jaffa, an all-Arab city bordering Tel Aviv with 100,000 population. The leading

Arab families had fled to Beirut, Cairo and Europe, leaving the community leaderless. As the Haganah and Arab forces faced off, a truce was kept until Arab irregulars came into Jaffa and plundered it clean, terrifying the population. Mass fear erupted while the word from Arab capitals was spread for the Palestinians to get out to clear a path for their armies. Before a single shot was fired between Jew and Arab, 75 percent of the Arab population of Jaffa had fled.

Several days after Deir Yasin, the Arabs got their revenge. A Jewish convoy of medical personnel left West Jerusalem in Mogen David (Red Cross) vehicles for the Hadassah enclave on Mount Scopus. Two hundred yards from a British post which supposedly guarded the road, the Arabs ambushed the convoy in broad daylight. When the firing had stopped, seventy-seven unarmed Jews, mainly doctors and nurses, had been slaughtered.

On May 14, 1948, a day before the end of the British Mandate, the Declaration of Independence of the State of Israel was read in Tel Aviv. Chaim Weizmann was named the new nation's first President and David Ben Gurion the Prime Minister of the Provisional Government. Its first act was to abrogate the White Paper and declare Israel open for automatic citizenship to any Jew in the world who wished to come. Dancing in the streets was modified by the shadow of war.

THE FALL OF THE JEWISH QUARTER

On May 1, a fortnight before the Declaration of Independence, Colonel David Shatiel, Haganah commander for Jerusalem, called a full mobilization that would net him some six thousand semi-trained militia with a thousand or so Irgun and Stern. He had rifles for a third of them. Shatiel was quite a colorful character, having earned his credentials in the French Foreign Legion. Before the Second World War he entered Germany on a secret mission, was captured by the Gestapo, and survived months of torture.

The heavily religious Jewish population of the city was not conducive to large numbers of volunteers. Thousands of the Hasidics followed religious beliefs that forbade them to take up arms as a mortal sin. As if Shatiel didn't have enough on his hands, a party of Hasidics known as the Neturei Karta would not even recognize the existence of the new state of Israel, declaring Israel's return could only come when the messiah appeared.

The Haganah defense line across the city north to south was stretched thin. Thus far the Arab Legion had remained in Transjordan but Shatiel could not depend on their staying there. He also faced the prospect of the regular armies of Iraq and Egypt coming after Jerusalem as the city shaped up to be the key and crucial site of the war.

Shatiel's greatest concern became the Jewish Quarter. Like Jerusalem itself, the quarter was a military liability but, also like Jerusalem, nothing symbolized the longings of the people more poignantly. For century after century, under the gravest duress and persecution, the Jews had clung to this little corner of their fallen nation close to the remaining wall of Herod's Temple. The quarter was occupied by sixteen hundred Jews, mostly Hasidics and deeply religious families. They were pinned in and cut off by thirty thousand extremely hostile Arabs.

Despite Jewish pleas for passage to and from the quarter, the British contended that the Arabs would not attack a neighborhood filled with unarmed and harmless old people. Memories of past massacres of defenseless Jews, particularly in Hebron, belied that contention. What the British offered was a one-way ticket out of the Old City so they could hand the entire place over to the Arabs.

When the British withdrew from the city, the Haganah realized it would only be a matter of days before the Arab Legion crossed the Jordan River a few miles away. A ragtag Haganah force, lightly armed, moved toward the Jaffa Gate and the Citadel. Arabs in the Old City rushed up to the wall and poured fire down on the Haganah from battlements built to accommodate the width of crossbows.

Uzi Narkiss had a hundred and twenty Palmach left from the Har El Brigade, which had been decimated in the Judean hills trying to keep the Bab el Wad open. At the same moment the Haganah tried to force the Jaffa Gate,

THE DIVIDED CITY, 1948-1967

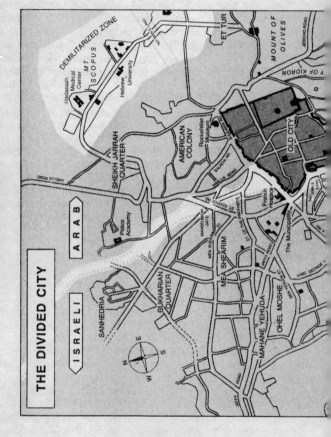

THE DIVIDED CITY

ISRAELI   ARAB

DEMILITARIZED ZONE

Hadassah Medical Center

MT. SCOPUS

Hebrew University

ET TUR

MOUNT OF OLIVES

SHEIKH JARRAH QUARTER

AMERICAN COLONY

Rockefeller Museum

NABLUS ROAD

OLD CITY

Y OF KIDRON

JERICHO ROAD

Police Academy

SALAH ED DIN ST

SALADIN RD.

NABLUS RD.

SANHEDRIA

BUKHARIAN QUARTER

MANDELBAUM GATE

MEA SHEARIM ST.

ST. OF THE PROPHETS

French Hospice

NO MAN'S LAND

NO MAN'S LAND

MEA SHEARIM

JAFFA ROAD

The Municipality

KING GEORGE V

MAHANE YEHUDA

OHEL MOSHE

BEN YEHUDA ST.

JAFFA ROAD

N E S W

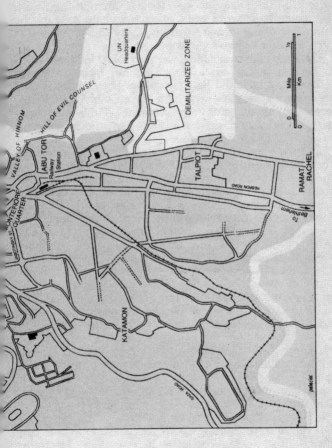

Narkiss stormed up Mount Zion and tried to open the Zion Gate. Both attacks failed but the Palmach had won Mount Zion.

The Arabs sent out desperate calls to Abdullah in Amman to send in the Legion to save them. Although the British had given their word the Legion would be kept on the other side of the Jordan River until May 15, Abdullah was hard pressed to break the commitment.

The Arab high command's war plan called for Transjordan to be responsible for a front that ran from Nablus to Hebron and included East Jerusalem. Both Abdullah and his military adviser, General John Bagot Glubb/Glubb Pasha, were soft on the entire involvement. Glubb Pasha was particularly wary of getting mixed up in a house-to-house street fight in Jerusalem.

Abdullah had no love affairs with the Arab leadership. The Grand Mufti Haj Amin al-Husseini was his archrival and enemy over Palestinian lands. He despised the despotic Egyptian monarch, King Farouk. He also hated the Saudis who had displaced his family on the Arabian Peninsula and cared very little for the irregulars, who were mainly in it for spoils.

The one irresistible lure was East Jerusalem. Abdullah was a Hashemite, the son of the Emir of Mecca. For him now to become master of the great Islamic shrines of the Old City would to go the roots of family honor and prestige. He felt that the Jews were palatable and an accommodation could be worked out with them which would allow his flag to fly over the holy shrines without a war but he was not the master of his own fate.

The war fever that had swept Cairo and the other Arab capitals spilled over into Amman. However, the mullahs in the mosques and Abdullah's own bedouin officers in the Legion were demanding he join the jihad to exterminate the Jews.

It was against this background that Golda Meir held two clandestine meetings with Abdullah. One was conducted in a foreign consulate in Jerusalem. The other found Golda, disguised as an Arab woman, making a dangerous trip to Amman in an attempt to temper the Legion's role. It was a perplexed ruler she met, a man caught up in a web of conspiracies and commitments to his culture.

THE ETZION BLOC

Six miles south of Jerusalem in the twisting Judean hills stood four kibbutzim of religious Jews in a settlement dating from the 1920s known as the Etzion Bloc. The Jews had been run out during the 1929 Arab riots and again during the 1936 riots. Both times the kibbutzim were leveled. Both times the Jews returned and rebuilt them. Because of their religious beliefs it was difficult to get them to fortify themselves or to train people for combat. But their position was one of the most strategic in the country as well as one of the most isolated. The always hostile Hebron was just five miles to the south. The Haganah moved in with a small unit, occupied a defunct Russian monastery which commanded the road and immediately began to harass Arab military traffic.

Before he was killed at the Kastel, Abdul Kadar attempted to take the Etzion Bloc without success. As the official war grew closer the Hebron-Jerusalem road became absolutely vital to Arab plans to link up the Egyptian army coming up from the south. The Bloc fell under heavy siege and Jewish relief convoys paid a brutal price.

Although the Haganah didn't have the manpower to send meaningful reinforcements, Abdullah and Glubb feared the entrenched Jewish positions which had proved so difficult to dislodge. The road had to be cleared and the agreement that the Legion not cross the Jordan was broken by moving them over the river and attacking the Bloc and taking it after a sharp and bloody engagement. On the eve of the Declaration of Independence the Etzion Bloc fell which came as a terrible shock to the Yishuv.

In the end the religious Jews of the settlements proved extremely courageous fighters, with many of their women dying on the line beside them. When the Arab Legion carted the Jewish prisoners off, hordes of Arabs from Hebron poured in and looted, then destroyed the place for the third time in thirty years. On this occasion the lovely orchards, nurtured by hand, were cut down in the false hope that the Jews would never return.

LATRUN

At the entrance to the Bab el Wad Palmach scouts from the Givati Brigade were surprised to find no return fire when they probed near the Latrun police fort. Finding it abandoned, they immediately occupied it with what was left of a battered Givati Battalion. What seemed absolutely incongruous was that the occupation of Latrun was not on the planning board of either the Jews or the Arabs, for it not only commanded the entrance to the Jerusalem road but was an important strategic location for both sides. Glubb's reason for not going in right away was the fear of overextending the Legion and sucking them into an all-out war which they didn't want.

The Yishuv had a different reason. A young Palmach commander, Yitzak Rabin, later to become chief of staff and Prime Minister, begged for sufficient reinforcements to be able to hold Latrun. Ben Gurion, in his mania to save Jerusalem, agreed.

Chief of operations was a young Jerusalemite in his early thirties, Yigael Yadin. He was already an eminent archaeologist, the son of E. L. Sukenik of Dead Sea Scrolls fame. Yadin's personal interest in Jerusalem could not have been more intense as his wife and family were in the besieged city. Yet he had to take desperate issue with Ben Gurion. The Palmach battalion needed to garrison Latrun adequately simply could not be spared. The more urgent of the two situations was in the south where the Egyptian Army was pouring over the border. Yadin's logic was that it was better to have a state without a capital than to end up with a capital without a state. Latrun went over to the Arab Legion by default. It was a gut-wrenching decision, one the Jews would have to make over and over, for they simply did not have the manpower to defend all the fronts they were fighting on. The Haganah would later try to regain Latrun but they were unable to dislodge the Legion after four attempts at the cost of a thousand men. The fort was to remain a bone in Israel's throat until 1967.

The cities of Nablus, Tulkarm and Jenin formed what was called the Triangle in Samaria, an area completely settled by Arabs. From Tulkarm over Israeli territory to the Mediterranean was a mere six miles. At this point the narrow waist of Israel is no wider than the San Francisco Bay Bridge is long. When Iraqi troops moved into Samaria they threatened to cut Israel in half. A more potent army would have made the situation dangerous for the Yishuv, but whenever Iraqi troops moved into battle, they proved inept.

Syria struck from the east, coming down out of the Golan Heights and hitting both ends of the Sea of Galilee. They captured two isolated Jewish settlements, then got stopped cold by one kibbutz after another. The Syrian drive sputtered and stopped after very little penetration.

From the south the Egyptians crossed out of the Sinai and split into two prongs. One column swung inland and up the middle of the Negev Desert toward Beersheba. The second column streaked up the timeworn path of battle through the Gaza Strip. The Egyptians overran two kibbutzim and advanced to within ten miles of Tel Aviv before being halted at Ashdod.

The Arab media broke open a large can of superlatives in their accounts of the first days of fighting, rattling off lists of "fallen" towns, including the "capture" of Gaza and Beersheba. What were being described as victories were merely entrances into Arab cities whose mayors and dignitaries were at the gates to greet the Egyptians.

What became apparent by the end of the first two weeks of fighting was that there was going to be no domino collapse of Jewish settlements or mass fleeing. After two weeks the Arab armies were running out of steam, had gained little and the Palestinian Arabs, seeing their hopes for quick victory vanish, abandoned their homes and fled by the thousands.

Jerusalem became the centerpiece of the war. An Egyptian column moved up from the south and the Iraqis down from the north. The most ominous development was the move of the Arab Legion into East Jerusalem. As they entered, they captured the Sheikh Jarrah suburb and effectively cut off West Jerusalem from Mount Scopus.

With the loss of the Etzion Bloc, the task of preventing a junction of Egyptian and Legion forces fell to Kibbutz Ramat Rachel in the south of the city on the road to Bethlehem. The battle for the kibbutz saw it change hands several times but in the end Ramat Rachel held and the Egyptians never reached Jerusalem.

Seeking one great victory, the Arab high command turned everything loose on West Jerusalem. It was still under siege and in the next few weeks Transjordanian artillery poured in over ten thousand shells with more thousands of incendiaries. The Arab lines of artillery and tanks fired at will with no danger to themselves, for the Haganah had no weapons capable of answering them. Jewish casualties on a per capita basis ran higher than British casualties had in London during the height of the German blitz. To add fuel to the fire, Count Folke Bernadotte, the Swedish-born United Nations mediator, proposed that all of Jerusalem be handed over to the Arabs. Bernadotte was later assassinated by the Stern Gang.

With Egypt and Iraq stopped at the doorstep of Jerusalem, the Arab Legion put a thousand fresh troops into the Old City through the Damascus Gate. They poured a withering barrage from the Haram esh Sharif into the Jewish Quarter, which had been subjected to round-the-clock fire for days. In the courtyards latrines were blown up, roofs caved in, walls split apart in a fearful concentration of gunfire. The Hasidics had been driven to living in the basements of synagogues. Supplies and food diminished to near zero. Defending the quarter were some eighty Haganah reservists who had managed to scale the wall and get in from Mount Zion.

Outside the Zion Gate, Mordechai Gazit, the senior Haganah officer, tried desperately to assemble enough men and arms for one last go at the gate. His people were as exhausted as the fighters inside the quarter and Gazit himself had not slept in five days.

Daddo Elazar, whose Palmach had just thrown the Iraqis out of the Katamon district, called for volunteers to go up to Zion. Only forty remained from the original four hundred and they were punchy from round-the-clock fighting. Gazit huddled with Daddo and Uzi Narkiss and hand-picked twenty Palmachmen and two women and gave them the task of dynamiting the gate. In what was a last burst of strength they managed to put up enough fire to drive the Arab defenders on the wall to cover, then blasted the Zion Gate off its hinges. For the first time since the days of the Maccabees, a Jewish army had breached the Old City wall. Daddo and Uzi Narkiss rushed through past the Armenian Quarter to the Street of the Jews. The Haganah, mostly dressed in civilian clothing, followed them with blood plasma and ammunition.

The over-all plan had called for Colonel Shatiel to send up reinforcements once the Zion Gate had been opened but history records they never arrived. Shatiel was having his hands full all over the city and once again the Jews were faced with the fact that their forces were stretched too thin.

Inside the Jewish Quarter, they were down to their last shekel. The Ben Zakai Synagogue, the final stronghold, had been turned into a hospital and resembled Bedlam. Blood spattered the walls and slickened the floors. The sanctuary was a shambles. A makeshift operating room was lined with bullet-riddled holy books. Lights failed and the corridors were jammed with old men whose last solace was prayer.

The Arab Legion pressed in blowing up each house and synagogue as they advanced. Desperate messages for help could no longer be answered. By May 27 there was no more food to be eaten, no more ammunition to be shot, no more water to be drunk, no more plasma to be transfused. On that day the Hurva Synagogue, the greatest symbol of Jewry in the Old City, was dynamited to the ground.

Narkiss had to make the excruciating decision to withdraw provided that an honorable surrender could be arranged for the inhabitants. Because the Legion had British officers, a massacre was prevented. First they stopped the Arab mob trying to get at the hundred and twenty wounded in the Ben Zakai Synagogue. Three hundred men of fighting age among the inhabitants were taken as prisoners. The balance were old women and children and were allowed to leave through the Zion Gate with their Torah scrolls and sacred books. Uzi Narkiss was the last of the Palmach to go through the gate.

The Jewish Quarter was then turned over to the mob which seems to be on the heels of every Arab army and it was looted clean. Afterward the Arab Legion systematically destroyed every building in the quarter, including fifty synagogues.

By June 1 the Burma Road had been cut through the Judean hills, bypassing Latrun and the Bab el Wad. Twelve hundred Palmach troops were shifted to Jerusalem and the siege was lifted.

The first of several truces was arranged on June 10 but for the Arabs the war was really over. Though there would be more months of hard fighting the Arab armies got no better.

In the interim the Jews found some artillery and received a large shipment of Czech arms. The air force was upgraded when some obsolete World War II fighter planes were purchased and flown to Israel "by the seat of the pilots' pants."

With inventiveness and daring a brilliant group of young leaders such as Allon, Daddo, Rabin, Dayan, Yadin and the rest, and fighting men of a quality that improved by the day, the Israelis routed the enemy from the land, seized the Negev Desert and claimed the outpost of Eilat on the tip of the Gulf of Aqaba. Ben Gurion particularly wanted Eilat, for he was already thinking of the future and a port that could be developed to give Israel access to the Far East.

The only Arab victor was Abdullah, who had seized the West Bank and held East Jerusalem and the Old City. For the first time in two thousand years, since the Maccabees held the Temple Mount and the Seleucids held the Upper City, Jerusalem was divided. An ugly gash of a no man's land ran down the Hinnom Valley past the Jaffa Gate. Sandbagged Israeli observation posts at the Notre Dame Hospice and the Church of Mary's Dormition on Mount Zion were to snarl at Jordanian posts on the Old City walls, with the two sides within touching distance. Narrow little streets around Mea Shearim, the American Colony and the Sheikh Jarrah Quarter came to abrupt halts at border points, usually denoted by high concrete walls. The Jewish facilities on Mount Scopus—their university, library and hospital—became a zone of no entry and fell into decay. The only connecting point between East and West Jerusalem was through a bombed-out plaza on St. George Road known as the Mandelbaum Gate.

The real losers were the Palestinian Arabs who fled. Those who remained were not only unharmed but now enjoy greater freedom and social and economic benefits than anyplace in the Arab world.

The refugees were greeted as lepers by their own people, debased and deliberately caged in festering camps to breed hatred of the Jews.

Writing in *Falastin al Thawra*, an official publication of the PLO, Abu Mazer, a member of the Executive Committee, stated what the Arabs have finally admitted is the truth:

The Arab armies entered Palestine to protect the Palestinians . . . but, instead, they abandoned them, forced them to emigrate and to leave their homeland, imposed upon them a political and ideological blockade and threw them into prisons similar to the ghettos in which the Jews used to live in Eastern Europe.

At the same time the new State of Israel welcomed over a half million Jews from the Arab world.

The Years Between

In late 1948 Operation Ten Plagues blew the Egyptians out of the Negev Desert and sent them scrambling in disarray back into the Sinai. At a place called the Faluja Pocket a young Egyptian officer was taken captive. Gamal Abdel Nasser was to reflect in his own bitterness the bitterness of the Arab world.

Since the Crusaders, every time the West had come into contact with the Arabs the result was war, occupation, exploitation, political trickery and an imposition of Western culture and technology, usually at the cost of Islamic values. The latest "intruder" was the lowly Jew. Here, at last, had been an opportunity for the Arabs to redeem their faltered manhood. Being outfought by the Jews was a crushing blow.

Nasser was to put his dark broodings into practice through a vainglorious attempt to forge a "greater Arab nation" with himself as its leader. From the day the various armistice agreements were signed on the island of Rhodes, the Jews were never to know a moment's peace.

The armistice with Transjordan called for free Israeli passage past Latrun, Jewish access to the Scopus facilities and, most importantly, Jewish access to their holy site of the Western Wall in the Old City. No sooner was the ink dry on the agreement than Transjordan broke it.

Access to Scopus was denied except for a changing of the guard every few weeks. At Latrun, traffic was blocked and a bypass road had to be used. Finally, the Jews were totally and completely denied access to worship at the Western Wall.

Pressure was put on Ben Gurion to compel the Transjordanians to live up to the armistice terms but he felt he had secured a viable state and there were too many priorities to risk taking up arms again.

The war had been costly; four thousand soldiers and two thousand civilians had been killed out of a small population of a half million. (Consider six thousand dead in a city the size of Columbus, Ohio, for example.) Financially, the new state was all but bankrupt. The detention camps in Europe had to be emptied. Jews in Arab countries needed to be freed. A national airline and merchant fleet had to be built. A parched desert had to be conquered. Armed forces had to be built to repel continued Arab aggression. Huge housing, farming and water projects had to be started. The list of problems was staggering and so the Transjordanian armistice violations were put on the back burner.

The end of the war had seen the smallest, poorest and least prestigious of the Arab nations, Transjordan, as the only Arab country which acquitted itself well on the battlefield and this stuck in the craw of the rest of the Arab world. Egypt, which had shown disdain for the Jordanians at the beginning of the war, was particularly humiliated. When Abdullah's Parliament attempted to annex the West Bank and East Jerusalem, the move met with opposition in the Arab world. Nasser and the Arab League made it clear to Abdullah that he was merely taking guardianship of this territory until the Arab armies could be rebuilt. Transjordan was always under pressure from larger and stronger neighbors and depended on economic aid from the rest of the Arab world, so it was forced to agree.

For two years Abdullah carried on secret talks with the Israelis until his assassination by a Moslem fanatic took place at the Al Aksa Mosque in 1951.

Transjordanian rule was never fully accepted by the West Bank Arabs although they were fellow Palestinians. Blocked from annexation of these territories, the Transjordanians came to regard the West Bank and East Jerusalem as something like vassal holdings. Troubles between Amman and the West Bank Arabs broke out periodically and, generally speaking, their rule was autocratic and unpopular. Progress in East Jerusalem was slight, with tourism the main base of the economy. Relative calm was maintained along the cease-fire lines in Jerusalem until a peaceful assemblage of archaeologists were shot down in cold blood by soldiers at a Jordanian outpost near Ramat Rachel. Pilgrims were allowed to enter Israel from East Jerusalem through the Mandelbaum Gate but it was a one-way route. No one with an Israeli visa in his or her passport was allowed to travel to any Arab country. Even those Arabs who had remained in Israel and were now Israeli citizens were denied the right to travel in Arab lands or even to make the pilgrimage to Mecca or pray at Al Aksa Mosque.

The rest of the West Bank became a staging ground for terrorist raids against the Jews.

The story of West Jerusalem was another matter. Thousands of new immigrants from one hundred countries poured in and the city expanded to the south and west rapidly.

A dramatic new explosion of construction was led by the complex of government buildings which was crowned in 1966 with a simple but stunning Knesset or Parliament building, a donation of the late James de Rothschild of Britain. Priceless Chagall tapestries were created and donated to the Knesset's main hall.

An entire new campus of the Hebrew University burgeoned in Givat Ram, drawing students from all over the world. A Henry Moore statue was donated as the centerpiece of the campus.

Mount Herzl was developed as a memorial park, lovely and wooded, a sort of Israeli Arlington with tombs of the great alongside tombs of her fallen warriors. Part of the mountain was used to develop Yad Vashem, a unique memorial dedicated to the victims of the Holocaust. Its archives, museum, sanctuary, woods and statuary cannot be visited without shaking the visitor's heart and conscience forever.

In the suburb of Ein Karem, a new Hadassah medical center arose as the largest in the Middle East and of world-class caliber. Chagall stained glass windows depicting the Ten Commandments in its small synagogue have become a world landmark.

A convention hall and fair complex was built to hold international convocations and exhibitions with an auditorium which has lured artists and orchestras from around the world. A smaller legitimate theater in the Rehavia neighborhood performs opera, ballet and stage plays.

Millions of trees were planted and large parks and tiny pocket parks came into being. A branch of America's Hebrew Union College opened and an Academy of Sciences and Humanities was built, as was a Chief Rabbinate. Office buildings, hotels, department stores, schools, research centers, artists' colonies came along with wide, flower-filled boulevards.

Monuments arose everywhere, usually embraced by woods and flowers: to John F. Kennedy, haunting the Judean hills, to the Danish people who rose to save their Jewish population, to America with a replica of the Liberty Bell.

The Israel Museum and its Shrine of the Book, holding the Dead Sea Scrolls, and the Billy Rose Garden of statuary, and its archaeological center rippled over a beautiful ridge like a series of Mediterranean villas.

West Jerusalem was a symphony of beauty tended with indescribable love. Jews from everywhere contributed to have their names on something in Jerusalem, an ambulance, a park bench, a hospital ward, a grove of trees.

THE SINAI CAMPAIGN

I recall my own first visits to Israel to begin research for my novel, *Exodus*. The spirit of the people was soaring in those days of 1956. The tempo of building was staggering. I would go up to Jerusalem often and, from my window in the King David Hotel, I could see over the garish no man's land to the Old City walls which were forbidden to me. On Mount Zion I could almost touch the gate but if one got too close the glint from the barrel of a Jordanian rifle in the nearby post came as a sorrowful reminder. Although I had never been raised or lived as an observant Jew, I became obsessed with a dream of going into the Old City and seeing the Western Wall before I died.

Although miracles of redemption were occurring all over Israel, the landscape was also filled with ugly temporary shack towns made of corrugated tin to absorb the flood of refugees, mainly from Morocco and Arab lands. The gritty little country was trying to juggle ten balls in the air while dancing on the head of a pin. Still, in a matter of a few years these eyesores disappeared as people were resettled in decent housing in the towns or moshavim and kibbutzim.

On the other side of Israel's borders there were also refugee camps but these did not disappear. They were filled with dispirited Palestinian Arabs whose illusions had been shattered by the lies of their leaders. Had there been any love for these people, the Arab leaders and the Arab people would not have permitted this condition to continue. They were mostly unwelcome in the lands of their brother Arabs. In the Gaza Strip, the Egyptians locked them in. In the camps around Jericho, the summer heat near the Dead Sea soared to 120°. There was no concerted attempt to relocate these people, to find work for them, to educate them, to do much but let them sit, stew, rot and build maniacal fantasies about the great castles and villas they had been forced to leave in Palestine. Their Arab brethren were content to let these people live off the scrapings of the world community, on handouts from the United Nations, with their own oil-rich states contributing virtually nothing to their welfare. The lack of dignity and concern for human life was disgusting.

Nasser saw in these festering human dumps the perfect breeding ground in which to build up a new generation predicated on hate and infused with paranoia and mania. Any serious talk of resettlement was squashed so Nasser could build his time bomb. The only Arabs to dissolve their camps and take their people out and provide meaningful lives were the Christian Arabs. The Arab refugee camps were needless, what with their enormous territories of unsettled land and resources. They were a sorry contrast to what the Jews were doing for Jewish refugees from Arab countries.

The litany of malevolence spewed forth from Arab capitals without abatement, every means at their command being used to berate Israel. Every international forum was convoluted to wring out condemnations against the Jews for imagined violations. The Jews were condemned by the World Labor Organization for their treatment of

Arab workers when, in fact, they worked under better conditions than they had ever enjoyed. At the same time the Arab laborer in Arab lands was little more than dirt and the Saudis continued to practice slavery. Members of Moslem nations refused to sit at a banquet table with Jews or shake their hands in public or allow them to compete on the sports fields. Jewish archaeological digs around the Old City have been condemned as "undermining Islamic shrines" when, only a few years earlier, Jordan had carried out the same excavations on the same sites. Singling out the Jew as the international leper became the high blood sport of the Arab nations. The United Nations itself was corrupted into a ridiculous forum bent on passing condemnations of Israel as the first order of world business. Israel's ships were kept from innocent passage through the Suez Canal and the Strait of Tiran. Her products and businesses were boycotted. Nations trading with Israel were blackmailed. The Arabs stopped at nothing, even attempting to poison her orange crop.

Israel's citizens were shot down in the fields and such military targets as schools were captured and innocent young hostages killed. These were not incidental isolated incidents but the policy of Arab governments to sponsor murder gangs. The Gaza Strip, the Golan Heights and the West Bank became staging grounds for these cowardly cutthroats to destroy, maim and butcher unarmed people. When they returned to their bases they were welcomed as heroes and liberators. Military targets have been studiously avoided by the noble freedom fighters of the PLO.

A vicious cycle of Arab murder squads and Israeli reprisal was set off and heightened. Nasser finally courted the Soviet Union for arms, then set up joint military commands with the nations on Israel's borders. Egypt moved more and more boldly building up her forces in the Sinai and Gaza Strip.

Israel was able to capture a political moment when Nasser nationalized the Suez Canal, ejecting Britain and France. While Britain and France wanted to regain the canal, Israel needed to halt the Egyptian threat on her borders. The partnership was formed and in November of 1956 Israel struck first, overrunning the Gaza Strip and the Sinai. She was at the canal within four days. In addition to obliterating the Egyptian Army, Israel achieved the secondary goal of capturing Sharm el Sheik. This outpost on the southern tip of the Sinai had been used to block Israeli and friendly shipping from the Strait of Tiran. In unlocking the Gulf of Aqaba and the Red Sea, Israel was able to develop Eilat and obtain a sea route to the east.

The British and French blundered in their part of the campaign. Hesitant and wishy-washy, they delayed their attack on the canal long enough for the big powers to move in and stop them. The canal was never taken and Sir Anthony Eden's government fell in what was to be the last hurrah for British imperialism in the Middle East.

Israel refused to leave the Sinai until a United Nations force occupied Sharm el Sheik to insure innocent passage of ships.

During the Sinai Campaign of '56, my cousin Jossi Yerushalmi was a paratrooper who was dropped behind Egyptian lines at Mitla Pass in the Sinai. He was the first of my family to go into battle for Israel. Several other first cousins followed in the paratroops and infantry in all of Israel's wars.

At the time of the Sinai Campaign I was living in Herzlia, a beach town north of Tel Aviv, with my family. I was compelled by the American Embassy to evacuate them. When this had been done during a rather wild night ride, traveling in a blackout to Lydda Airport, I became a correspondent and immediately went into the Sinai. I later joined my family in Rome and returned to the States dead broke, but at least I had the notes for a book, a book named *Exodus*.

The Temple Mount Is Ours!

It was more than the simple perverse joy of destroying Israel that Nasser had in mind. In the decade that followed the Egyptian thrashing in the Sinai Campaign, he continued to pursue a demented dream of pan-Arabism. Israel's continued existence was a perfect foil, a constant sore point he could press to unify the otherwise disunified Arab world.

By keeping the Palestinian refugees locked up and converting them into a cancer force of terrorism, he had also created a political mechanism to holler and yell for world attention. At the same time he saw to it that Jordan did not annex the territory nor would he allow the Palestinians of the West Bank to declare their independence.

The Soviet Union, which nurtured the old czarist ambitions to get a toe into the Mediterranean, was only too happy to join in an unholy alliance by supplying the arms and experts. While billions were spent to create a military machine, the size of which had never been seen in this part of the world, the Egyptian peasant and laborer continued to live an impoverished existence.

Oil-fat Gulf states poured billions into Egyptian, Syrian and Iraqi arms. As for the Palestinian refugees, there was a lot of breast beating in the Arab press and at the United Nations, but the oil states' contributions to them were paltry. The refugees were left as wards of the world, with America the principal source of funds for their care and feeding. Had the Arabs spent a fraction of what they spent for arms on resettlement of these people, there would have been no Palestinian problem. But Nasser didn't want that.

The attitude of the Arab world was reflected in *Al-Akhbar*, the official Egyptian newspaper, when it stated, "Arab unity will serve as a hangman's rope for Israel." This sentiment was echoed and re-echoed by every Arab head of state, publication, radio and TV without exception.

The Israeli response was simple: "When Hitler said he was going to exterminate the Jews, no one believed him. When Nasser says it now, we believe him."

The first deadly move came from Syria, which attempted to divert and cut off the principal source of Israel's water supply. Israel put this move down but by 1966 Syria was constantly and indiscriminately cannonading Israeli settlements in the Galilee from the Golan Heights. Assad, who was then Syrian Defense Minister, declared, "We will drench this land with your blood, we will throw you into the sea."

By May 1967 Nasser felt he had the military strength and the allies for a go at Israel. He had become enamored of this Russian military hardware and the ability of his troops to use it in training exercises.

At the last minute King Hussein, the ruler of Jordan, was summoned to Cairo to put the icing on the cake. Like his grandfather Abdullah, he was ramrodded into a last-minute alliance. With Hussein's signature on a "mutual defense pact," Nasser now had a second front against the Israelis.

The Iraqis agreed to attack from Lebanon and in addition Nasser had at his disposal troops from Saudi Arabia, Kuwait and Algeria to go along with the principal armies of Egypt, Jordan and Syria. As these forces deployed, a hangman's noose had been placed around Israel's neck.

A hundred thousand Egyptian troops in seven divisions with a thousand tanks and five hundred pieces of heavy artillery, the greatest Arab military force ever assembled in the Sinai, crossed into the buffer zone and moved toward Israel's borders.

On May 16, 1967, Nasser ordered the United Nations Emergency Forces to clear out of the buffer zone and also take leave of Sharm el Sheik. They obeyed and immediately whimpered off as the world community went into a confused rhetoric. After taking over Sharm el Sheik, Nasser closed the Strait of Tiran on May 22 and blockaded Israeli shipping, an overt act of war. Israel continued to seek avenues of peaceful settlement but at the same time she was forced to mobilize her reserves, a costly operation during which all normal life and business in the country ground to a halt.

By early June, Nasser felt he was ready. His last words on the subject were "We intend to open a general assault against Israel. This will be total war. Our basic aim is the destruction of Israel." This was followed by the issuance of a general order by the Egyptian commander in the Sinai, General Murtagi, to wage a war of destruction.

What could be clearer?

Israel hit first. What happened when Israel made her pre-emptive strike must go down in military annals as among the most perfectly executed battle plans in history. Kicked off by a brilliantly conceived air strike, Israel had all but demolished the Egyptian Air Force within hours. Although outnumbered, outtanked and outgunned on every front, Israel went onto an offensive that flattened the combined Arab armies in six days in a masterpiece of military achievement.

In the early hours of the fighting, as news of the disaster reached Nasser's ears, he was on the phone to King Hussein in Amman, lying in his teeth about Egyptian "victories" and exhorting Hussein to get the Arab Legion into battle.

The Israeli Prime Minister, Levi Eshkol, sent a message to Hussein stating that Israel would not attack Jordan if Jordan stayed out of the conflict.

JUNE 5, 1967

Israel's pleas to Hussein to hold his fire were answered loudly and clearly as Jordanian artillery vomited all along the torturous and vulnerable border with Israel. The citizens of West Jerusalem found their morning screamingly punctuated by the wail of sirens and the crashing of Arab shells which slammed indiscriminately into non-military objects all over the city such as the Israel Museum. An Arab Legion brigade moved up to the Hill of Evil Counsel and, after a few choice words with the United Nations people, sent them packing.

By one of those incongruous historical coincidences the commander of Israel's Central Command, which included Jerusalem, was Uzi Narkiss, who, two decades earlier had been the last of the Palmach fighters to leave the Old City.

By midday the Israeli high command was aware that the Jordanians were not putting on a little song and dance exercise to appease Arab unity but were full partners in the war.

In Jerusalem the Arab Legion's taking of the U.N. headquarters posed an immediate threat from the south. A hastily assembled reservist unit, made up mostly of older men of the Jerusalem Brigade, immediately went into an attack and succeeded in throwing the Jordanians off the Hill of Evil Counsel.

At the same time an armored unit which carried the name of the old Judean Palmach, the Har El Brigade, was rushed up from the coast with orders to seize the three vital ridges north of the city. The Legion's positions on these ridges were ponderously fortified with reinforced concrete bunkers protected by minefields and barbed wire. The Har El under Uri Ben Ari found, as the Romans had, that neither chariot nor tank were particularly creatures of the hills and operated in that terrain with great difficulty. All the best mine-clearing equipment was in the Sinai. While fire from Israel's tanks tried to pin down the Legion in their bunkers, sappers and infantry cleared paths by hand, a messy business. Once the lanes were opened, the tanks lumbered in and by the end of the first night Jordanian positions on the ridges were collapsing.

A brigade of paratroopers under the command of Mordechai Gur, later to be chief of staff during the Entebbe rescue operation, had been kept on hold at an airfield down on the plains, scheduled for a drop into the Sinai to help in the capture of El Arish. Things were going well in the south, so the decision was made to shift the paratroopers to Jerusalem. By the end of the first night they were already moving toward the most heavily fortified Arab positions in the city, a thick defensive belt which protected the northern and most vulnerable side of the Old City.

Entering the fight late at night, the paratroopers had before them a roll call of the 1948 battles at the thickly entrenched Police Training School, Ammunition Hill, the American Colony, the Sheikh Jarrah Quarter and the Rockefeller Museum. This shield had to be penetrated if the Israelis were to get at the vulnerable northern walls of the Old City. The Arabs always did their best fighting from fixed defensive positions and collapsing this area would constitute some of the bitterest fighting of the war.

JUNE 6, 1967

Morning found Uri Ben Ari's armored brigade in complete control of the northern ridges with the fall of Nebi Samuel, that historic and lamented hill within sight of the city. His people were astride the Ramallah road leading north and cutting off reinforcements from that direction. Ben Ari quickly moved some of his units to make a swing around the back of the city to cut off the Jericho Road and get them into position to blow the bridges over the Jordan River.

On the southern side of the city, the Jerusalem Brigade consolidated their holding on the Hill of Evil Counsel, captured an Arab village and linked up with Kibbutz Ramat Rachel and sat astride the Bethlehem Road.

These Israeli maneuvers north, south and east of the city had effectively cut off the possibility of Jordanian reinforcements. The noose was now on the hangman's head.

With the Egyptian Air Force destroyed on the ground, the Israelis shifted their own air power to pick up selected targets as they expanded operations into the West Bank. Among the key positions to fall to Israel was the Latrun police fort, a sweet victory after a twenty-year hangover of the '48 war.

To Motta Gur's three battalions of paratroopers fell the unenviable task of crossing the Jerusalem armistice line and sweeping the fortified northern Arab suburbs. They had to cross into the teeth of magnificently prepared defenses: a perimeter which had a wide and devastating

field of fire, a maze of bunkers and trenches laced with a
blizzard of land mines and cascades of thick rusty belts of
barbed wire.

The assignment of taking the Police Training School and
Ammunition Hill fell to the northernmost of the paratroop
battalions. The center battalion was to move through the
Mandelbaum Gate and against the Sheikh Jarrah Quarter
where every housetop and alleyway was a defended
position. The southernmost battalion also had a street
fight on hand with their line running from the American
Colony to the Old City walls.

No one had seriously expected Jordan to attack, so
plans for East Jerusalem were largely conceived on the
spot. The paratroopers were not familiar with either the
terrain or the fortifications they would face. The plan for
the northern Arab suburbs was plain old bread-and-butter,
pay-as-you-learn, infantry work. Victory or defeat would
depend on the ingenuity of smaller units, leadership,
co-ordination and determination.

At two o'clock in the morning the paratroop brigade
crossed the armistice line toward East Jerusalem. Casualties were immediate and heavy as the Legion perimeter
laid down a torrid fire. As the northern battalion inched
in, it became involved in a hand-to-hand piece of trench
warfare. Israeli bangalores and other charges opened the
barbed wire reluctantly while deadly land mines killed
and crippled dozens of attackers.

Hour after hour throughout the night the paratroopers
battered in, having to take every post and position by
hand. With the coming of dawn, Israeli armor rushed up
to offer artillery support. Bloodied and decimated, the
northern battalion broke through Ammunition Hill and
the Police School by 0700. One company had but four
men still fighting.

In the center of the line, the middle battalion effected a
breakthrough that gave them the entire Sheikh Jarrah
Quarter by 1000. Just about the same time the southern
battalion had captured the pivotal position at the American Colony and wheeled south to the Rockefeller Museum.
Noon found the northern suburbs of Arab Jerusalem
fallen, with tanks on Suleiman Road opposite the Old City
walls.

Although the heart of the Jordanian defenses had been

smashed by this sheer-guts assault, the Legion still held the Old City and an eastern ridge that ran from the Church of the Ascension on the Mount of Olives to the Augusta Victoria complex. A small Israeli unit held out on Scopus waiting for relief.

The command decided the paratroops were too exhausted to try to link up with the Scopus enclave or attack the Mount of Olives, so the day was spent mopping up, consolidating and reorganizing. Uri Ben Ari's Har El Brigade was already moving north toward Ramallah.

South of the city the Jerusalem Brigade captured the village of Abu Tor just below Mount Zion in what turned out to be another hand-to-hand, house-to-house struggle.

Nightfall of the second day found the paratroop brigade rested and regrouped. Under cover of night they deployed at the bottom of the slopes of Scopus and Olives.

JUNE 7, 1967

For the Jewish people it was the twenty-eighth day of the month of Iyar of the year 5727.

The largest remaining obstacle other than the Old City was the Legion's position at the Augusta Victoria, which offered a clear view down on the Temple Mount and the Dome of the Rock. The paratroopers' dawn assault was brazen and direct with no fancy maneuvering. They came straight up the hill into Jordanian volleys while sniper fire poured at their backs from the Old City. For the first time in the battle, the Israelis had the luxury of being able to single out a target and call in the air force, which streaked out of the skies with the coming of daylight. Coupled with artillery fire, the paratroopers went to work.

Having witnessed their bulwarks at Ammunition Hill crushed in a single night's fury, the Arab Legion had little stomach left. The Augusta Victoria was in Israeli hands within a few hours. A second battalion linked up with Scopus and attacked along the hogback of the ridge and cleared the entire Mount of Olives of the enemy. The vista along the ridge was stunning and taunting in the mid-morning light. Below them was the Old City, to the east the Dead Sea. Ezer Weizman, chief of operations and author of the air strike, and Moshe Dayan, Minister of Defense, had rushed up to Jerusalem and streaked past the newly captured Sheikh Jarrah Quarter, still subject to occasional sniper fire, and up to the Mount of Olives to join Uzi Narkiss for a grandstand view of the assault on the Old City. The tension became excruciating, for within their grasp was one of the greatest Jewish military victories in six thousand years.

While two of the paratroop battalions had smashed their way up to the ridges, the third was deployed in a line from the Rockefeller Museum along Suleiman Road and probed at Herod's Gate. As the final phase of the battle opened with firing to and from the wall, the paratroopers on Olives and Scopus left a small security force and shifted down to the finale against the Old City.

The Jews knew they had to be tenderly careful of how they attacked this, the most sacred square mile of soil on earth. Any damage to the Dome of the Rock or the Church of the Holy Sepulchre would have made the Jewish people accursed for centuries, although, through the ages, the Moslems and Christians had shown poor little respect for one another's holy sites, and none whatsoever for sacred Jewish places.

An arc of fire poured into Jordanian positions on the wall running from Herod's Gate around to the Lions' Gate. Although the Lions' Gate was on the eastern side of the city and could be entered only by negotiating a fairly steep road with tight walls binding it on either side, a direct hit from a tank blew the gate off its hinges and changed the course of events.

Up on Scopus, Motta Gur, the paratroop commander, was in full view of everything from his post at the Intercontinental Hotel. When he saw the Lions' Gate blown, he leaped into his half-track and tore down from Olives, exhorting his driver, and his driver responded with a speed and recklessness that earmark the Israeli driver. Gur reached the opening first, squeezing past a burning bus and driving right over the top of the fallen gate. As he burst onto the Via Dolorosa, his three battalions poured in after him and fanned out to quell what was to be nothing more than a whisper of resistance.

A few moments before ten o'clock, Mordechai Gur

stood before the Western Wall and flashed the magic word up to Dayan, Narkiss and Weizman and the world, "The Temple Mount is ours!"

The paratroopers, who had been the epitome of professionalism for nearly three solid days without rest, were suddenly consumed in a wave of emotionalism. They flung themselves against the Western Wall weeping aloud and without shame and they prayed incoherently and kissed the stones. They cried long and they cried hard, for within each of them was the spirit of millions of Jews who had died by abuse during seventeen centuries of pain.

The rest of the campaign saw the Jerusalem Brigade strike south, taking Bethlehem, the old Etzion Bloc and Hebron. Jericho fell to the Har El Brigade and the Jordan River bridges were blown to cut off the East and West Banks. At Nablus, Uri Ben Ari's people were joined by Daddo Elazar's troops coming down from the north, and with the capture of Nablus the entire West Bank was in Israeli hands.

The amen of the Six-Day War came as an afterthought. Daddo was able to convince the high command at the last moment that the troops of his Northern Command could take the Golan Heights. Their forward positions were a monument to defensive planning, yet they were cracked in hours. The Syrians were thrown off the Golan and the settlements below were free from artillery harassment for the first time in two decades.

Needless to say, the Arab states began a choir of howls for a truce.

A swell of humanity from around the country and around the world converged on reunited Jerusalem. The plaza before the Western Wall became a mass of exalted, emotional people twenty-four hours a day. Throughout the land a song was heard, a song that had been presented at a festival only a few days before the war's outbreak. It was called "Jerusalem of Gold," and it would become a second national anthem. The incredible high of the moment was soon to be tempered with a realization that the struggle with the Arabs would continue and continue. But for the moment no joy had ever been like it.

ARABS AND JEWS

The euphoria that resounded in a billion reprises of "Jerusalem of Gold" dimmed only too soon, as the sounds of cannon fire were to be heard again. Israel's feat in the Six-Day War ranked among history's military epics. Most of the world rejoiced too.

As the shattered remnants of Nasser's army crawled back over the canal, Nasser offered to resign. In one of those orchestrated demonstrations that the Arabs regularly employ to prove solidarity, millions of people in Cairo took to the streets to demand that their revered leader, who had plunged them into two disasters, remain as the head of state. As the scenario called for, the people's outpouring "convinced" Nasser to remain. He died a few years later, an embittered man embalmed in his own hatred.

The Soviets, mortified once more by the defeat of Russian weaponry and training, still dreamed of breaking through to the West's sources of oil and were determined to keep their foothold in Arab lands. Their presence was more important than the loss of a few billion dollars in tanks and planes and the Arab arsenals were quickly replenished.

What resulted was the "War of Attrition," a continuing exchange of fire, raids and escalating unpleasantries between the two sides. Most of the action took place along the Suez Canal.

The Israelis constructed a series of observation bunkers along the canal mistakenly called the Bar-Lev Line, named after the chief of staff at the time. These bunkers were never intended to halt an attack, only to absorb the first shocks to give the main Israeli forces farther back in the Sinai time to get into action. Often the bunkers were manned by reservists.

The daily exchanges of fire along the canal drew Israeli casualties but they nearly wrecked the fragile Egyptian economy. The canal cities of Ismailia and Suez were pounded silly. Many of the inhabitants gave up and left, the oil refineries were blown up, Soviet radar equipment was seized on a raid, the canal remained closed to shipping, and on one occasion six Russian-piloted MIGS were shot down by the Israelis.

Nasser's death brought to power Anwar Sadat, a man few believed would last. A cease fire went into effect in 1970 but Egypt, Russia and Syria went into deep and meticulous planning for the next round, practicing constantly and perfecting bridging equipment. The planners knew they could never match the Israelis in the air, so in order to protect their armor and the battlefield a system of mobile, interlocking missiles were perfected to move right along with the action.

T he fourth war began on Yom Kippur of 1973, with the Arab forces achieving a stunning surprise on the holiest of Jewish days. Attacking with five divisions crossing the canal at ten places along a hundred-mile front, the Egyptians caught the Israelis unmobilized. They stormed over the canal, overran the Bar-Lev Line and penetrated several miles into the Sinai.

On the Golan Heights, the Syrians struck with two columns of five hundred tanks each closely protected by the mobile missiles. The Israelis did manage to knock out many of the missiles but paid a terrible toll in aircraft. Their undermanned units caught the brunt of an attack which saw the Syrians come perilously close to a break-through which would have sent them pouring down into the Galilee. Another prong of five hundred tanks backed up by a thousand artillery pieces hammered away to split the thin Israel line. It turned into a furious eyeball-to-eye-ball battle, point-blank, savage as combat can be envisioned. In the end, the Israelis held, but only by a micro-scopic thread, until enough Russian missiles had been cleared to give the Israel Air Force room to operate and time for the reserves to get into battle.

The Egyptian advance into the Sinai faltered after its initial success but the fighting was to remain bloody. The tide swung Israel's way when their brilliant armored commander, Arik Sharon, found a hole between Egyptian

316 *Jill and Leon Uris*

units, exploited it and made a spectacular crossing of the
canal to the Egyptian side. The Egyptian Third Army was
suddenly enveloped, trapped and in danger of total disin-
tegration as the Israelis captured Suez City, cutting off
their retreat. The Israeli beachhead widened and the road
to Damascus was opened on the one front and the road to
Cairo on the other. The Arabs screamed, "Truce!" Loudest
of the table pounders were the Russians, whose years of
planning had gone for naught and whose prestige was
now bent on saving the Egyptian Third Army.

Officially the Yom Kippur War was declared a draw. The
fact was that both sides had battered each other into
exhaustion. Certainly the Egyptian Third Army would not
have survived, except piecemeal. Israel had the superior
strategic position but whether she could have mounted a
knockout counteroffensive on both fronts is conjectural.

The Yom Kippur War sobered the nation terribly. In
addition to several thousand casualties the cost was
staggering. The performance of the Arabs in the initial
days shook up Israel's notions of invincibility. Worse, it
meant Israel would have to continue living under the
pressures of their astronomical military bill and have no
peace in sight. It also meant the Arabs could continue to
engage in these limited and draining wars and call for a
truce at their convenience. No matter how Israel won on
the field, the nation would never be able to occupy Egypt
or Syria or compel a peace treaty.

If there was a winner, it was Sadat. He was able to
convert his modest initial success into a fantasy of monumental victory, thus "proving" the Arabs had won back
their self-respect and some of their sacred soil. Machismo
in battle is all-important to an Arab male. Now, having
"beaten" the Israelis, Sadat was able to talk on an equal
footing.

The entire exercise was a sick kind of game but it gives
a tremendous clue to the Arab character. Losing the war
and taking devastating losses in men and equipment were
not nearly so important as saving face, a value they place
at the top of the list, and so their "victory" was blown up
out of all proportion.

Sadat alone among the Arab leadership fostered no
further illusions about defeating Israel militarily. Egypt,
the largest and strongest of the Arab nations, had all but

destroyed itself in a quarter of a century of engaging in a fight generated by some kind of Islamic mental aberration. Egypt never had a real quarrel with the Jews, Zionism or Israel, which never posed a threat of any kind to Egypt's existence. Yet they had thrown themselves into four wars in an infantile game of macho and religious bravado with absolutely nothing to gain.

Egypt now teetered on the verge of bankruptcy. Her main sources of revenue, the canal and the Sinai oil fields, were lost. Her cities along the canal were wrecked. She was becoming more and more indebted to the Soviet Union, which had used her as a pawn for Russian ambitions. Sadat decided he could get what he wanted in other ways. He rid himself of the Russians and unilaterally canceled Egypt's debts of billions to them. Using the peace process, he was eminently successful, regaining his oil fields, opening the canal and winning back much of the Sinai without firing a shot.

Sadat's great miscalculation was his belief that he could negotiate on behalf of the whole Arab world. He found himself completely abandoned. The reason was basic. The fate of the Palestinians was not and never has been the central issue. Islam is incapable of making an accommodation for co-existence with anyone, much less the Jews. The only issue has been and still is the destruction of Israel. Looking at the entire range of Arab history, peace has never been a value in the Arab world.

THE ASSASSINS

The origin of the terrifying word "assassination" stems from a Moslem sect out of Syria called the Assassins who operated between the eleventh and thirteenth centuries. Their creed was that it was a sacred religious duty to murder one's political opposition. The network of Assassins worked through clandestine cells throughout the Fertile Crescent and murdered hundreds of political enemies. Before they struck down an opponent, they doped up on hashish to give them dutch courage and at the same time a vision of heaven. Unfortunately, the Assassins were not unique or a passing oddity, but represented a mainstream of behavior that has continued unabated in the Arab society.

Sir John Bagot Glubb, certainly no devotee of Zionism, makes an interesting observation in his autobiography, *A Soldier with the Arabs*. After the assassination of his boss, King Abdullah, a Cairo newspaper published a list of Arab public men who had been assassinated between the years 1946 and 1951. The list included two kings, one president, four prime ministers, one military commander-in-chief, a leader of the Muslim Brotherhood, a ranking sheikh, a cabinet minister, several police chiefs and judges as well as innumerable unsuccessful attempts made on other Arab leaders.

Little has changed in the way business is done. There has never been an Arab government since the inception of Arab nations that has not been an autocracy. Nothing resembling a democracy has existed or ever will exist in the Arab world.

The PLO, created by the Arab governments for the assassination of the state of Israel, has proved a worthy successor to the ancient Assassins, but with a twist. It has gained the fear and recognition of much of the Western world.

The Arab world has contributed almost nothing in the way of advancement for the human race for a thousand years. Work is not an Arab ethic. The Arab ideal is centered around the bedouin, the man who sleeps beneath the stars and epitomizes the free spirit. It is far more heroic in the bedouin life style to steal from one's neighbors, to raid and to avenge family honor than to bend one's back in toil. The city dweller and the peasant are looked down upon as people of a lower order. Many of the "real Arabs" of the Arabian Peninsula don't even consider the Egyptians to be true Arabs.

The lack of industriousness coupled with a reactionary religion has made this a sterile part of the world which would scarcely be heard from except for its oil reserves. There is centuries-old dull repetition in their architecture, music, poetry and a lack of initiative that shows an inability to get out of the mire of the past. Technology confounds them and, unable to cope with a modern society, they sink deeper into Islamic fundamentalism, which tells them to live in the past and hate the people who are bringing the future into their part of the world.

Islam, as practiced for the internal peace of the Moslems, is almost a billion strong. The Arabs are certainly entitled to live by their own values and standards and practice their own religion. The problem has come when they have left their own borders to live among the rest of the world's peoples.

T he question is not how Islam gets along with itself but how it gets along with the rest of mankind and the answer has been: Not very well. Their ideas of justice, democracy and equality are antipathetic to Western values. Their major gifts to the civilization of this century have been the introduction of international terrorism and an ongoing attempt to gain financial control of the planet for the corrupt purpose of lining the pockets of a few thousand feudal princes and businessmen.

The basic principle of modern terrorism is the indiscriminate murder of innocent people. In bringing their ancient ways out of the desert, the Arabs have turned Western Europe into a shooting gallery.

We are admonished to forget right and wrong. The only kingdom that runs on righteousness is the kingdom of heaven; the kingdoms of the earth run on oil. Our technology is so dependent on oil that the morality we have built for thousands of years is fast being eroded by Arab blackmail. It takes no genius to read the simple facts that tell us that, without Arab oil, the technology of the West may not survive. We have glutted ourselves into a position of extreme vulnerability and we now have to deal with the past masters of the art of extortion and blackmail. The West is quickly conceding what little is left of its conscience to assure its flow of oil. The bottom line of European thinking is that the Jews are expendable but oil isn't.

If we have learned one lesson from the past, we ought to know that tyrants cannot be appeased. Yet the PLO has gotten away with atrocity after atrocity without so much as a slap on the wrist and through the subtle skills of blackmail this gang of killers has been upgraded into respectability.

There is some truth to the PLO's claim to legitimacy in representing the Palestinian people. It is a large organization with banks, business enterprises, schools and hospitals. The Mafia has also purchased respectability but, as in the PLO, the inner circle is run by gangsters. They have terrified and bullied the world by bloodletting on city streets, hijackings, kidnapings, mail bombings, and they carry on innumerable underworld operations such as the hashish trade. Terrorism feeds and breeds on moral cowardice and the PLO has been able to make its dastardly behavior a permanent new fixture of Western life. As its operations get bolder and with no one to stop it, it has expanded terrorism so that it infects the bloodstream of democracies and endangers them everywhere.

At the same time Arab oil and financial interests have gotten the none too subtle message across to timid Western leaders and is using the West to impose a unilateral settlement on Israel that would be the first step in that nation's destruction. We are fools to think that the Arab leaders will not continue to try to dictate the foreign policy of the Western nations on other matters by holding them hostage to their oil. If the net result becomes a Russian-supported PLO state established on the West Bank with Europe's coercion, it would permanently legitimize blackmail and terrorism and only whet the appetites of the intimidators.

As the PLO spits in the faces of those who grovel before it, its arts of terrorism are openly sponsored by the Soviet Union and have now expanded into Western Europe, the Caribbean and Central and Latin America. Even as the PLO publicly berates the United States as the world's Satan, *Time*, the *Christian Science Monitor* and the Washington *Post* have adopted a policy of glorification of the terrorist as some sort of freedom fighter and one of the world's magnificent creatures.

Through the joint use of cunning and thuggery the Arabs have managed to extort a good part of the nations of the world into joining their vendetta against Israel. At the same time the leaders of the PLO must be laughing their socks off, for they have never renounced the use of terrorism, they have refused to join the peace process or to change their declared sacred goal of destroying the Jewish state.

The ultimate irony of all this is that most of the Arab states despise the PLO. The organization has been thrown out of Jordan, Egypt and even Libya. Its members are kept under tight control in Iraq and Syria. They have wrecked Lebanon, where more Arabs have killed their brother Arabs than had Israel in four wars. They strike fear into the Saudis and oil sheikdoms via a large Palestinian work force.

Continuing to yield to Arab blackmail will only encourage an expansion of PLO operations until its tentacles have reached into every festering corner of the world. Anyone who believes that the United States is immune to PLO terrorism, is living in a fool's paradise.

THE DOUBLE STANDARD TANGO

No one can deny that the Palestinian Arab, particularly the peasant, has a deep love for his native soil. Nor can anyone deny that the Palestinian people have legitimate human rights. But the Palestinian refugee problem has been blown out of all proportion by a mentality that glorifies the assassin.

In the first instance, the refugee problem was largely initiated and deliberately perpetuated by the leaders of the Arab world. It has been continued by people who don't have the dignity to get up and better their own living conditions but are satisfied to live off the scrapings of charity and whose main thrust is the perpetuation of hatred.

In the second instance, the Palestinian people, who consider themselves elite among the Arabs, have never had the ambition to rule themselves. "Self-rule" and "legitimate rights" are jazzy catch phrases that are hollow drums, but if you bang an empty barrel it can make a lot of noise. One would be led to believe that the Palestinian has a tradition of democracy which has been ripped away from him and that his fight for freedom is the principal cause of man's improvement in this century.

Since World War II there have been over a hundred million refugees. Today, over a million refugees live on the brink of starvation in Africa. The tragedy of Ethiopia and Somalia scarcely gets an inch of news space. A million refugees, more than twice the original number of Palestinians, have fled Afghanistan and are living in squalor in Pakistan. The second half of this century continues to be filled with terrible testimonies to man's inhumanity to man: the genocide of Cambodia and Nigeria's Ibo tribe and the boat peoples of Vietnam and Cuba.

Other people have diasporas beside the Palestinians. The Jews invented the diaspora. Millions of Irish were forced to leave their homelands and so were more millions of Chinese, Italians, French, Greeks, Russians. The world has been in constant upheaval because people have been driven out by wars, political circumstance and privation. Yet if we are readers of such terrorist endorsements as the *Christian Science Monitor* we are led to believe that the Palestinians present the greatest cause for freedom, justice and human dignity since the planet was formed. Nothing could be farther from the truth. When the PLO tell us of forming a "secular democratic state" in the West Bank they speak hogwash. They don't and never will have the slightest notion of how a democracy operates. Allowing these people to form and operate a cancer state shows a world ready to use ostrich tactics of pretending not to see and hoping it will all go away. The moment such a state comes into existence, the Middle East, the West and the world will be in serious danger.

No military occupation has ever been known for its benevolence but some are better than others. Be assured that it is better to be an Arab under Israeli rule than the other way around. Since Israel assumed military governorship over the West Bank and Gaza, they have instituted an open-bridges policy to allow the Palestinian Arab complete freedom to travel into the Arab world. The Palestinian is free to get an education in Cairo or Damascus. By contrast, the Jordanians wouldn't even allow Israeli Arabs to cross the Mandelbaum Gate and pray at the Al Aksa Mosque.

Since 1967 Israel has done away with many of the refugee camps by providing new housing and jobs. It should be noted that the United Nations relief people, in order to sustain an unneeded bureaucracy, retain directorship of many totally abandoned camps so they may continue to receive funding.

In places like Gaza, where every man who wants a job can work at decent wages and under decent conditions, the United Nations still passes out monthly rations although they have not been needed for a decade. Nor has the U.N. been able to keep an accurate count of the number of refugees still in the camps. Palestinians who have built new homes or have gone to other parts of the world still retain a refugee camp address so as to remain eligible to collect handouts. There is one classic case of three brothers, who have built a half-million-dollar complex of three villas, driving up to the refugee camp in a Mercedes each month to get their rations.

Education in the occupied territories is completely run by West Bank Arabs who use the Jordanian system and textbooks. A new Arab university has opened despite the fact it is a hotbed for PLO recruiting.

The courts are run by West Bank and Gaza Arab judges who handle all legal problems except security and they use the Jordanian legal system. As a matter of special interest, the West Bank courts are bogged down trying to straighten out landownership. It appears that some Arabs living overseas have sold their sacred soil up to a dozen times to a dozen different parties.

The West Bank and Gaza Arab has enjoyed the best economic conditions as well as the best medical care, social benefits and working conditions of any time in Palestine's history.

The greatest irony is that the Arab governments, all of them and without exception, are demanding political freedom for the Palestinians that they don't give their own people. If the same freedom of expression and dissent the Israelis permit were tried out in Saudi Arabia, Syria or Iraq, the dissident would be dead, in prison or have his tongue cut out.

The Saudis in particular have led the choir of bleaters for the return of East Jerusalem and their holy places, yet no Arab monarch set foot on the Haram esh Sharif or prayed at the Al Aksa Mosque during the nineteen years of Jordanian control.

In its weekly love sonnet to the PLO, *Time* magazine never fails to select the most gruesome story and photographs to illustrate Israeli tyranny. While it is pitiful to see an Arab mayor with two stumps for legs which have been blown away by a car bomb, this is exactly what the Israeli people have had to endure for four decades on a daily basis without respite. I recall one particular day when the headlines screamed out about the Israeli military who had tear-gassed some Arab school children. There was scarcely a mention that on the same day in Lebanon six hundred Arabs had been butchered by each other.

It has been, and is, the double standard tango.

Suppose, for example, it had been Jewish terrorists who had been running amuck in Europe, hijacking planes, holding embassies hostage, fostering terrorist groups, conducting massacres in public airports and at sports events. Be assured the Europeans would not have turned the other cheek as they have done with the PLO.

Suppose, for example, it had been Israel instead of the PLO who refused to talk peace for over thirty years and suppose the Jews had a covenant to exterminate the Arab people . . . as the PLO has against the Jewish people.

Suppose, for example, Arab armies were overrunning Israel and Israel called for a truce. Does anyone of normal mentality believe the Arab armies could have been stopped?

Suppose, for example, Jordan had captured West Jerusalem. Does anyone really believe Jordan would have agreed to a divided city or would Jordan have thrown the Jews out?

When Israel reunited Jerusalem in 1967, Jews had been denied access to the Western Wall for nineteen years. Suppose, for example, that Israel denied the Arabs the right to worship in the Al Aksa Mosque.

Suppose, for example, when the Arabs were using the Haram esh Sharif as a military post the Israelis had opened artillery fire on it! Suppose, for example, Israel had dynamited to the ground the Dome of the Rock as the Jordanians dynamited the Hurva Synagogue.

When the city was reunited, Israel confirmed not only the total and deliberate destruction of the Jewish Quarter of the Old City but desecration of the ancient graveyard on the Mount of Olives. Gravestones had been torn up and used as building blocks in Jordanian constructions, including an Arab Legion barracks.

The late Pope Paul and the Vatican gave the Jews weekly advice on how immoral it was to make reprisals against the PLO, which was murdering their citizens. The same Vatican kept a sterile silence over the attempted genocide of the Christian population of Lebanon.

While the Islamic world has harangued tiny Israel for four decades, it has kept a discreet posture toward the Soviet invasion and destruction of Moslem Afghanistan. It is one thing to pick on a few Jews and another thing to tell the Soviet Union where to go.

To divide this city again would be the most heinous crime the world could perpetrate. Jerusalem has been honored with a reverence, dignity and greatness where none existed before. Centuries of Arab neglect culminated in a broken promise in which the Arabs completely proved they have no respect for another's religion. So long as the Jews rule this city, everyone's holy sites will be protected and respected and no one will be barred from worship.

Yet the only kingdom of right is the kingdom of heaven; the kingdoms of the earth run on oil. What will be the final price for that oil? Our morality? Our freedom to conduct our own affairs without outside extortion? We had better think about it. This isn't the story of New York, Paris or London. This is the holy city. Christian nations which have refused to account for some of their barbaric behavior to the Jewish people in this century are quick to rush to judgment of the Jewish nation in order to protect their oil supplies.

But in the end the West can only give so much of itself away. If there is a world of conscience left, it is a prisoner of Auschwitz just as the Jews were its victims. Once the West lowers its flag of humane standards, it has sealed its own fate and demise as well.

Teddy and Jerusalem of Gold

T he municipal minibus was filled with American report-
ers awaiting the tour guide. In a few minutes a fatherly-
looking, pudgy, sixtyish man dressed in the Israeli manner,
without tie or jacket, took the seat next to the driver,
swung the microphone around and, as the bus pulled out,
began his spiel.

Population? Approaching a half million with a hundred
thousand Arabs.

A Film Institute is under way with the special job of
preserving whatever Jewish history there is on film. We
have just recently completed a Music Center with an
ultramodern recording studio and the latest TV remote
unit, the kind used as a monitor at American football
games. In the studio we videotape master classes and
send them around the country. Artur Rubinstein will be
teaching a class later this month. You just missed Alexander Schneider. He was wonderful working with the
Beersheba Symphony. It is mostly made up of Russian
immigrants. They are excellent technical musicians but,
like everything the Russians do in art, they are sterile.
Sasha was trying to get them to put a little soul into their
music.

What else is new? Liberty Bell Park will be dedicated on
the fourth of July. The park is part of our master plan that
calls for greenery to break up the monologue of stone.
When enough trees are planted, we can work to keep the
parks green all year round. You will see the green belt we
have planted around the base of the Old City walls. No,

projects never stop. A good part of the development comes from donations to the Jerusalem Foundation. Jerusalem is the only Jewish capital and all Jews have a special love for the place. The results of their donations are everywhere: Hadassah, the Knesset, parks, museums. I have arranged to have a bus take you around to see the night illuminations. We have lit the walls of the Old City as well as a number of ancient sites. In West Jerusalem the principal buildings of art and government are lit. It's spectacular.

Are you going to retain two university campuses? For certain. The crown of Mount Scopus has been lowered several yards to form a plateau. A hundred-million-dollar development is well under way.

A stadium is on the boards but it has been a struggle. The Orthodox are very much against it, putting up cries of "Hellenism," but Jerusalem sports fans are no less excitable than those in Glasgow or Madrid and we'll eventually get it built. Israel fields world-class basketball and soccer teams, the guide adds proudly, and tennis is not far behind.

We see a lot of new hotels going up. There were a half million Christian pilgrims last year as well as two hundred thousand from Moslem countries. Of course, we permit Arabs from anywhere to enter Israel. Some of our beaches have become quite popular Arab resorts, especially with the troubles in Lebanon.

We also have a lot of new permanent residents, immigrants from affluent cultures as well as impoverished ones. We have hundreds coming in from America, Scandinavia, South Africa. They've come to live here for spiritual reasons but they insist on first-class housing. Otherwise, many people around Israel want to live in Jerusalem. It's not only caused a housing shortage but we have a problem with space. We've stretched the city and every time we do it always brings protests from the Arabs. That and trying to retain the beauty have been difficult.

The tour guide rattles off a list of present and upcoming events in response to a question. Zubin Mehta, the permanent conductor of the Israel Philharmonic, will be giving a pair of concerts. A Romanian opera group is in town.

String quartets, recitals, special films, a rock concert are scheduled. A multi-screened video show at the Citadel shouldn't be missed. A new play in Hebrew is opening at the Jerusalem Theater with the national ballet company coming in afterward. Yes, there is a bit of night life, small group theaters and some acts at the Khan, a converted Turkish inn. The Convention Hall is preparing for an international book fair and with the holidays there will be dozens of special events for Christian pilgrims; a Lutheran choir from Germany will be doing excerpts from "The Messiah" and an international organist will be giving a recital at the YMCA. Next month the events include the annual march up to Jerusalem of thousands of people in dozens of organizations. There are several scientific seminars at the Van Leer Institute. And there is always a lot of activity around the Knesset. This is the nation's capital. As an afterthought the tour guide needlessly adds that no city of this size in the world has as much going on.

The minibus has swung past the old Montefiore windmill, a landmark that was built in the last century when the Jews ventured out of the Old City. The original Mishkenot Sha'Ananim building has been converted into lovely apartments by the Levitt Foundation. Invitations to use one of the ten accommodations is made by committee. Special invitations are given to writers, musicians, artists and photographers to come and discover the city and just to meditate.

Who is there now? Sara Davidson, a fine American writer, and Saul Bellow, whom I think you know. Isaac Stern is a regular. He's done as much for the culture of the city as anyone. Jill and Leon Uris are working on a Jerusalem book, although Uris has a few unkind observations about the place. Next week Claude Frank and Lilly Kallir, the husband and wife concert pianists, will be in to give a recital.

They pull to a stop before the Paley Art Center for Youth near the Rockefeller Museum built by the renowned

Israeli architect, Moshe Safdie, of Habitat fame, who has put an indelible stamp on the new Jerusalem. A roomful of Jewish and Arab children are receiving an archaeological slide show about their city.

No, the tour guide says, this isn't typical. Outside of business contacts and a few formal and artistic events, the Arab and Jewish communities have little social contact nor the desire for it. We have individual Arab friends and co-workers but we don't push people together artificially. Jerusalem is not a melting pot, it is a mosaic. The Arabs and Jews have entirely different needs and we respect the differences. Take the matter of housing. The Arab simply cannot function in a high-rise apartment. His culture is structured around the extended family, three or four sons and their families living with the father and mother. We have tried to design and build housing suitable for them.

He continues. When the Jordanians ran the school system in East Jerusalem the curriculum, even for Christian Arab children, was based on the Koran. We give their educators all the assistance we can but we don't interfere. Arab schools have to be constructed differently so boys and girls are completely separated. They even have separate entrances. One of the most important things is that we have numerous cultural differences, even among the Jews, and we can co-exist if we don't try to impose our culture on theirs. We don't seek converts, only peace.

Are the Arabs really getting a fair share of the pie? The tour guide is thoughtful but he doesn't hesitate. The Arabs have been on the lower end of the economic scale as have been our own oriental Jews. No one is deliberately keeping them down. The Arabs have received tremendous economic benefits by reunification and more and more Arabs are acquiring skills and professions. Many work in West Jerusalem. Besides the tourist industry you'll see them working in banks and offices but it will be some time before there is a significant body of white-collar workers. One of the problems is that none of the Arab countries operates the social state as it is practiced in the West. We pay high taxes and in return we expect high-quality civic services. The Arab has traditionally paid little or no taxes and receives few social benefits from the state. Things like quality education and medicine are only part of it. Take paved streets, proper street lighting, police service without bribery. These are new to the Arabs. Once inside an Arab home, you are in his womb, his fortress. You'll see few playgrounds or any other form of public communal life other than the mosque and coffeehouse. There was a problem of people living in walled villas, expensive homes on the Nablus Road. They'd simply throw their garbage over the wall and complain when it wasn't picked up. We tried to explain that garbage collection must be paid for somehow but they have no sense of neighborhood.

In a few minutes the entourage crossed into the Old City through Herod's Gate. Although the tour guide was a Jew, he seemed uncommonly popular among the Arabs. Turning a corner, they came to a street-building project in a narrow alleyway.

Here is what I'm talking about, the guide continued. When we reunited the city in 1967 only ten per cent, the wealthiest ten per cent, of the Arabs had access to water in their homes. The rest received it by carrier every ten days. They allowed this system to continue for centuries. The only neighborhood pride you'll see is in the Christian and Armenian Quarters and, of course, the new Jewish Quarter.

Now there is so much water since we've installed it, the sewers can't handle it. What you see being dug up is a drainage system from the fifth century. We are also installing permanent light cables so every home will have electricity.

The guide looked up to the blizzard of TV aerials and mumbled something about progress. We are getting rid of that disgusting sight by a central signal tower in the Citadel.

Can the Arabs receive programs from Arab countries? Yes, of course. Many of us watch the news from Jordan as well as some of the American serials. TV, books, newspapers, anything they want. There is virtually no censorship.

They all slide past the street project. We must be extremely careful how we build and repair around here because we never know what's under the ground. Every building project is also a potential archaeological dig. We first dug up the past when we reconstructed the Jewish Quarter, then covered it up very carefully. We can't use trucks in most places, so everything has to come in and out by donkey. Yes, it's expensive. It is also expensive to keep facing all the new buildings with Jerusalem stone but even the poorest neighborhood has the dignity that comes with stone.

After a visit to the Western Wall, perennially filled with people at prayer, tourists, or some sort of celebration, the tour guide stopped at the Dung Gate to check the progress of the dig along the southern wall, which was part of the original City of David. As soon as one dig stops, another starts. We don't have the money but we can't quench our thirst to keep discovering our past.

Problems? The same problems every city has these days and maybe a few unique ones. One day the ultra-Orthodox will barricade their neighborhood or protest a new disco or throw stones at cars that pass too close on the Sabbath. On the next day the Arab shops might shut down in protest while Arab school children lay wreaths where the Jordanians fell. There are slums and angry young men, our own Black Panthers. In addition to our own city council, we have all kinds of governments in absentia, the Vatican, the United Nations. Everyone looks over our shoulders.

The Arabs refuse to get involved in the political process. They are being intimidated by Hussein and the Jordanians on the one hand and the PLO on the other. The Palestinian Arabs have shown very little political initiative in the past. As the tour guide explained, the catalogue of problems seemed endless. The main thing, he said, is that, for all the different stripes and breeds, people here get along extremely well.

Obviously this was no ordinary tour guide, although he acts as one often. His name is Teddy Kollek and he is the Mayor of Jerusalem. When Sadat was greeted on his arrival, he knew in advance of the world's most famous mayor, the one who often gets up at five in the morning to do chores like riding with the garbage trucks to see if the system is working and whose day invariably ends long after midnight. He is the mayor who stops at a restaurant on his way from one function to the next and gets his dinner by simply taking food off the plates of his friends while standing and chatting with them, and the mayor who has won international recognition for falling asleep at public affairs. He eats too much, is out of shape, overworks, undersleeps. He speaks to each person as though that person were the only one in the world at the moment. He sloughs off compliments as though he didn't hear them.

He lives in a modest flat filled with a passionately achieved collection of antiquities. Teddy Kollek is the greatest single person to have benefited Jerusalem since the days of the Bible. His place among the Jewish immortals is secure.

Jill was among the journalists on tour with Teddy, as he is universally addressed. She returned with him to the City Hall opposite the northwest corner of the Old City. When he assumed office in 1964, the City Hall was the last building in West Jerusalem smack on the frontier. He canceled plans for a new City Hall in a safer location so no one would get the idea that the divided city was an accepted fact. The building is bullet pocked as a testimony to the recent past.

His office door is open and there is a homey, informal atmosphere. Teddy likes beautiful women around him as the outer office will testify. One of the secretaries was without a baby sitter for the day, so her infant crawled about on her desk top. Teddy patted the baby on the head and entered his own spartan office. It is decorated only with a few pictures and ancient maps of the city. The door remained open to a stream of comers and goers as he alternately signed papers and answered the phone. Business was conducted with the casualness of the marketplace. He treats everyone with uncommon ease, taking time and patience for the daily stream of foreign Jews who merely want to come and shake his hand.

An old artist on the skids entered without knocking. Teddy reached in his pocket and handed him a bill, a regular monthly handout.

A secretary reminded him he was due at the President's Residence for a formal reception. "Do I have to wear a jacket?" he asked.

She looked at him with disdain, "Well?" and took his coat off the rack, folded it neatly and placed it on the corner of his desk so he wouldn't forget.

At six o'clock the staff drifted off. Everyone worries out loud that Teddy works far too hard but he doesn't listen. There were four more engagements to attend to out of the office, including the one at the President's where he had to wear the jacket. As Jill left with him she was astonished to see him punch a time card. She sneaked a peek. Almost every check-in time was around 6 A.M. and many of the checkouts were around ten or eleven o'clock.

The next evening Teddy picked us up at Mishkenot Sha'Ananim, driving a beat-up Volvo several years old. His son Amos, a fine novelist, was along. Teddy has suffered some guilt feelings because his life and work have often prevented him from giving more time to his family. A number of other great men, including his mentor Ben Gurion, have been burdened with the same problem. Teddy listened to my complaints about Mishkenot Sha'Ananim's many shortcomings without anger, then asked me to put it in a letter.

Before heading for a restaurant, he insisted on driving us around to show us the new illuminations at the Monastery of the Cross and the Russian Church of Gethsemane. On the boulevard near the monastery he suddenly hit the brakes, jumped out of the car and raised absolute hell with a woman picking roses in the boulevard's divider strip, then waited for a passing police car to give her a citation.

We drove over to East Jerusalem and stopped at an Arab hotel. Everyone broke into a smile as we passed through the lobby to the elevator and rooftop restaurant. Here, in one of the most volatile locations on earth, its most prominent citizen walked freely without bodyguard or arms. One cannot help feeling the reverence the Arabs have for this man. Although the Arabs have refrained from taking part in the political running of the city, thousands vote for him in each election.

Teddy Kollek was born in 1911 near Budapest, the son of an official in the Rothschild bank. He was named after Theodor Herzl, the father of Zionism. When he was bar-mitzvahed, he made a pitch for contributions for his youth group so they could buy a canoe. Teddy has never stopped pitching for funds ever since. It is an ancient Jewish art called "schnorring" but he has never "schnorred" for himself, only for the Jewish people and, mainly, for Jerusalem.

Arriving in Palestine in the mid-thirties, he was a founder of the Ein Gev kibbutz on the Sea of Galilee and, incidentally, a fisherman. He married his childhood sweetheart Tamar a few years later. Arthur Koestler, who lived and researched at the kibbutz later, dedicated his book, *Thieves in the Night*, to the Kolleks.

Teddy's talents for leadership soon became apparent and before World War II he was sent to Austria on a rescue mission. After a meeting with Adolf Eichmann at the former Rothschild mansion in Vienna, Teddy was able to get exit visas for three thousand Jewish youngsters.

About that time his association with Ben Gurion began and he was there at Lake Success when the United Nations voted for the partition which led to statehood. During the War of Independence Teddy went on the vital mission to establish an illegal arms pipeline from America. With headquarters in a fading mid-Manhattan hotel, he enlisted a highly unlikely group of arms suppliers and gun runners from among respectable members of the Jewish community which included rabbis, bankers, manufacturers, Jews with military backgrounds and the maverick newspaper publisher, Hank Greenspan. He also cavorted with Irish dock workers, the unions and even the Mafia to get the hardware to his beleaguered countrymen. His office was mainly phone booths to avoid FBI detection.

After the War of Independence Kollek's career was interwoven with Ben Gurion's as director of the Prime Minister's office. From that vantage point and later as Mayor of Jerusalem he saw and participated in the passing parade of Israel, its struggles, its achievements, its legion of great and near great men, the inner workings of Ben

Gurion's tumultuous reign. With the years he has gathered probably more personal friends than anyone in the world, most of whom would travel halfway around the world for him without giving it a second thought.

He was into a bit of everything from starting up the Israel Bonds group to director of tourism, finding the money to keep dozens of enterprises of the new country from going under, to starting dozens of new enterprises. He was in on the spy story purchase of the Dead Sea Scrolls, the founding of the Israel Museum, the Eichmann trial, the formation of the state coins and medals company, the intelligence failure scandals, the near miss in trying to arrange a meeting between Nasser and Ben Gurion, the Pope's visit.

With all his public service, Kollek had remained largely a behind-the-scenes man until he became mayor. When Ben Gurion split away from his party and formed a new one, Teddy went with him in a move that could have ended his political career. When Ben Gurion's public career ended, he made the decision to run for Mayor of Jerusalem. His party only won a fourth of the council seats but he was able to form a coalition and has remained ever since.

In a manner of speaking, Jerusalem is not only a precious and precarious post for a mayor, it is like a small unique state of its own. And like Ben Gurion, he has become a prime minister of sorts. Many people believe he should lead the nation itself.

During the Six-Day War the man was a paragon of strength in keeping up the city's discipline and morale. Because radio silence could not be broken, the population had only Arab news to listen to. Kollek went on a nonstop mission from neighborhood to neighborhood, bunker to bunker. In the sudden and unexpected reunification and flush of victory he found himself the mayor of an expanded city with two separate sets of municipal functions, a wary Arab population and an outpouring of exultation by the Jews that brought hundreds of thousands of them pouring up to the city to see the Western Wall.

By June 10, the last day of the war, Zubin Mehta had arrived and a victory concert was staged. A few days later another concert, conducted by Leonard Bernstein, with Isaac Stern and Jennie Tourel, was held in the amphitheater of the old Hebrew University on Mount Scopus.

T eddy gives full credit to Moshe Dayan, the Minister of Defense, for the decision to tear down the walls that separated the two cities. Kollek personally favored a more cautious step-by-step reunification, not knowing how the two populations would react to each other plus the imponderables from the international standpoint. But Dayan insisted and he had complete authority. And the ugly barricades, fences, barbed wire and concrete walls that had mutilated Jerusalem for two decades came tumbling down!

Suddenly Jews and Arabs were intermingling in the Old City which the Jews had longed for and Arabs ventured into West Jerusalem. There was more curiosity than rancor, more of a desire to get along than to continue the fight and Teddy Kollek has seen to it that things have stayed that way.

The problems of putting the two pieces together were mindbending but when one is motivated by love there is no stronger or more passionate driving force. From June 29, 1967, onward, Jerusalem marched to greatness under the relentless energy and creativity of this great man.

Living together and fusing two economies and cultures required not only great judgment and decision but fairness. If any single feature has dominated Kollek's terms, it has been the winning of the Arabs to the notion that they are being treated with decency, dignity and consideration.

In acting on one problem after another in his dawn-to-dusk schedule he has accomplished the miracle. Nonetheless, it will be a long time, if ever, before the Arabs accept

Jewish rule. Although Christian holy sites are meticulously guarded and respected and relations with them are excellent, many Christians, including the Vatican, have their noses out of joint because their holy sites are protected by Jews.

But they have all come together, pray God, never to be separated. Not that the Arabs have accepted their share of responsibility for the city, but if the world is to survive, there are those places where different people must learn to share the same turf and live side by side with mutual respect and give peace to one another. Thus far sporadic terrorist activity has failed to turn the communities on each other and, generally speaking, Jerusalem is one of the friendliest, safest and most openhearted cities in the world. Jerusalem has never been as free and as liberal as it is today under Jewish rule.

Mayor Richard E. Carver of Peoria, who is president of the American Conference of Mayors, wrote in his 1980 report:

> I, and some other American Mayors, recently visited the City of Jerusalem. In this community we found virtually every problem that could ever confront any city in the world, literally a divided population which until recently was in part committed to the destruction of each other. These two peoples were separated by nationality, religion, culture and ethnic background, and yet, under the magnificent leadership of Mayor Teddy Kollek, have come together as one city. Mayor Kollek has proven that committed leadership, strategic planning for the future, and a willingness to bring total community together to deal with their collective problems, can overcome almost any obstacle.

It is correct, is it not, to leave our visit to Jerusalem with the words of Teddy Kollek, as told in his autobiography, written with his son Amos.

Today Jerusalem is a beautiful city, and I often wish I could take people back in time and show them the city before 1967: the sadness of no-man's land, the walls, the barbed wire, the deserted streets, and the deteriorating areas along the frontier. For whatever reason, this city has only flourished under the Jews. Nobody else ever paid a great deal of attention to Jerusalem. The Crusaders had a high regard for the city and were willing to sacrifice their lives for it. The British had a historic feeling for it. But only under the Jews—both in ancient and modern times—has it been the capital of a nation. When the Arabs had the choice, they bypassed Jerusalem and built Ramle as their capital—for the brief period they had a capital in this country at all. They never really developed Jerusalem and grew much attached to it only when others ruled it. The Arabs expressed their passion for Jerusalem when the Crusaders ruled it and again since we have governed it. In between, there was very little feeling for the city, and it suffered conspicuous neglect.

. . . it is the soul and heart of the Jewish people. A body can live without a limb; it cannot live without its head, heart, and soul . . . now the unity of Jerusalem is an irreversible historic fact. The shock of the Yom Kippur War, which we still have not overcome, is nothing compared to the trauma that the Jews of Israel and the Diaspora would experience if Jerusalem were divided again. I cannot imagine how the Jewish people and the State of Israel could survive such a blow intact.

And Teddy ends his autobiography with these words . . .

We are like ants building the most beautiful ant hill that was ever created, and we hope it will continue to exist undisturbed. But who knows? Maybe a man with a stick will come along, poke into our masterpiece, and part of it will be destroyed. If so, here we are, like ants. And we will build it again and again as well and as beautifully as we know how.

It was another day, it was late, and Jill was chasing after Teddy for one last set of pictures. He punched his time card and tucked his jacket under his arm, to be put on later when he reached a reception for Oral Roberts, Jr., whose father's church had heavily endowed an orphanage for Arab children in the Old City. As the two waited at the stop light before crossing and entering New Gate a bus filled with West Bank Arabs passed by. "We live together," Teddy said and, as they crossed the street, he repeated, "We live together."

Chronology of Jerusalem and Related Events

B.C.

3000	Earliest discovered remains of habitation at Jerusalem on the hill of Ophel
1850	Jerusalem referred to in Egyptian Execration Texts
1280	Exodus from Egypt
1250	Conquest of Canaan under Joshua
1013–973	King David makes Jerusalem the capital of the united kingdom of Israel
973–933	King Solomon builds the First Temple
928	United kingdom splits into Judah and Israel
715–687	King Hezekiah of Judah builds tunnel from Gihon Spring to Pool of Siloam and strengthens the city walls
587	Nebuchadnezzar, King of Babylon, conquers Jerusalem, destroys the Temple and exiles Jews to Babylonia
538	Cyrus, King of Persia, conquers Babylon and allows Jews to return to Jerusalem
537–332	THE PERSIAN PERIOD
515	Completion of the Second Temple
445	Nehemiah, governor of Judea, rebuilds the walls of Jerusalem
332-167	THE HELLENISTIC PERIOD
331	Alexander the Great passes through Palestine and perhaps visits Jerusalem
198–128	RULE OF THE SELEUCIDS OF SYRIA
172	Jerusalem becomes a Hellenistic polis named Antiochia

visits Jerusalem and names Christian sites. Building of the Church of the Holy Sepulchre begins

543	Jerusalem at the height of Christian splendor
614	Persian conquest of Jerusalem
638–1099	THE MOSLEM PERIOD
638	Caliph Omar enters Jerusalem; city falls to Arabs
691	Dome of the Rock completed
996–1020	Church of the Holy Sepulchre destroyed
1037	Church of the Holy Sepulchre rebuilt
1099–1187	THE CRUSADER KINGDOM
1099	Crusaders capture Jerusalem; Jews and Moslems banned
1099–1187	Jerusalem capital of the Latin Kingdom
1187	Saladin captures Jerusalem from the Crusaders
1229	Christian Emperor Frederick II gains Jerusalem by treaty
1250–1517	THE MAMELUKE PERIOD
1250	The Mamelukes, slave kings of Egypt, seize the city
1517–1917	THE OTTOMAN TURKISH PERIOD
1516	Ottoman conquest of Jerusalem
1538–1540	Sultan Suleiman rebuilds the walls of the city (the same walls are in existence today)
1827	First visit of Sir Moses Montefiore
1838	First consulate (British) opened in Jerusalem
1861	First Jewish settlement outside the city walls
1883	Beginning of Baron Edmond de Rothschild's help to Jewish settlements
1898	Visit by Dr. Theodor Herzl, founder of World Zionist Organization

1917–1948	THE BRITISH OCCUPATION AND MANDATORY PERIOD
1917	November 2: Balfour Declaration; December 11: British conquest; General Allenby enters Jerusalem.
1918	Dr. Chaim Weizmann lays foundation stone of Hebrew University on Mount Scopus
1921	Arab riots in Jerusalem. Sir Herbert Samuel appointed first British high commissioner
1923	British Mandate confirmed by League of Nations
1925	Hebrew University dedicated in Jerusalem
1936	Arab general strike and riots
1946	Irgun blows up the King David Hotel
1947	United Nations resolution recommending the partition of Palestine into Arab and Jewish states
1948–1967	THE DIVIDED CITY
1948	British Mandate ends and state of Israel proclaimed
1948–1949	Israel's War of Independence (May 1948–January 1949), the first Arab-Israeli War, ending with a divided city. New City of Jerusalem remains intact but Jewish Quarter in Old City falls (May 28, 1948). Signing of Israel-Transjordan armistice agreement in which Jerusalem is divided between the two countries (April 1949). West Jerusalem declared the capital of Israel
1964	Teddy Kollek elected Mayor of Jerusalem
1967	THE NEW ERA
1967	Six-Day War in which Israeli troops capture the Old City from the Jordanians. Jerusalem liberated and reunited
1973	Yom Kippur War
1979	Israeli-Egyptian peace treaty signed

ABOUT THE AUTHORS

JILL URIS studied photography at Colorado College, Harvard, and New York University. She served as Associate Director of The Center of the Eye, a photography school in Aspen, Colorado.

LEON URIS is the author of *Battle Cry, Exodus, Mila 18, Topaz, QB VII* and *Trinity*. The Urises live in Aspen.

QUANTITY PURCHASES

around the world '1

Leon Uris

TRINITY

a novel of Ireland

☐ 24864	**THE HAJ**	$4.95
☐ 24964	**JERUSALEM, SONG OF SONGS** with Jill Uris	$4.95
☐ 24154	**EXODUS**	$4.50
☐ 23547	**TOPAZ**	$3.95
☐ 24160	**MILA 18**	$4.50
☐ 23907	**TRINITY**	$4.50
☐ 20991	**BATTLE CRY**	$3.95
☐ 22697	**QB VIII**	$3.95

<u>Prices and availability subject to change without notice.</u>

Buy them at your local bookstore or use this handy coupon for ordering:

By the year 2000, 2 out of 3 Americans could be illiterate.

It's true.

Today, 75 million adults… about one American in three, can't read adequately. And by the year 2000, U.S. News & World Report envisions an America with a literacy rate of only 30%.

Before that America comes to be, you can stop it… by joining the fight against illiteracy today.

Call the Coalition for Literacy at toll-free **1-800-228-8813** and volunteer.

Volunteer Against Illiteracy. The only degree you need is a degree of caring.

SPECIAL
MONEY SAVING
OFFER

Now you can have an up-to-date listing of Bantam's hundreds of titles plus take advantage of our unique and exciting bonus book offer. A special offer which gives you the opportunity to purchase a Bantam book for only 50¢. Here's how!

By ordering any five books at the regular price per order, you can also choose any other single book listed (up to a $4.95 value) for just 50¢. Some restrictions do apply, but for further details why not send for Bantam's listing of titles today!

Just send us your name and address plus 50¢ to defray the postage and handling costs.